RUNNING INTO ME

A MEMOIR OF RESILIENCE, RELATIONSHIPS & RECOVERY

By

elisemarie

RUNNING INTO ME

A MEMOIR OF RESILIENCE, RELATIONSHIPS & RECOVERY

By
elisemarie

DEDICATION

To my children
Jacob Vincent, William Louis, Nicholas Samuel,
and Kate Madison Marilee

To my parents

Vincent S. DiCarlo and Marilee Frances Mitchell DiCarlo

You are the bookends that support and sustain my life

I love you

TABLE OF CONTENTS

ARISE I

HEALTH IS WEALTH II

ROOTS III

FAB FOUR IV

BELOVEDS V

UNDER HIS WING VI

LEELEE VII

Lessons From The Course VIII

Sunset IX

ARISE I

SHINE

LIFE IS ABSOLUTELY oozing with beauty and grace, but there are still tough days, weeks, months, and even years. They are out there for all of us. But the more I face the truth, the better I feel. Even if the truth is uncomfortable or downright ugly, it's okay if I can see the monster in front of me. There is no value in shadowboxing; I need to look that villain straight in the eye and know that no matter what, I am okay. And you are, too. I want you to press on, even in the darkest of times. The sun will burst forth for you as it has for me.

I know that moving forward on a dream can feel overwhelming. Still, I cannot let go of them even if I try. One of mine has been to write a book. From grade school, I knew I was a writer.

My third-grade teacher instructed us to start a journal. I can still see the cover of mine, pink with purple dots. This is where I got the idea to call our school newspaper *The Purple Dot*. I was the editor of the school news in elementary school. I was editor of my high school newspaper and editor of the yearbook. And what did

I do all this time? Write, write, write. I wrote stories and reported on dances and sports events. I wrote almost every caption in the yearbook during my senior year. I have heard of writer's block, but it's foreign to me. If anything, I have writer's flood. I have so many things I want to write about that I cannot get them on paper fast enough. The more I write, the more the ideas come. It seems they are endless. Many teachers and professors have told me I am a writer. I am grateful for their encouragement.

Words contain the very kernels of truth that sustain my life. They embody my hope for tomorrow, which I desperately need today. They are the conduits that carry my messages of good news to you. This is the hope I share with my patients, my family, my friends, and everyone who needs to be uplifted.

From a young age I knew that I would write books. It has been a deep longing in my heart. With all this evidence from God and those around me, you would think I would have jumped right in at age eighteen and written my first novel. However, I only had the confidence to say that I would do this when I was twenty-four years old. I am more than embarrassed to tell you that three decades have elapsed since I made my intentions known. Why the delay? Why the seemingly reckless procrastination?

First, I needed to learn that if I was going to live my dream, I must do it. No one else can hold me accountable. I told my brother, "I need to write a book. I've got to do it. I want to have it done by Christmas. Please hold me accountable." It was February of 1995! Why didn't he do this for me? I cannot blame it on him. He's a busy person. He's not my gatekeeper. *I* needed to help me with this. *I* needed to hold myself accountable. As I went along, *I* needed to find people to read and provide feedback.

It's my responsibility to get this book to you, and I am serious about it. I jump out of bed to start writing. I am not blocked nor stumped for what will come next. My hope is to use my God-given talents and abilities to help you by taking all the horrible, tragic, and unfortunate things that have happened in my life and use them for your good. I am sharing my experience so that you can do it another way. I want spare you some serious pitfalls. I tell my kids, "You can learn from your own mistakes, that's smart. Or you can learn from the mistakes of others. Now, that is genius."

When I was twelve, I begged my mom to take me to Los Angeles to become an actress. She proceeded to tell me how few actors make it, how most are just 'starving actors' who never make it big. My mom is an absolute saint and an incredible woman. She had reasons for everything she ever said to me, and these reasons came out of love. I want to be clear about that. Marilee DiCarlo is an absolute jewel in the world. I blame her for absolutely nothing and give her credit for the good.

I bring this up because, sometimes, the people who love us the most won't support us. It's not that they want to hurt us; they come from their own fears and insecurities. My mom wanted to see me become a doctor. She is a highly determined woman, and so am I. With this combination, medical school graduation came to pass for me. I buried this book and my desire for it. The busyness of my life pressed it down flat in my soul. It was still alive just silent like a dormant bear waiting for a warmer climate.

About three years ago as I began a quest to fiercely manifest my goals. I told a friend, "I am going to write a book."

"A book, why would you want to write a book? Who even reads books? Do you know anyone reading a book? Take that Michelle Obama book. Do you even know anyone who has read it? No one is reading books," she asserted.

I was crestfallen. I did not have a pulse on the climate for book reading. I did not say anything about reading it. I said I wanted to *write* it. That is my part. I am not in charge of the results. I am writing, and obviously, I hope you read. But that is entirely up to you.

Much later, she gave me a book her client had written. Shocked, I said, "You told me not to write a book."

"Did I say that? If you want to write a book, go ahead. If it's just something you need to do. I don't have a problem with it."

She said this with as much enthusiasm as a wet cracker. Please keep in mind that these are people I love and respect. Why were they dismissive? Because they are not me. The dream is planted in *my* heart, not theirs. It's not on their radar, it's on mine. It's my job to listen and act on the still, small voice of God inside of me. Many people are not risk-takers. They are firmly planted in numbers, percentages, and rates of return. They are logical, orderly, procedural thinkers. They are who God made them to be, and you are who God made you to be. I have a friend who reminds me, "We are not statistics and numbers; we are individuals with our own paths." I needed to get quiet and set aside the opinions, fears, and well-meaning advice of others.

I figured out what I wanted, what I was meant to do, and began accomplishing it. Do not wait for someone to green-light you. I realize now that I am the someone I have been waiting for. Give yourself permission. Only you can green-light you. That is what I am doing, and it feels amazing. I want this for you, too. I want to see you shine. Hold nothing back. Now is the time.

As we become our true selves, we liberate others to be themselves.

I hope you will find encouragement, strength, joy, love, and understanding on these pages.

I hope you will forgive yourself and others for all mistakes and shortcomings.

I hope I can help you find your way when it seems there is no way.

As you find parts of yourself within these pages, I encourage you to live more fully and love more deeply. I hope you will realize you are enough and always have been. Give yourself permission to be the person God has always intended you to be.

The world needs you. I need to hear what you have to say. Your voice counts. You count. You are precious. The Bible says, "He knit you in your mother's womb." God made you and He loves you infinitely. He wants to see it come to pass for you. He is for you. You and God are a majority. He wants to give you the desires of your heart. He is the one who put them there. Let nothing stand in your way.

I hope you will shine.

I love you.

Elisemarie

"Her own thoughts and reflections were habitually her best companions." Jane Austen

"Stay away from those people who try to disparage your ambitions. Small minds will always do that, but great minds will give you a feeling that you can become great too." Mark Twain

"You are the light of the world. A town built on a hill cannot be hidden. Neither do people light a lamp and put it under a bowl. Instead, they put it on its stand, and it gives light to everyone in the house. In the same way, let your light shine before others, that they may see your good deeds and glorify your Father in heaven." (Matthew 5:14-16 NIV)

FACE THE SUN

I GREW UP in Kansas City, Missouri. For those who have not lived there, there is not a great area of land that defines the end of Missouri and the beginning of Kansas. There is, in fact, a line dividing the two states, and it runs down the middle of a street, aptly named State Line Road. My childhood home was three blocks from Stateline, so we lived close to Kansas. One can literally be in Missouri and walk across the street to Kansas.

As a child, I often went with my parents to look at land. My dad was in construction and was an entrepreneur, always looking for possibilities. I knew we owned a farm out in Kansas, and we visited the farmer to see how the crops were growing. I have long been infatuated with sunflowers. If I had to guess, I would say this started when we would drive by huge fields filled with sunflowers on the way to the farm. They seemed so hearty and strong on their stalks, not like daisies or even roses. Those stalks held great disks of seeds that were sometimes two feet wide.

"Keep your face to the sunshine, and you cannot see the shadows. It's what the sunflowers do," wrote Helen Keller. She was not just using sunflowers as a metaphor. The head of the sunflowers do turn throughout the day to continuously face the sun. They are brilliant.

While our backyard was not a sunflower field, Dad grew a beautiful garden. The entire place was stamped with his green thumb. There was nothing he could not grow. We had an apple tree and a cherry tree. We also grew tomatoes and an array of flowers. But what Dad loved most was his rose garden. He meticulously tended the roses with food, water, and the best soil. If they were leaning, he carefully tied the stem to a stick for support. When they were 'ready,' he would cut them individually and put them in little vases. The vases sat on the kitchen table and the windowsill near the kitchen sink. From there Mom could see me and my neighborhood pals playing in the backyard. Many times, I found a small vase with a tender pink rose sitting on my bedroom desk.

Sometimes on Saturdays, Dad took me to the nursery and occasionally let me pick out a rose plant. The American Beauty Rose was a favorite of mine. They are classified as a hybrid perpetual rose. This means that they repeatedly bloom throughout the spring, summer, and fall. That is probably why Dad also approved; this bush would give him plenty of blooms to bring to Mom. While I don't like crimson roses, American Beauties can also come in a deep pink that I love.

Then I learned that American Beauties are also known for their strong fragrance. Suddenly, I was catching a scent. As I was a toddler, I walked by the rose bushes and smelled them. Time was all mine, so I smelled as many roses as I wanted on each bush and delighted in their sweetness. Another favorite was the snapdragon. I loved that when you opened the 'mouth' of the flower, it looked like the maw of a beautiful dragon. We also grew a honeysuckle bush. Dad taught me how to pick just the right blooms to get a drop of honey to eat. Being a father of six, he improvised about what was food. He would bring home mushrooms he found around town. Although they *might* be poisonous, they also might *not* be. How did we find out? Very scientifically, Dad would taste them first. If he lived, it was safe for the kids.

Sometimes, we bought small plants and seeds to grow. On one of our Saturday outings I was looking through seed packages and spotted sunflower seeds.

"Dad, may I get these?" I asked as I held up the package.

"Sure, you want to grow those? I don't see why not?"

We planted those seeds along a wall in our backyard. I was amazed as they grew and grew. They were as tall as the wall and soon surpassed it. The strong stalks, now six feet tall, held up their massive heads. Then one day, the stalks collapsed. The huge heads of seeds plummeted to the ground. I was so disappointed. My young mind questioned, "Why didn't they keep growing? What made the stalks fall down? Why did this happen without warning?" I demanded to know.

I was learning about a relentless taskmaster that is always silently lurking close by. He never takes a break, and he never gives one. He keeps his march as a perfectly trained soldier, never wavering in his mission. I constantly desire more of him and loathe his passing in equal measure He's the runner I never catch up with; he only seems to go faster with each strike of his foot. When I'm worn down to a pulp, exhausted and suffering, he slows his pace. He seems to taunt me and decelerates to a sluggish crawl. Is there no escaping him? I finally let my eyes close for what seemed like a moment. I awake to find he is now miles ahead, almost out of sight. I call out, "Thief! Slow down! I need to catch up." My pleas fall on deaf ears. I am continuously tortured by him. Can he never stand still? Can he not be a gentleman and wait?

Like all the greats, it seems there is no beating him, save for one thing. Like a world record that is finally smashed by .01 seconds, there is only one place where he does not reign supreme, and it's right here, right now, with you. It's hearing your laugh and seeing your smile. It's when my daughter stretches out her arms and says, "Huggie?" When my son walks in from practice and cracks me up with his joke of the day. It's when I lean down to pet an adorable dog or when I am lucky enough to be on the back of a horse. It's when I look into my mom's eyes. Yes, in those moments, he stops. He can't possibly speed by. He glances back for a second, but then, like any experienced athlete, he faces forward with new determination.

What am I left with? The satisfaction that I made him look. The fact that my life is so marvelous and precious that for even one second, he went unnoticed. Although he marched over my sunflowers, letting them fall, and looked on as my father wasted away, there is hope. But his unrelenting dominance crumbles under the weight of the present moment filled with laughter, tears, beauty, and celebration. He is wholly defeated by the one thing that proceeds with equal determination and even more strength: The love and beauty we contain in the moment. All the goodness that has been poured into our souls by loving people. All the joy, forgiveness, and service we give cannot be stopped by time. No, Time, I will not let you touch these. When I write, I assure myself that these thoughts of mine stand still on paper. They exist, and so does love. Not even time can take these away.

"Time and tide wait for no man." Geoffrey Chaucer

"Fall seven times, stand up eight." Japanese Proverb

"Teach us to number our days aright that we may gain a heart of wisdom." (Psalm 90:12 NIV)

IMPOSSIBLE YOU

DID YOU know that the odds of you being alive are zero?

Ali Binazir, M.D., trained physician and business consultant, elaborates, "Imagine there was one life preserver thrown somewhere in some ocean, and there is exactly one turtle in all of these oceans, swimming underwater somewhere. The probability that you came about and exist today is the same as that turtle sticking its head out of the water — in the middle of that life preserver, on one try."

Researchers thought that the odds you'd be born were 1:400,000,000,000,000.

However, that estimate is entirely too generous. Luke Devo, computer programmer and author, has concluded that "The odds of you being born are way, way, way less than 1 in 400 trillion. Try 10 with 2.68 MILLION zeros behind it. That is 850 or so pages of all zeros in a notepad. This statistic makes the number of atoms in the known universe feel insignificant, at a mere 10."

The likelihood that you even exist is infinitesimally small. The fact that you exist defies logic. The numbers were stacked against you, but that could not stop you from making your appearance here on planet Earth.

The miracle of human life drew me to work in obstetrics and gynecology (OB/GYN) in a hospital before I began medical school. I would get an even more intimate look during my rotations. I witnessed many beautiful outcomes of pregnancy and some genuinely tragic ones.

When I was doing a rotation in OBGYN, a man was standing at the nurses' station. He was intensely angry, saying, "Why? Why? Why does that person have healthy twins, and we have no baby? Our baby died. How is that fair?" Indeed, no one had an answer for this shattered man.

I wish this outcome were rare, but I saw several variations in my work. There is no logic to apply. There are no words save for the fact that our very existence defies all logic.

Four years after witnessing that man's heartache, I was elated to be pregnant with my third child. This pregnancy had come after many nights of crying out to God:

Please send us another baby. Please, Lord. Please, oh please, Lord, hear and answer my prayer, in Jesus' name. Amen.

This one was a miracle, just like the two pregnancies before it. The hand of God was upon me, and I was grateful. The moment I found out I was pregnant, I would begin praying every day:

Please, God, let this be a healthy child, and let me be a healthy mom. If the baby is cute, that would be a bonus too.

It was a bitterly cold February morning, and I decided to attend a church closer to our home. It was five minutes away instead of the twenty-five-minute journey to our home church. I love our church;

I think I was looking for an easier way rather than God's way. God's way is not always more manageable, but it is infinitely better. Still, this Sunday, I decided it was so cold that the baby boys, Jacob and Will, could stay home with Daddy while I went to church. I drove the five cold minutes to Life Chapel and went in for the service, sitting on some benches in the back. I was curious about this church. The pastor was talking, and within two minutes, I knew this was not the place for me. I listen to the leanings of God, and I trust that in my life.

Usually, I would feel the need to be people-pleasing and polite, but I hold my Sundays sacred. I need to be in a place where I can hear from God. So, I did something very uncharacteristic. I got up and walked out, politely and discretely, of course, but I did it. I thought, "My soul can't be here a minute longer." I returned to the bitter cold with its biting wind on my face. I quickly drove to Kansas Blessings Church. At this time, the church was in Overland Park. I was now late for the 9:00 am service.

There was never enough parking at this church, and if you were late, parking was on the side streets far from the entrance. I found a spot on the street and began walking briskly to the church, my feet pounding on the frozen cement. I felt utterly relieved as I walked into the auditorium for the service. Now, I was peaceful. I listened intently to the service, which was beautiful, as always.

Standing in the back of the church, I suddenly felt something warm and wet in my underwear. I thought I was losing some urine, a common occurrence during pregnancy. When I felt this wetness, I thought, wow, I am losing control of my bladder this time. I dashed into the bathroom and pulled down my jeans and underwear to find no urine but bright red blood gushing out of my body, not coming in drops but pouring out of me like water from a pitcher. I prayed.

No, God, no, this cannot be. I am out of my first trimester. I am supposed to be in the clear. I am in week 14. I have heard the heartbeat and know this baby is alive within me. God, the first trimester is over, so I must be okay. This cannot be happening.

But it was happening. I quickly pulled my clothes back on and dialed my cousin Collin Johnson. He is an OB and one the best in his field anywhere.

I said, "Collin, I am bleeding, bleeding, BLEEDING! Oh my God, what do? What do I do?"

By now, I was back outside, making the long, freezing walk back to my car. I was audibly crying.

Collin said, "You need to try to calm down and stop crying. I can't understand what you are saying."

I tried to quell my tears for a moment and said, "I am bleeding. I am gushing blood. What do I do?"

Collin is a calm and wonderful human being, which makes him ideally suited for his profession and life in general. His patients, friends, and family love him. He is willing to drop Everything to help someone, and today; I was that someone.

He said, "Everything will be okay. You need to calm down and take a breath. Where are you?"

"I am leaving my church at 83rd and Lamar."

"Who is with you?"

"No one. Jeff is home with the kids."

"Okay. Are you okay to drive? I mean, can you meet me at a hospital?"

"Yes. Which one?"

"Let's meet at Saint Joe's South. Park in the back by the emergency room. I am working out and will get there as soon as possible. Please look for my car and wait in it until I arrive. Just sit tight. I will be there soon."

"Thank you, Collin."

We hung up, and I began the drive. Everything looked distorted and blurry through the vast, wet tears in my eyes. I called Jeff and told him what was happening and that I would meet with Collin. He wished me well.

I looked out my car window and saw the brightest sunlight possible. The light was clear and pure white at that time of morning. I could feel the rays of the sun profusely pouring over me. Although I was afraid, this beauty, this grandeur of creation, enfolded me entirely. Peace amidst the storm.

I arrived at the hospital and sat in my frigid car to pray. I experienced an aloneness that I felt most acutely during pregnancy. It was not that I felt lonely; it was just that my husband couldn't truly grasp the magnitude of the experience. Pregnancy is a solitary journey. I alone carried each of my two boys in my body. It was the same this time. I was the 'house' for this unborn person. There is no other feeling like that. Every day, I was growing a human inside of me. That was the work of my body, to make another person. I must eat healthy foods, exercise regularly, rest adequately, and take care of myself. Then, I let the miracle take place. I understand Mary's words, "Let it be done unto me." She did not say, "Okay, thanks for the instructions on growing the Messiah. I'll get to work on this right away." No, it's a miraculous process occurring second by second. Everything has got to go perfectly. In the embryonic period, all the baby's major systems and structures develop. As cells multiply, they begin to take on specific functions. Every cell must split and act as the precursor for the next cell. This process proceeds with exact precision.

As I waited, I called a friend, but she was on the phone with her kid's doctor and quickly hung up on me. God was clarifying that I need not lean on people right now. I needed to go to God with this crisis. God only knew my feelings and my journey with this pregnancy. He was with me during all the nights of crying, hoping, and praying. He alone "formed me in my mother's womb." He alone has "counted every hair on my head." He would be with me in this darkest moment of fear.

I was sure eternity had passed as I waited for Collin to arrive. Blood was still running out of my body. Collin came in his usual manner: strong, confident, and lighthearted. He is always laughing and joking with people, and this was to be no exception. We went in some back doors through the ER to his office upstairs. This smart move allowed us to bypass the whole ER check-in protocol. Collin never rushes.

I had shadowed Collin before medical school. He got a call that one of his patients was ready to deliver, so we dashed across to the hospital. When we got to the door, he promptly stopped on a dime. He often said, "Never run into a delivery room. You don't want to bring that rushing energy into that room. Stay cool." He let me stand so close. The baby made his triumphant cry as he entered the world. Altering us to his arrival in life. It was a quick and easy delivery. He said, "Don't ever tell them it's that easy, or I might be out of a job. I stand there, and they do all the work. It's amazing, really."

After that delivery, we ducked into a secret room containing little juices and crackers for patients to get a snack. Collin offered me juice. I was still really choked up from seeing this life, a perfect baby, come into the world. He said, "I know; I was like that, too."

This time was different. *I* was a patient—fourteen weeks into a pregnancy and saturated in blood. When we got to the office, I asked if there was a clean pad. He smiled, "Of course, an OB office without pads would be like a McDonald's with no French fries."

The blood was slowing now. I was calming down, mostly from being in the presence of a caring person, and we crossed the hall to do an ultrasound. Perhaps my only look at this baby. I just prayed that there would be a heartbeat. I asked Collin to tell me the sex. I wanted to know if I had an impending farewell with my son or daughter. Collin found the heartbeat, a reassuring sign. He said, "It looks like this one is a girl." He explained that the best-case scenario was that a blood vessel was pressed on and exploded. It was emptying like a little hose, and it would stop. He told me, "Lie down and be on bed rest for as long as you can. Don't pick up, push anything, or exert yourself in any way. Don't go to the grocery store and push a cart. Don't pick up your kids. Nothing. Rest as much as possible."

I knew this was nearly impossible, so I called someone for help. This individual had time on her hands and was capable. When I told her what was going on, I said, "Can you come out to help me?"

"I can't. Couldn't you hire a nurse or something?"

I was devastated. I was in a crisis! I wouldn't be asking for help if I could hire a nurse. Again, my reliance on God proved to be my only steady anchor in this storm.

With two- and three-year-old boys, I was unsure how to succeed in my 'rest only' assignment. Once home, I placed myself gently on our kitchen's little green and yellow couch. I lay there and prayed,

God, let me stay pregnant for the next five minutes…God, please let me stay pregnant for the next ten minutes…God, let me stay pregnant for this next hour…please let me stay pregnant today.

Collin sent me home with a small portable Doppler machine. With this, I could listen to the heartbeat every hour to make sure the baby was still alive. I was so thankful for that sound. I can still hear its reassuring cadence. I kept listening for that thrum, thrum,

thrum, swooshing sound on the tiny speaker. It told me Everything was okay, if only in that present moment.

Collin told me to see my regular doctor in the morning, his colleague, Doctor Jones. All was going well, and then just after midnight, more blood, more bright red life began pouring out of me. I called the on-call doctor. She told me, "Lay back down and rest. There is nothing more we can do." They could not stop the bleeding. It would need to cease on its own or not. It slowed again. I called the office in the morning to tell them I was on my way.

When I got there, they did another ultrasound. I told the tech, "Collin says it's a girl." She responded, "Not from where I am standing. That's a penis right there." She pointed at the monitor, which displayed a beautiful silhouette of a baby. She laughed. The heart was still beating. They were ready to send me on my way, so I stopped at Doctor Jones's office. I said, "Is this baby going to live?"

"We don't know. You need to keep resting and see what happens."

"Isn't there something you can do? Something to stop the bleeding?"

"No. There is nothing to do but wait."

That hung heavily on me. Do you mean to tell me that in all of medical science, with all the advances and research in treatment, the best you can offer is 'wait and see'? That is just not good enough. I am not a 'wait and see' type of person. I want something done. We are talking about my unborn child, and you say, 'Wait and see'! Wait and see!

But I had to accept it as the only available option. All I could do was pray. Why do I say that as if it's the absolute death sentence, a last-resort thing to do? All I can do is pray. Isn't that Everything? All I can do is have intimate contact with the Creator of the entire universe. I act like that is my last choice. Why wouldn't that be my absolute first go-to move all the time? Why wouldn't I say, "No one can help me now, but thank you, Jesus. I know you and God can do all things. All things are possible with God."

It doesn't say, "All things are possible with the best medical care in the world," or "All things are possible if you can afford it," or "All things are possible if you can just get to the Mayo Clinic." No, it's "All things are possible with GOD."

I have access 24/7 to Almighty God. The one true God and I act like it's a consolation prize when it's Everything. It's a gold medal; it's priceless, and I always hold it in my heart. When all human powers have failed me, medical science has nothing to offer, no one understands, and friends seem far away, I need to find joy. I need to rejoice that I can go to the Father of us all, my Heavenly Father, and go boldly with my needs as a child going to her dad. I am blessed, not when I am relying on all things outside of Him, but when I rely on being *in* Him. That is when He shows His power in my life.

I had two more bleeding episodes in the middle of the night during this pregnancy.

I was given the same message, "Either it will stop or won't. There is nothing we can do." The simplify and finality of this statement was utterly unsatisfactory. Again, it was my only option on the material plane, so I humbly relented. I wanted a sure thing, not a this or that. I reached my sixth month. Still pregnant, I abandoned the reassuring whoosh of the doppler. I accepted my daily surrender to God and his good and perfect will.

In my seventh month, I underwent a routine check. This time, on the ultrasound, there was no heartbeat. I was, of course, terrified. Dr. Jones explained, "Sometimes babies' rest.' They don't need to work their heart constantly because they get Everything from Mom. Perhaps it's because you've been lying down or being still. It will likely start beating again." This line of reasoning was entirely unpalatable for me, and he saw that on my face.

He offered, "Or we can have you eat something, wait about thirty minutes, and see if that wakes up baby and we find a heartbeat."

"Yes, let's do that."

I prayed as I ate and rested:

God let this baby's heart begin to beat.

Again, God met me in the darkness when I could not find my way. He showed up powerfully in the form of my baby's beating heart. He bestowed the peace that passes all understanding. That is when I knew I could rely on God and his infinite love.

God brought peace this time and countless others. The Prince of Peace reigns in my heart, mind, and body. People will let me down, but God never will. God kept my heart in perfect peace. One day at a time, I continued to have a viable pregnancy until August 5, 2007. That is when our son, Nicholas Samuel, was born full-term and a perfect baby boy.

Thank you, God, for the miracle of my son, Nicholas, whom I know was destined before the beginning of time by you, and for you, in Jesus' name, Amen.

Your existence is incredibly unlikely. The planet has never seen and will never see another you. A miracle is astoundingly rare and precious, and I've just proven you are a miracle. Please adjust your life accordingly.

Be spectacular.

"I praise you because I am fearfully and wonderfully made; your works are wonderful; I know that full well." Psalm 139:14, NIV)

"And He has said to me, 'My grace is sufficient for you, for power is perfected in weakness.' Most gladly, therefore, I will rather boast about my weaknesses, so that the power of Christ may dwell in me." (2 Corinthians 12:9 NASB)

"Of all the things my hands have held, the best by far is you." Andrew McMahon

HEALTH IS WEALTH II

THE NON-NEGOTIABLE

3.15

HEN I WAS in sixth grade, Mr. Edwards took us outside for P.E. class. Our task was a simple one: run around the block while he timed us. Simple does not mean easy. Running around that huge city block was a bear for me. I was sucking wind and hating it. I was one of the last to make it around and felt chagrined when Edwards shouted out my time as he stared at his stopwatch.

Flash forward to my sophomore year in high school. A dear friend of mine was tragically shot in an armed robbery. She survived but with serious injuries. A run was held to raise money for a charity for others with similar injuries. It was a 5K run, meaning 3.15 miles in distance. Everyone I knew would be there and I wanted to look good. I had a boy to impress. What I learned was that successful running is not done through preparation on how to look attractive. Runners are made by consistent practice and dedication. Lacking insight for that challenge, I was again sucking wind after about a mile. It was impossible to look good while walking in the second half. My ego was bruised, and my legs were sore.

I did, however, decide that it would not stay that way.

I became a dedicated runner.

At first, I ran several times a week, and as years passed, I became a daily runner. I lived in New York and ran Central Park in sunshine, rain, heat, sleet, snow, wind, and every other environmental challenge. I disciplined my eating to have better fuel for my running. I asked God to direct me to the best nourishment for my body. I saw food as fuel, so I chose to eat what would make me more efficient and faster.

I ran to keep in fit condition and to have an attractive figure. The other benefit I noticed was in my mind. Running made me feel good about myself. It didn't matter what I looked like, what I was wearing, or if I had makeup on. I felt good about being me. Only running gave me that and kept me alive in the darkest times. It solidified for me that I could do hard things, whether I wanted to or not. I didn't have to feel like running. What I had to do was put on my running shoes and get out the door. Whether or not I felt like running had very little to do with it. I simply had to run. I told a friend, "I am trying to figure out what day I can take a break from running. I just can't find a day that I want to feel like crap."

I have run various distances over the forty years that I have been a dedicated runner. My longest races have been half marathons, or 13.1 miles. I trained hard and finished them satisfactorily. For a long period of time I ran ten miles a day. I thought nothing of this distance, it felt good. However, it did take up some serious time each day. As my life has become increasingly full, I have reduced my minimum daily distance to 3.15 miles. This is the distance of that first race in which I could not even run the entire course. Now, when I do run a race, I run from start to finish. It's part of my bottom line. If I am going to do a race I am going to finish, and I will run the whole distance. I reap more benefits mentally than physically from running. I run when I feel good and when I don't. When I am seriously ill, I will take off maybe one day, or I go a shorter distance. Maybe two days of the year I don't train.

"What are you training for?" my neighbor called out to me one day as I ran by. I really didn't have a quick answer, so I waved and smiled. I do have an answer. I train for life. I train to push past the physical fatigue and exhaustion that my life brings. I train to elevate my mood and allow new, creative, and beautiful ideas to flow in.

I tell my daughter Madison, "I run because I need to be here for the long haul with you." Training is my anti-stress, anti-depression, anti-cancer, anti-negativity, anti-illness, anti-mental confusion answer. It is my pro-health, proactive, pro-solution, pro-clarity, pro-God, and pro-me time of day. For the love of all that is good and holy, do I not deserve to carve out 27 minutes each day to improve my life?

Do I always 'feel' like it? Heck no. But I know at this point that the days I really don't want to run, the days I feel too tired, too defeated, too frustrated, too down, and too overwhelmed are nonnegotiable days for running. People who don't run say things like, "Your spine will compress. You will need knee and hip replacements. Your joints will suffer from the pounding." To which I respond that maybe those things will happen, but I will be able to handle it because my body will be strong enough to endure the trial. My mind will be well enough to make a clear-headed decision, and I will have many happy years in my pocket I would not trade for anything.

Most importantly, I am living in the present, so no future catastrophizing is allowed. When I run, I live right here and right now in this moment. Step, step, step, and breath, breath, breath. There is nothing in the way of right now. The only way I am defeated is if I quit, and that is not an option. I have a friend, Dr. Bob, who has gone to the VinFast IRONMAN World Championship several times. The event is more commonly referred to as Kona, as it takes place in Kailua-Kona, Hawaii. As an event, it represents a competition among the most elite athletes in the sport of triathlon. Bob consistently places at the top of his age group there.

I asked him, "What is the trick to accomplishing all that you have achieved physically?"

He responded, "Just don't stop. If it's running, keep going. If it's a swim, go. Keep the forward momentum going and don't stop until you cross the finish line."

I learned from him that I cannot allow the option to stop to exist for me. I tell myself, "I can slow down if I absolutely must, but I may not stop altogether."

This is great mental training for me. In life, things happen, and I may need to make a detour or slow down my pace for a time. When given careful consideration, that may be okay for a day or even a week. But stopping? That is out of the question. I must press forward. I live with the urgency of a tornado. Meetings and wasted time? Those I can barely endure. I know that life is urgent. I have seen it slip through the cracks all too easily, too soon, and too unannounced to think there exists an endless supply of days. Each one must be lived intentionally and deliberately. Wasting time gossiping, drinking, or bingeing on anything is not an option for me. I can't afford to spend my energy there. If I identify a problem, it has got to be addressed and extracted as a surgeon urgently removing an infected appendix. I cannot let if fester. I cannot deal with it tomorrow. I need it eradicated. I need my energy for the important tasks at hand.

I see this contrast most distinctly with my nine-year-old daughter. I can ask her to do something like get out of the tub. She will say, "I will." 'I will' can mean five minutes or fifty minutes. I have started to tell her, as I stand there with a towel for an undetermined amount of time, "This is my life. I can't afford to waste it. You have plenty of time, and that is great. I'm going to put your towel here so you can get out when you are ready, and I can use this time." While this may sound 'un-positive,' a word we use in our family, it's quite the opposite. In natural circumstances, a nine-year-old has more time ahead on planet Earth than a fifty-year-old. I am just looking that fact in the eye and asking myself, "Is it the best use of my time to stand here with a towel, frustrated, waiting for my daughter to exit the bathtub? Or might I see this as twenty to fifty precious minutes of my life and choose to spend them wisely?"

I have never understood when people say, "I have an hour to kill." What does that mean? Is your time so unlimited that you can afford to kill some of it off? The fact is that the answer is unknown. None of us know, for sure. Nothing is promised. As far as I am concerned, I got a second shot at this game of life. That is exactly one more than I bargained for. I am living on 'house money,' so I better spend it wisely. Every minute I am awake, I'm in it to win it.

When I run, I am right here in that present moment. I am sure I am doing the right thing with my time. I get 28 minutes in which I can be sure I am doing the right thing. Those 28 minutes inform the rest of my decisions and my entire day. It seems a small price tag for a great life.

I grab that nonnegotiable 3.15 miles and never look back.

"Success is not final; failure is not fatal: It is the courage to continue that counts." Winston Churchill

"Nothing in the world can take the place of persistence. Talent will not; nothing is more common than unsuccessful men with talent. Genius will not; unrewarded genius is almost a proverb. Education will not; the world is full of educated derelicts. The slogan 'Press On' has solved and always will solve the problems of the human race." Calvin Coolidge

"Brothers and sisters, I do not consider myself yet to have taken hold of it. But one thing I do: Forgetting what is behind and straining toward what is ahead, I press on toward the goal to win the prize for which God has called me heavenward in Christ Jesus." (Philippians 3: 13-14, NIV)

I Need A Miracle

MY SKATING CAREER began at six years old. The ice rink was my 'happy place.' I was thrilled to get out on the ice the second the Zamboni finished cleaning it. I stood there shivering and chomping at the bit to be the first to put my blade down on the glistening ice. I can still hear the tiny cracks being made in the smooth ice as the sharp metal traveled across it.

I loved the feeling of pressing down on the blades and skating fast. Doing back crossovers quickly makes a sound that I can only describe as strength, as the blades push into the ice to create momentum. Then there is the sound of the pick entering the ice before a jump. When the Winter Olympics were televised, I loved to listen to the ice. It talks as the skaters jump and spin. My favorite sound is that of a fast scratch spin. This leaves lower-case cursive e's etched into the ice. The closer the e's are to each other, the tighter and better the spin.

I had a very fast scratch spin and loved the spiral in which one leg is down and one leg is kicked up high, while gliding and doing something beautiful with your arms. On the ice, I was completely free. I could go as fast as I liked and stop on a dime.

Adjacent to the rink was an indoor area covered with carpet. There were large boxes covered with industrial carpet. We practiced our jumps from the boxes. It was easier to practice where falling on the industrial carpet was not soft, but at least we were not injured. In my teens, I began to have swelling in my knees. It was quite painful and could not really be eradicated. I saw many different doctors who failed to diagnose what was wrong. My mom took me to the best doctors in the city. The last orthopedic doctor I saw was one of the team doctors for the Kansas City Chiefs, who concluded that this was not an orthopedic issue. I was sent on to a doctor who specialized in the treatment of rheumatoid arthritis (R.A.). When we arrived at Dr. Cool's office, one thing was strikingly apparent: this was a disease of the elderly. As a teen, anyone above sixty was considered elderly in my book. The other patients were primarily using walkers or, worse, wheelchairs. I did not fit in. How could I have this disease? Wasn't I too young for this diagnosis?

Dr. Cool took several X-rays and determined that I had two major things working against me. The first was that I had scoliosis of my spine to such a degree that if it curved even one more degree, I would require a back brace. He took a string with a steel nut tied to the end. One end was tied to the top of the light box, showing the X-ray of my back. When the nut was dropped it pulled the string straight. "That is the line your spine should follow," he explained. My spine was closer to an S than a line. My mom wanted to try something else before jumping to a back brace. She took me to classes every Saturday. We called them Saturdays with Lola. I knew we did things such as learning to walk properly. We walked around with books on our heads. We did what I now know was yoga. We did exercises to strengthen our pelvic floors and gluteal muscles. My body and my spirit began to align. I was tapping into my spiritual being, who was healthy and well, although this is not what my body yet demonstrated.

Dr. Cool also shared the results from my bloodwork. I did indeed have rheumatoid arthritis (R.A.) causing my knees to constantly swell and become excruciatingly painful. Dr. Cool gave me the news that I would not be skating competitively that season, nor any other season in the foreseeable future. I was devastated, but I was also out of choices if I wanted to walk again without pain.

"What you have is juvenile mono-articular rheumatoid arthritis," he explained.

What that meant in English was I had this disease in my knees. The cure? There was no cure, only management, so I would begin taking twelve aspirin a day. I took a special kind called Ascriptin, as these were less likely to burn a hole in the lining of my stomach. I was to rest the leg that was hurting the worst by walking on crutches and using my best leg to do all the work. In about four weeks, the leg I rested felt better, but now weak. The other leg throbbed from overuse. I lived in this cycle, switching legs and staying on crutches for six or eight months at a time. The 'icing on the cake' was that I periodically needed to have the fluid drained off my knees. No deadening the area, just a large-bore needle stabbed into my knee. The fluid would pour out, and my knee would look normal again for what seemed only a moment. This became so routine that my mom would just drop me off at my appointments. On one occasion, Dr. Cool looked at my leg and said, "We need to drain it. Let's call your mom in and we will get started."

"My mom is not here," I replied.

"Who brought you?" he asked.

"My mom, but she is not waiting for me."

"Well, I guess we will begin without her," he submitted.

The pain was wicked. The nurse allowed me to hold her hand, and I knew I was squeezing it tightly once the needle was in. I am still grateful for her kindness.

One day, I went in feeling downtrodden. I looked at all the other people in the waiting room using walkers and wheelchairs. They did not look like they were going to beat this disease anytime soon. When I went out to get in the car with my mom, I decided to ask her a burning question. A question that I was scared to ask and scared not to ask. I pulled together all my courage and said, "Mom, I am going to die from this?"

"Die from this? No, not at all. You are going to get better," she confidently assured.

End of story. I believed my mom, not what I read in books or journals. Not what my doctor said. I knew if she said I was getting better, well, then I was. Mom never lied. I thank God for her unwavering belief. My parents decided to take me to visit my cousins in Dallas. Aunt Judy had five girls, so I had kids to hang out with. I think my parents thought it would cheer me up to see my cousins. However, it had the opposite effect.

I was crushed when a wheelchair greeted me at the Dallas airport. This was made worse by not having a cast or brace from which I could lay claim to a heroic soccer stop or daring ski run. No, outwardly ,I looked fine. People stared at me and said with their eyes, "Oh, that poor girl. I wonder what is wrong with her. Maybe it's a developmental problem. Maybe she was born that way, so sad." If I were going to have all eyes on me, I wanted it to be for something great, not this lame wheelchair. I was humiliated.

As a backdrop to what was happening with my knees, I was also insanely insecure in my freshman year in high school. I did not know who I was, nor did I grasp my own gifts and purpose. My goal was to be in with the popular crowd. It was as if my life depended on being a part of the 'inner circle.' I was willing to do anything to fit in, and that meant partying and drinking. This also helped me to blot out all the pain, both physical and emotional. My body seemed to be in the process of betraying me. One outcome of being struck with an illness as a child or teen is thinking it's not *supposed* to be this way. As a teen, I believed it was my right to be healthy. It was my right to have legs that worked and took me wherever I wanted. But that is not how God works, at least not in my experience. That is the thinking of entitlement, that I deserve this or that just because I exist. However, if there is less than a one in a trillion chance that I was ever even brought into existence, then really, do I need to cash in my 'I deserve this or that card'?

This is not to say that God gave me rheumatoid arthritis; He allowed it in his infinite wisdom. God sees the end from the beginning. He knows what we need and when we need it, even if we disagree. I had free will, and I had a part in my sickness. I was 'eating' Diet Coke for breakfast every day. Then, at lunch, I would have more Diet Coke and a package of HoHos. On the weekends, I lived on alcohol and ice cream. This was not helpful for my mind or body.

Now we know that alcoholism has both genetic and environmental precursors. This was certainly true in my case. There is a long line of alcoholics in my family, and it's being passed on to the younger generations at Mach speed. In my case, I acquired the genetic component both fraternally and maternally. My environment was chock-full of alcohol. We had a wine cellar with hundreds of bottles of wine. The main 'bar' in the house was locked, but one of my brothers revealed its location, and I was off to the races. Alcoholics in recovery are not bad people getting good, they are sick people getting well. I believed alcohol freed me from my psychological and physical discomfort, as nothing else would. Alcohol was the companion my loneliness embraced. I also believe it's a physical allergy. My first sip of wine was my first communion at age six. I became violently ill. My body was trying to tell me, "No more of this ever." But alcohol left me deaf to that still, small voice. As much as I hated alcohol, I wanted the effect of fearlessness and belonging that only alcohol gave me.

One time, Dr. Cool asked if I drank alcohol. I said, "Yes, just socially. I am a social drinker." Now, if my sixteen-year-old son told me he was just a 'social drinker,' it is likely he would earn a chair in rehab. Dr. Cool didn't say anything more about this. Why did he ask? Was my bloodwork off? He could have at least said, "Do you know that is illegal and that it's toxic for your body?" I would learn much later that alcohol is a toxin processed by the liver. Ongoing alcohol abuse causes fatty liver disease and ultimately liver failure. It was a problem I was not going to address on my own, and his silence gave me a free pass for the time being.

For a trained medical professional to ignore the alcohol consumption by any patient, and especially a teenager, is negligent, or, at best, careless. The World Health Organization explains that as the alcohol breaks down, it's harming the body. For me, the harms of what I was ingesting, along with my insecurities, depression, and anxiety, gave me an autoimmune disease called rheumatoid arthritis.

For better or worse, I did not have the luxury of looking up this diagnosis on the internet. Now that I do, I still have not studied it beyond what was required in medical school, and I don't want to. I don't want to be informed on all the studies and possible pitfalls out there. I was my own study of one. My 'World Health Organization' was my mom.

She said I would get better, so I would. That was the fact. I did not need to look up eighteen articles and watch YouTube. I had to tap into something far greater than a doctor's prognosis. Job one was to put down the alcohol. It was killing me, however slowly. I needed to set down the alcohol and Twinkies to hear God's voice. Medical science and twelve aspirin every day cannot tell me what the Divine purpose is for my life. No, for that kind of direction,

I needed to go to the Source of all healing and all knowledge. I needed to let go of the alcohol and soberly receive my inner guidance for healing. However, I also needed to hit rock bottom, and I was on my way there.

When my mom told me that I would get better, I believed her. I trusted her entirely and did not let any other thoughts about future negative possibilities enter my mind. I focused on a cure, although one did not and still does not exist. I had to find other people who had healed without medical explanation. I read Louise Hay's book, *You Can Heal Your Life,* where she cured herself from incurable cancer. I embraced the mantras I learned there, saying them daily.

I listened to stories of people we knew who had been healed from every possible malady. One that stuck with me was our family friend, Libby. She was diagnosed with pancreatic cancer. The recommendation for her was extensive chemo and radiation. She had the boldness to say, "No, thank you. I am going home, and I will get better." That is precisely what she did. My mom explained to me that Libby had incredible faith and prayer alone kept her in daily health. Libby lived another ten years. Five years of survival after diagnosis is considered a cure in the world of cancer.

These are the people I focused on, ones who had overcome the odds, where it appeared that all hope was lost. I began listening to healing meditations as I drifted off to sleep. I put my cassette tape player on the ground, next to my head. Night after night, I heard, "All is well. All is well in your world…" I had to train my brain to think like a healthy person and take the actions of a healed person. I was laser-focused on what I could do, not what I was not yet able to do. If all I could do was walk around one block with this pain, then I did it. Then I went two and four blocks, and so on. I started to eat healthy foods. I learned to look in the refrigerator and pray:

God, help me intuitively know what to eat and drink today to keep my body healthy. Help me make the choices you would have me make as I select my food. Thank you for healing my body.

I realized that I would not put a bunch of trash in the tank of my car and hope it would run efficiently. The same was true for my body. Food equaled fuel, it was that simple, and what I ate determined my day. I could not afford a broken-down body any longer.

As I created beliefs of health and healing, my own body followed suit. I was released from the crutches. I was not overly jubilant because I had been released from them before and had been forced to take them up again. This time, my right leg was so weak from lack of use that I hobbled along. I had a limp that could be spotted a mile away. This is where my dad came up with a genius plan. We had season tickets to the Kansas City Royals. Back in those days, the stadium had a glassed-in area called appropriately the Royal's Stadium Club. It included upscale dining on prime rib, grilled chicken, salad bar, beautifully prepared pastas and vegetables, along with dessert. My favorite dessert was a Napolitan dessert that had layers of chocolate cake alternating with pink and white filling. I wouldn't touch it today, but loved it then. You could take the escalator straight up to the stadium club, and that is what most people did. Or you could walk up via the twisting ramps that led up to all the levels of stadium seating. Dad would walk closely beside me in the parking lot, trying to give me a gait to follow for 'normal' walking. He would occasionally bend down and whisper in my ear, "You don't want all these people thinking you are crippled, do you?" As a teenager enslaved to what others thought of me, this was the perfect fear-driven technique to get me to walk 'correctly.'

At Kaufmann stadium we had four seats inside the club and four seats outside for each game.

Many times, we would go to the stadium club to eat, and then I would beg Dad to take me to the outside seats. They were behind home plate. There are two levels in the field section, and we were in the first row of the second section. I did not appreciate those seats with a perfect view of the field like I do today. Like many special blessings, I can see them in hindsight. I realize how precious they are when they no longer exist, and this homeplate view of Royals Baseball was one of these.

My insistence on going outside, even in the summer heat, gave me a tremendous view of every single batter and many steps of walking practice. Over that summer, Dad took me to game after game. I overcame a limp that was so ingrained that I was not even aware it existed. I learned to walk normally again. I was able to walk and play tennis that summer. There was hope.

I examined my knees every single night before going to bed. I felt my patella, longing for the reassurance of feeling only the curvature of the bone and none of the distortion of swelling and inflammation. I searched for the slightest evidence of inflammation. Only then, satisfied that I bought freedom from RA for another day, did I drift off to sleep, saying the rosary.

Sadly, I began to feel the pain and swelling returning to my knees. I dreaded the sound of Dr. Cool's ballpoint pen as he drew blue Xs on my knee that showed where the needle was to puncture my skin. The large-bore syringe would fill again and again. Dr. Cool and the nurses marveled at the amount of yellow fluid they removed from my joints. While the needle remained in my leg, I did not make a sound or shed a tear, although the pain was excruciating. I would sometimes break out in a sweat. I told myself, "No use crying. It's not like that would keep them from doing this procedure." I knew that any drama on my part would only prolong the time it took to be done. I wanted to be back in Mom's Honda Accord, heading home. I set my sights on the completion of the draining marked by the sweet removal of the needle from my leg. The payoff was a pain-free use of my legs for an undetermined amount of time. By the grace of God, these unpleasant treatments became farther and farther apart. By my freshman year of college, I ran with regularity and was enjoying a problem-free time with my knee joints.

Yet I continued to pour the toxin of alcohol into my body. I was 100% convinced that I needed alcohol. It was the only way to have fun. It gave me the freedom to talk to people. With alcohol, I believed I was funny and charming. Drinking was my way to escape pain and suffering. *None of that was true, but the disease of alcoholism told me these lies.*

At age twenty, I put the drink down and have not picked it back up since.

If I can put alcohol down one day at a time for over 30 years, then so can you. Junior year came, and I was running in a different kind of race, for the President of the Undergraduate Government at Boston College. In my typical fashion, I went all out for this. My wonderful friends made every effort to make this happen. We met in the middle of the night to spray paint sheets and hang them in the quad the next day. I worked tirelessly to keep up with my studies and canvassed every single dorm room on the entire campus to ask for votes. When I was down to one week before the election, my knees started swelling again. I was forced to abandon my nightly campaigning and instead rest my knees. I didn't have a rheumatologist in Boston. However, Dr. Cool set me up with one of the best at Mass General, the first and largest teaching hospital of Harvard University.

My boyfriend, Alex, went with me on the harrowing errand where my knee was drained and injected with steroids. The doctor instructed that there would be no walking on that leg for at least a couple of days, including the flight of stairs to my second-floor apartment. "Would you be able to carry her up there?" The doctor inquired of Alex, and he agreed. I was grateful that Alex stopped with me to pick up my medications. These acts of caring helped me in my time of need.

No act of love or kindness is ever wasted.

Immediately following graduation from Boston College, I began a year of volunteer work with the Sisters of Elizabeth Ann Seton. By this time, I was sober and really didn't know what I wanted to do with my life. I definitely felt I needed to give back to the world for all the times I was less than my best in my drinking. I lived in a convent with twelve nuns, which is a book in itself. All the nuns and volunteers worked in Catholic elementary and grade schools in the New Jersey Area. Our neighborhood was not particularly safe, so I ran inside the Catholic high school next door to the convent. After being a runner for most of the previous six years, I needed to run for my sanity as much as for my health. Again, my knees began to flare with familiar aches and pains.

One of the sisters was able to direct me to a rheumatologist in the area. The doctor came into the room and said, "I am sure your knees may be hurting, but we are not sure why you are here." I looked at him quizzically, and he continued, "You don't have rheumatoid arthritis. You don't have any markers for it in your bloodwork. Are you sure you had rheumatoid arthritis? Maybe you need to check back with your doctor to see if that was your diagnosis. Either way, it may be something that can be addressed surgically. My nurse will give you a referral to a surgeon who can take a look at it for you."

I can tell you with complete certainty that I did not need to revisit my diagnosis with Dr. Cool or my doctor at Harvard. There was no question that from twelve to twenty-one, I had rheumatoid arthritis. Laboratory results announcing the absence of this villain were welcome news. Was this the miracle cure I was praying for all these years?

I gladly left the doctor's office with my X-rays in hand and went to see the surgeon he recommended. In medical school, years later, I learned two mottoes of surgeons. The first was, "Surgeons cut." Meaning that if you go to a surgeon, they are going to be ready to cut you, it's what they do. Just like if you go to an herbalist, you will get teas. I have rarely been to a surgeon who did not want to directly schedule a procedure. Another mantra of rising doctors on the surgery rotation was, "When in doubt, cut it out." The surgeon I saw was much the same. He had zero bedside manner as he talked at me, not to me.

He briefly looked at my knee and said, "We are going to go in and clean up that joint laparoscopically. It's a straightforward procedure. We will just see if cleaning it up helps it feel better. My nurse will schedule with you. See you then."

I wanted to say, "I don't even know you. I would not have a cup of coffee with you, much less let you cut open my knee and 'clean it out.'"

When the nurse pulled up the schedule to find a date for my surgery, I said, "I'll pass." I could not get out of that office fast enough. I trusted the uncomfortable feeling in my gut that told me to leave and never go back. That was precisely what I did.

When I returned to the convent, one of the sisters told me about her doctor, Dr. Haven, and suggested I make an appointment. As it turns out, Dr. Haven had *invented* the artificial knee joint. I could not have set this up if I tried. This time I did not have my X-rays with me, as I had accidentally left them with the previous surgeon. I was interested to see what Dr. Haven would glean strictly from examination without images. It's more challenging to ascertain what's going on without films. Dr. Haven did not disappoint.

He said, "You don't have your films? We may not need them. Let me look at your knees."

Dr. Haven talked *with* me about my exercise routines and examined my knees. "Well, I understand that you don't have rheumatoid arthritis. You also do not need surgery. What you need to do is strengthen the muscles around the knee joint to support the stress you are putting on this joint as you pound the pavement."

Finally, this plan made sense to me, and I followed the doctor's recommendations of daily strengthening exercises. I was able to start running again, building up slowly. I started with five-kilometer races, then ten kilometers, then ten miles, and half marathons. I have completed several triathlons as a team and individually. Currently, I run at least thirty-five to forty kilometers a week, depending on my other training demands.

Sometimes I will encourage one of my kids to run, and they will say, "I don't really feel like running today. I think I'm going to skip it." They say this casually. For me, I consider running a privilege and a gift, as I remember when I was shackled to that wheelchair and the years of on and off crutches.

After all, the National Health Service in the United Kingdom states, "There is no cure for rheumatoid arthritis." One of the prominent researchers in the treatment of RA said, "Remission is attainable for a good number of people – if you get diagnosed early and treated aggressively – *but sustaining a drug-free remission for more than a year or so is unlikely.*"

What do I make of my over thirty years without a trace of RA? A miracle of God. I believe God blessed me with a total cure because all things are possible with God. God is in the business of performing miracles: it's what He does. My healing was extraordinary to me, but effortless for God.

I was deeply grateful for my gift. I began seeking a deeper relationship with Jesus. Now, I knew His infinite power and love personally.

I was told, "If you want to know Christ better, read the Gospels and pay special attention to the words in red; they belong to Christ." I began reading the gospels continuously. Matthew, Mark, Luke, John, Matthew, Mark, Luke, John, Matthew... Each time, God showed me something different. Each time, I learned more about the essence of Jesus Christ. I found His love for me was beyond comprehension, and it brings me to tears even as I write. I realized that He died on the cross for me. Jesus did this for me; He suffered unimaginably for *me*.

"Hope is like the sun, which, as we journey toward it, casts the shadow of our burden behind us." Samuel Smiles

"By His wounds you have been healed." (1 Peter 2:24)

"Heal me, Lord, and I will be healed; save me and I will be saved." (Jeremiah 17:14)

FOR WOMEN ONLY

THE DANGERS THAT exist for women are real. At eighteen, I began traveling alone to college in Boston. Airports, bus stops, subway rides, cab rides, and walking in the dark were included in my journey. One of my travels back to Boston College from Kansas City after Thanksgiving break stands out. My habit was to land in Boston, get my bags, and go directly to get a cab back to school. At this point in my life, I was wearing expensive clothing, carrying luxury brand suitcases, and intent on looking my best.

On this evening, I exited the airport and hailed a cab. One cab quickly pulled over, and the driver jumped out and rapidly threw my bag in the trunk. Immediately, I felt uncomfortable. If this happened today, I would simply say, "I need my bag back, thank you." However, at this point in my life, I was very much a people pleaser. I did not yet have the voice of a clear and confident woman that I enjoy being today. I thought, what would this person think of me if I don't take his cab? What would that look like? I don't want to hurt his feelings. I learned later that if you are a woman and your intuition says to run, do it. It's your body, mind, and soul trying to protect you. But at age 21, I didn't have the words to express my needs and take care of myself.

Now it was late at night, and the sky was a dark shade of gunmetal grey. The driver was radioing in another language and talking to another man. After a few minutes, we cut off the main highway and onto unfamiliar roads. This was odd because I had made this trip countless times. I was growing more and more nervous with the unfamiliar surroundings. I squirmed uncomfortably in the back seat. Finally, he said, "I am stopping for gas over here." We drove so far away from any main roads that it seemed an eternity before we got to the gas station. There were no big buildings, nor residential areas of Boston, that were familiar to me. All was dark and quiet except for his voice talking to the man on his radio. We came to a stop. I knew I had no escape. Where would I run? There were no other stores, houses, or anything. We had driven for miles on a dark, two-lane road. Was he going to attack me and leave me here hurt, or worse?

I immediately took out my cell phone. It was the early 90, so there was no Life 360, no tracking devices. My phone was dead, so I just pretended. I faked calling my roommates. I said I was on my way home and that I would be there in 15 minutes. I described over the phone, to the silence, about how strong my boyfriend and all his friends were. I talked about how they were waiting for me and wondering what was taking so long. I promised to arrive there promptly. I spoke loud enough that I was sure the driver heard every detail. It was then that he radioed the other man again. He started the car and took me home.

To this day, I still vividly see his face; I believe something was very wrong. I don't know if it was my fake conversation or the prayers of my mother or both that got me home safely. I thank

God. Sadly, this was one of many instances of poor decision-making on my part.

Another time, I was sober, attending Pratt Institute for my MFA, and living in New York. The dangers for a single woman, lost and alone, are even more real. I met Giovanni in an art gallery. He was from Italy, and in New York on a grant he received to study art. The award included a gorgeous condo in New York along with a stipend and travel expenses. Giovanni asked if I wanted to go look at a few more galleries with him. I was planning on going to a few shows in Soho that day, so I agreed. He was quite charming, well-dressed, and well-versed in the arts. Toward the end of the day, he asked me to join him for dinner. He talked all about the view from his condo, and how it provided the backdrop for a gorgeous painting. I am a trusting person, and I was also a naïve twenty-something. We made the journey to midtown to see this 'view' from his condo.

As we walked toward his building, it all looked completely legit. It was a beautiful building with a doorman wearing a black coat and white button-down shirt as he opened the door for us. "See, there," I thought, "This guy is not some mass murderer. I am sure the doorman would do something if he didn't see me again soon." Well, I learned that is just 100% wrong. Doormen are not looking out for young women who enter with male residents. Quite the opposite, they are paid to look the other way and mind their own business.

When we walked into his condo, it did not disappoint. The view of New York City lit up at night was breathtaking. But that was not the only breathtaking topic Giovanni had in mind. He soon made it clear that he had brought me here to have sex with him. I panicked. The front door was a dark, thick wood with a big silver bolt lock. I went toward it. But I was no match for Giovanni's frame, which stood between me and the door. Behind me and to the right was another sleek, dark, wooden door with a silver handle. He told me, "Relax, you just need to relax." He pushed me back into the door, and it swung open to reveal a stunning white and silver bathroom. Once we were in there, he handed me a robe. It was thick and dark like his sudden turn in mood. Giovanni pressed the robe to my chest and said, "Here, why don't you take a nice, hot shower and relax?"

"No, really, I don't want to shower. I want to go," I insisted. Turning, he exited the bathroom and closed the door behind him. Giovanni was too strong, too big, and too forceful. What on earth was I going to do? Suddenly, headlines flashed before my eyes: "Woman found dead in luxury midtown condo." I was a dead woman walking, and I knew it. He was going to rape me and kill me, no question. I had to get out of there. But where? There were no windows in the bathroom. There was no phone. I didn't even have my bag with me in there. The doorman was not going to protect me. What kind of stupid idiot would think such a thing anyway? I asked myself.

An urgent message broke through my thoughts, repeating, "I've got to get out. I've got to get out. I've got to get out." Okay, my only hope was to get to the door. Clearly, I did not have the strength to push through him. I had to be at the door first and I needed to buy some time for my plan to work. I needed to make him think I was going along with his instructions if he was going to let his guard down. I opened the shower door and turned the water on to make it sound like I was getting in. I waited and assured myself he was not going to be in front of the door the next time I opened it. I kept the shower running. I prayed. I panicked; I prayed some more. All of this happened within about five to ten minutes. Then I decided to make a run for it. The plan was to get to the door, rush out, and immediately go over to the elevator. Once in that hall, I would be safe. I could make a racket and hope someone came out in the hall. I cracked the bathroom door ever so quietly. Peering out the crack, I could see that the main door was unguarded. Everything needed to be faster than the blink of an eye, so I dashed across to the door. Instantly, Giovanni was there, protesting and trying to pull me back. I flew to the elevator and somehow got it shut before he was able to stop me. I ran through the lobby, by the silent doorman, and down the street, never looking back. My next thoughts battled between shaming myself and thanking God I had escaped unharmed.

A few years later, I met Vicki in AA. She drove a Jeep. I was sitting in the passenger seat, attempting to find something in the center console. That's when I saw it, Vicki had a gun in her car. I was shocked that she was 'packing heat.' I asked her, "Why do you have a gun in here?"

"It's for protection. You may not know it, but I was kidnapped."

"No way! What happened?"

"I was grabbed and thrown into the back of a van. They blindfolded me and bound my hands and feet. The only thing I could do was talk, so I did talk, lots of it. I told them all about my family, my niece and nephews, my parents, anything to humanize me. Eventually, they let me go. I believe it was because I spoke so much about my parents and how they would be destroyed if anything ever happened to me."

I was suddenly back in my drinking days, going to Westport, the site of many of my major sprees. On this occasion, I went out with my cousins. There was a bartender that I was infatuated with, so I proceeded to do what I thought was best: get very drunk. After hours of dancing and drinking, my cousins were going home. I told them, "I'll stay. I can find a ride." They made sure and double sure I was fine with this plan. So as the bar was closing, I made it clear to Mike, the bartender, that I needed a ride home. Mike agreed to this plan. He knew how much I had been drinking. Saying I was wasted is an understatement. The next thing I remember is that he was not taking me home at all. We were going to his place.

That was my pattern. Staying out too late, getting wasted, trusting untrustworthy men to get me home safely. I'm not a victim, but a volunteer, as they say. I have a huge part in this and likely gave this man the wrong idea. Violence against women is at all times unacceptable and cannot be overlooked.

When we arrived at his place, I was struck sober. What was I doing here, and how could I get home? Keep in mind, this is before cell phones were a thing. I had no way to communicate with anyone but Mike. It was clear what he wanted. I just wanted to go home, desperately so now. Previously, I learned from Oprah what to do in an abduction scenario. Oprah had shared many wise things for women in these circumstances. She interviewed a woman who had been abducted. The woman, Joanna, was walking in a dark parking garage, alone, late at night. She saw a man who was also walking to his car. Joanna felt uneasy about him, although she did not know why. It was just an inner feeling that this situation was unsafe, that *he* was unsafe. Did she run to her car as fast as possible? No, she told herself how offensive and ridiculous that would be and listened to her brain. It told her, "Joanna, get a hold of yourself. What is wrong with you? Do you want that guy to think you are crazy? Do you want to totally offend him by looking ridiculous and sprinting to your car? Just calm down." Before she could finish her thought, his hand was over her mouth, and she was being dragged to a nearby van.

Oprah told the terrified viewers, "As women, we are intuitive. If you get the feeling that something isn't right, you need to trust that gut feeling and run. It does not matter if you offend someone. If you're right, you may just save your life. If you are wrong, oh well. You cannot worry about offending anyone. This is your life we are talking about."

Oprah offered a list of women who experienced this very same sense of danger and ignored it. The things that happened to these women were tragic. I have already taught my eight-year-old daughter to trust that feeling. I do this by telling her, "I just have a bad feeling about that. I trust my intuition." Maybe we walk a different route or leave a location promptly. I have explained to her, "We have feelings inside that are trying to speak to us and protect us. When we have those feelings, we need to respect them, listen, and take appropriate action. Don't worry about hurting the other person's feelings. God will take care of them. That is not our responsibility; our responsibility is to take care of ourselves."

In my situation with Mike, I did what Oprah had advised. I humanized myself. I talked about my family. I made up this bogus story that I was going riding early that morning. I pretended I still thought the best of him and told him he could come ride, too. I told Mike all about my three very protective brothers and how they would be very concerned about me by this time of night (really morning now, close to 3:00 am). I described them in detail, their size, stature, and temperaments. I didn't need to make anything up here. They were all tall and well-built, and I told Mike as much. After what seemed like hours, Mike finally agreed to take me home. What was the tipping point at which he made his decision? I'll never know. I don't know what will work for you, just that something will.

My mom told me of a woman in New York City who was being chased down an alley by a strange man. All she could think of was the Bible verse that said, "He will cover you with his feathers, and under his wings you will find refuge; his faithfulness will be your shield and rampart." (Psalm 91:4 NIV)

She began screaming, "Feathers, feathers, I'm covered in feathers," while flapping her arms like wings. The man began to think she was insane, and soon she was alone in the alley. We don't know what our saving grace will be. I encourage you to trust what your mind and body tell you.

I want all women to know that if you are ever in this sort of predicament, you must never give up. My escape from these situations is more the exception than the rule. If you were physically, emotionally, or spiritually harmed, I am truly sorry. It is not your fault. I know women who did their absolute best but did not escape. I hope you are without shame and judgement for yourself. Any violence against women is always unacceptable and cannot be overlooked.

The important thing now is that you receive the help and support you need to work through your trauma and heal. For every woman, it's important to have an emergency plan in place that you can execute to keep yourself safe. Travel in numbers and ask for help. I commonly ask security guards and police officers to walk me to my car in dark parking lots. On most college campuses, you can call for an escort. I am asking for someone to do their job, and that is okay. I used those in medical school when I crossed campus late at night. Part of taking care of yourself is availing yourself of possible sources of protection. I am not embarrassed when I do this. I cannot tell you how many dark parking lots I sprinted through in my teens and twenties, and still do when I feel it's necessary.

In any circumstance, have a plan to ensure you will see your friends and family again. Be certain that you will find a way or that God will make a way for you to get out. When He does, take it. Run, fight, kick, and do whatever you need to do to get out. Act. If you can talk, talk. If you can run, run. Be persistent and fearless. If I can escape, so can you. Tell friends, moms, sisters, and daughters what to do in this situation. For having the courage to do so, you might save a life.

"Although the world is full of suffering, it is also full of the overcoming of it." Helen Keller

"You intended to harm me, but God intended it for good to accomplish what is now being done, the saving of many lives". (Genesis 50:20, NIV)

"If you say, 'The Lord is my refuge,' and you make the Most High your dwelling, no harm will overtake you, no disaster will come near your tent. For he will command his angels concerning you to guard you in all of your ways." (Psalm 91:9-11 NIV

Hold Me Tight

THE MORE HE PUSHED, the more I resisted. I was determined to make it without you. I did not want to depend on *you* to make me feel okay. I refused to need you. I wanted to silence you on my own, so I ran harder, swam faster, and prayed longer. The thought of needing you was repulsive. I was worried that I would be stuck with you forever in a sick codependent relationship. A relationship based on fear and need, not freedom and choice. I did not want you to dominate me, the me I worked so hard to attain. I thought I would become a quiet, passionless, and unmotivated wallflower. The thought of it disgusted me. So, as two powerful and parallel lines we lived, never intersecting. I made you *all* bad. But in life, the extreme is rarely the truth. Yes, there exists a vicious dog, but also a benevolent one. The stronger one is the one I feed.

All the while, I was repressing the voice that knew I needed you. The scary part? If you were the last stop and even you were unable to help, then what? That defined hopeless, so I chose fighting over despair. I would rather be angry than feel emptiness inside. Yet, I have long held that anger is a cheap shot, delaying confrontation of the real pain underneath. My brain will divert and divert and divert my attention to keep from confronting the truth right in front of me. The longer I deflected, the more the neighborhood in my head dilapidated. Paint chipped, toilets flooded, and entire floors buckled. A rundown area cannot thrive again without effort, intention, work, and a plan for going forward successfully. This was also the case with my necrotic headspace.

My self-destructive thoughts were spiraling out of control. I lived in a state of overwhelm. I kept myself in constant motion like a spinning top. Like that top, I succumbed to friction, loss of momentum, and not until I collapsed, motionless, did I stop. The banter of my brain presented me with a smorgasbord of self-sabotaging story lines. My thoughts felt intolerable and antithetical to my entire belief system. In the words of one of my favorite counselors, "That is so painful!"

I was desperate, but it wasn't until the young ones started speaking about it that I knew it owned me, and I needed your help, no question.

The littlest one would look at me and say, "Mommy is sad today." There was no denying her observation. She saw the tears running down my face. She read the anguish in my expression. She was so tiny, but she knew the truth. It's common to hear the truth from the mouths of babes, and this was no exception.

I wanted to say, "No, Mommy is good," as I wiped away the tears, but I resisted. Lies only add another layer of dysfunction to a damaged system. I was *not* fine, not at all.

I told my baby girl, "Yes, I am sad," because what was the point of denying her ability to read me? I refused to say, "No, I'm fine," and let her feel like *she* was the crazy one. This 'mommy is sad' scenario played out daily, like the hurt of a thorn puncturing my skin as I grabbed for my beautiful bouquet of life.

Then came the eldest. I didn't know he was suffering because he is my understated, brilliant, peacemaker with a heart of gold. But not even he was able to quell the relentless pushing, pushing, pushing of my disease. So, like an unwilling fighter, backed into a corner, against the ropes, in self-defense, he threw a crushing blow. He told me how he hated the disease and what it made of me. He wanted to be far from me, and he would get there as soon as possible.

His display of bravery and resilience saved my life. I only had love for him. But like a rancid cup of old milk, this illness tainted my nourishing love. Making it unrecognizable to my own beloved son.

This was unacceptable.

I needed you now, so I asked for you, only to be told I was 'fine.' I didn't have the energy to explain further. It was hard enough mentioning my life slowly being strangled by thoughts. If this professional was unable to see me gasping for air, I would not waste my little remaining oxygen trying to prove it. I walked out of the office, dismayed, starting to turn purple from lack of O2 saturation. Black spots started forming in front of my vision. I was fading into utter darkness.

"I can't let this happen," I told myself. I need help.

I dragged myself across the floor to the phone. I would make one last call, one last try to get you, now my only hope. It took me an entire appointment to mention you. Even then, I minimized the misery of a life hijacked by depression and anxiety. I said I could take you or leave you. I'd be 'fine' either way. She was ready to dismiss me, and I saw myself sinking deeper into quicksand in my brain. With darkness falling, time was running out, so I stopped short of the door. I said I'd give you a try. What did I have to lose? Everything, but I was out of options, so I surrendered.

I would become your slave if I needed to. I bowed to you every morning, and in response to my worship, you executed your job.

You brought me back from the edge and performed your work quickly and meticulously, like the hand of a skilled surgeon extracting a tumor. I was grateful for you and your provision. For all my resistance, I found I needed you. There, I said it, and there was no shame in it. Just as a diabetic needs insulin or a broken bone needs casting, I needed you. No judgment. I was ill, and you were my crucial cure.

We got along swimmingly. If I were consistent with you, you were consistent with me. We worked in sync, the illness receded, and health returned to my mind. All was well for many years. I thanked God for you.

But there was a catch.

Along with the utter darkness, you took the brightest lights in my sky. I no longer fell into the unexpected hole leading to the sewer. However, the satisfying summit at the top of the mountain was also denied to me. It was as if I walked continuous switchbacks across the middle of a mountain. I no longer descended into the muck and mire. I also was denied the beauty of the mountain top. As I lost the anguish of the freezing nights, I lost the warmth of pure sunshine. There is one point in the day that has always felt strange to me: dusk. It's no longer light and not quite dark. It lies in some bizarre in-between place that holds the beauty of neither. It's neither terrible nor wonderful. It just is. It exists as neither hot nor cold but is as exciting as soggy cereal.

Another cost of having you was the extra tax you charged. With this charge, you stole my energy, leaving me depleted. Not just a bit sleepy, but stop-in-your-tracks and go-no-further exhaustion. This wave would completely knock on my behind into the sand. Again, I needed you, so I accepted the inconvenience of a sandy suit as the price I paid to keep you in my life. I didn't blab about your downsides, and I did not want you to go away. Far from not wanting to need you, I *knew* I did; the spoils of victory would be yours for almost ten years.

Finally, I mentioned the exhaustion and took the suggestion to move your assistance from morning to night. Only the unexpected happened. I felt wonderful. I didn't miss you at all or even notice your absence. Night came, and I went to bed peacefully without you. Days started to pass like this. My energy returned, and exhaustion left. My emotions were more present, but instead of feeling like dying, I felt more alive than ever. I feared the monstrous dark thoughts would seize me, but I was untouched by them. The dogging barks were silent. I did not tell anyone of my newfound freedom, fearing it would suddenly evaporate if I shared it. Like a wish that would not come true if I told anyone. But I knew that was a fallacy.

My health did not arrive by fortune cookies and fairy dust. It's the product of twenty-nine years of consistent, not perfect, effort. Research now illustrates that neural pathways have plasticity. This is excellent news to anyone who has a brain. This wonderful organ can now change and adapt. One way to change that hard wiring is to exercise with intense physical exertion. And two of the top contenders? Running and swimming, my loves. Further, prayer, meditation, continued personal growth, and service are foundational to me. All of these are protective for mental health. Why did my healing come as such a shock? I must have forgotten about miracles. I thought I used all mine up. There were already cures, healthy babies, and numerous diverted tragedies. I accepted this illness was my forever cross. For years I prayed the self-damning thoughts would be lifted out of me. On my knees, I cried out to God for his protection and healing. The thoughts trudged on day after relentless day. I assumed this was an unanswered prayer. Was I angry with God? Of course not, if He allows it, it's ultimately for my good. After all, suffering is the surest way I know to His heart. It's within the suffering that I must reach for the protection of my Father. With Him I am loved so that I may endure and even find joy in my suffering.

However, I dismissed a crucial factor: time.

The fact is that I am bound to earthly time, which is arbitrary in God's perfect and eternal world. I think the healing took forty tough years. It was my own personal journey to the promised land. In God's eyes, this is a second in eternity. Now I see that the passage was perfect. As my mom likes to say, "No pain is ever everlasting." My wellness was not a fluke but a miraculous result and blessing stemming from my commitment to grit and God.

I'm not encouraging anyone to quit medications, especially without speaking with a doctor. This can be dangerous and life-threatening. I want you to know, stopping this medication came to me unintentionally. Initially, I forgot to take my medication. In the past, my brain felt this sudden shift and that served as a reminder for me that I needed help. However, on this occasion, those feelings were absent. I felt good, and even better than I felt in a long time. I stayed on this trajectory for a while, and I was elated.

However, I did notice the struggle rearing its ugly head again in my brain. I started resenting the people in my life who were 'forcing' me back onto meds with their bad behavior. This went on for a period of time. I ended up realizing it did not matter how 'they' acted. What I needed to feel good about was *my* actions and *my* words. I brought one of my boys to tears with my sharp words one morning. He was devastated by my tone, and it made him feel worthless. This is not the person I could allow myself to be. No matter how much I loved my reclaimed passions and soul-stirring emotions, I needed to allow my mind reprieve so I would not hurt anyone I loved.

A thought was introduced to my black and white mind. It was the idea that maybe I could go on a different medication or a different dose. I am delighted that I found a new normal. It's one I can embrace and feel good about myself and my interactions with others. I realized I was trying to be like some very faithful friends I have who have abandoned their medications. It rarely serves me to compare and despair. I need to live my journey and my truth. I judged that maybe my faith was not good enough or strong enough. This, I don't believe. My mind is made by God, and I trust what I need to keep it well. I firmly believe God uses people to accomplish tasks. He uses people to make all sorts of amazing medications that heal many diseases. For all that is, I am thankful.

I still believe that I have encountered a miracle of healing. In recovery, I have been restored to sanity as only God can accomplish.

I am rejoicing because God granted me yet *another* miracle of healing, this time in my mind. I kept myself accountable and told several people close to me. I asked them to let me know if they noticed anything out of character in my behavior. I have a rock-solid commitment to do whatever is needed to maintain my mental well-being. No more pretending I'm fine. No more suffering like a martyr trying to do it on my own. No, there are no points for style in maintaining health.

For today, since I need medicine, I will take it without shame or guilt because that is the smart thing to do.

I am explaining this because after two major depressive episodes, and I have had more than two, the DSM (Diagnostic and Statistical Manual of Mental Disorders) recommends staying on an antidepressant. This is where I find myself now.

My healing is still rare and miraculous. Healing can mean the disease no longer exists. However, frequently with mental illnesses, healing can mean the ability to recognize what is needed to live a healed life and to take action in that direction. I cannot tell you why God has chosen to bless me in this way, only that He has willed it for me, and I gratefully receive it. That is an awesome responsibility in my eyes. I want to shout from the housetops about what God has done for me. Since this is not Jerusalem in thirty-three A.D. I shout from these pages. I am so grateful for my illogically blessed life. My major illnesses did not follow protocol; they followed the benevolent will of God.

This is not to say that if illness remains for you or me, God has discounted us. I don't believe in a vending machine God where I can press a button, and what I want simply drops down in a tray, although God can do that, too. I need to stay open to miracles and always accept God's will.

I used to read my Bible as a young person and think, *Why did God do all the cool stuff then? Of course, people would believe if they saw the lame walk, the blind healed, and the dead raised.* I now believe that miracles are more about the eyes that behold them than the occurrences themselves. This is a time, where those without legs walk. Many of the blind do once again see. We have paddles and electrodes to raise the dead. Didn't Jesus Himself tell us we would do greater things than even He?

> *Very truly I tell you, whoever believes in me will do the works I have been doing, and they will do even greater things than these, because I am going to the Father. And I will do whatever you ask in my name, so that the Father may be glorified in the Son. You may ask me for anything in my name, and I will do it. (NIV, John 14:12-14).*

As I see it, the problem is not the lack of miracles, but my inability to recognize their commonplace form. Glasses and contacts for vision, running water and soap for hygiene, antibiotics to cure illnesses, speeding cars, planes defying gravity, oxygen tanks for breathing, pacemakers for beating hearts, medications to control high blood pressure, cholesterol inhibitors, fat absorption blockers, and organ replacements. There are plenty of miracles occurring perpetually. God keeps producing these wonders. I fail to see them.

Healing from a forty-year-long depression is unlikely. You can call it a fluke or a coincidence, but as I tell my kids, "This is for believers, and that's you." The 'scales' have fallen from *my* eyes, and I am endlessly grateful.

I love you, God. Thank you. I love you.

So, why this lavish outpouring of miracles in my life? While I can't say for sure, I believe it's at least in part, so I can share and give you hope. These incredible happenings are to demonstrate *God's power through* me and not visa-versa. God did not bless me because I am a flawless follower. On the contrary, God uses the weak and broken to confound the powerful and strong. I openhandedly received my blessings with the trust of a child. No one is beyond the grasp of God's hand.

I am grateful and I feel amazing! I feel the best I ever remember feeling physically, mentally, and spiritually. I'm running faster and feeling better in my body. Mentally, I feel strong and positive. I'm not taking things so seriously. I hear myself laughing more. I laugh with you or at me with equal pleasure. My sponsor, Diane, used to tell me, "They say to wear life like a loose garment. You are wearing it like a strait jacket. You've got to lighten up."

Finally, I am light and free. When things occur that I can't control or change, I say, "Oh well, what next?"

I have internalized my mom warmly saying with a wink, "Don't sweat the small stuff, and remember it's all small stuff." Deep inside, I believe there is nothing to worry about. I have peace that I have worked very hard to attain, and it's a peace that surpasses all understanding. My overarching belief is that my life is in the hands of a God that loves without limits and forgives beyond what is reasonable. For these graces I am thankful.

"But God chose the foolish things of the world to shame the wise; God chose the weak things of the world to shame the strong." (NIV, 1 Corinthians 1:27).

"At that time Jesus answered and said, 'I thank You, Father, Lord of heaven and earth, that You have hidden these things from the wise and prudent and have revealed them to babes.'"(NKJV, Matthew. 11:25)

"Do not be anxious about anything, but in every situation, by prayer and petition, with thanksgiving, present your requests to God. And the peace of God, which transcends all understanding, will guard your hearts and your minds in Christ Jesus." (NIV, Philippians 4:6-7)

ROOTS III

HEY COWBOY

MY BROTHER JOHN is Mom's oldest child. He arrived after several miscarriages and years of waiting. Mom was not about to let anyone speak to her little Johnnie in an unkind way. My mom was always smart and assertive. She would speak up for her kids to anyone who needed correction. Her kids were more important than pleasing people or doing things against her moral compass.

My grandfather, Jasper DiCarlo, was a tenacious man. Determination and grit were his trademarks. He immigrated from Italy as a young teenager. I imagine it was terrifying to arrive in New York City without money, in a country where you do not speak the language, where you don't know anyone, and knowing you're never going back home. This must have taken incredible courage. I met my grandfather some 60 years later. Even as an older person, he was strong and resolute. Dad lovingly referred to him as hardheaded. Was he strong-willed? Yes.

This grit is likely what inspired him to start his own business and make it a success. Jasper was a bricklayer. This suited him well.

Although quite intelligent, he did not need to be able to speak eloquently for his job. He needed to be able to measure, mix, estimate, approximate, delegate, advise, and negotiate contracts. These tasks could largely be accomplished with numbers. Jasper learned the words that were essential for his career, and enough other words to get by.

Jasper was not a man you wanted to cross. Rosie, my grandmother, had a brand of spunk that was all her own. Their arguments, which were in Italian, were passionate displays of emotion. I never argued with Grandpa, so I was shocked to hear about Mom and Grandpa having words about anything.

She told me this story. "When John was a little guy, your grandpa, Jasper, used to call him 'Bad Boy.' Finally, one day I had had enough of that and put it to a stop. I said, 'Jasper, you get what you call in. If you keep calling that little guy 'bad boy,' then guess what we will have on our hands? A bad boy. I need you to stop calling him that and figure out something else you want to say when you greet John."

"What did he say then?" I asked.

"Well, from that day on, he called him 'Cowboy.' He would come into the house and say, 'Hey, Cowboy, how are you doing?' You can see what happened. John loves riding horses."

I knew Jasper greeted all men with, "Hey, cowboy." After LeeLee's correction, he was diligent about calling all boys 'cowboys' and all girls 'cowgirls.' Many times, I heard his heavy Italian accent calling out, "How are you, cowgirl?"

As for me, from as far back as I can remember, Mom called me 'Miss Love.' I can still hear her calling, 'What are you doing, Miss Love? What do you want for dinner, Miss Love?' and so on. This was the appellation I took on for all my childhood. Who did I become? I was the loving child my mom proclaimed I would be. I learned kindness, and I attribute that to Mom. She is the most kindhearted and generous person I have ever known. She told us from when we were young children that we were smart and talented, and she expected great things from us. She stood up for us when needed.

If I did not understand something going on in school, Mom would promptly meet with me and my teacher to investigate what was happening. When I was in first grade, I missed about half of the answers on a math assignment. I took it home and made the corrections. In my mind's eye, I can vividly see that math paper. It was manilla-colored with two rows of ten problems each. I had to fill in the 'greater than' and 'less than' signs. When I took it home to correct, it was apparent to me that if I missed one, I just needed to turn it the other way for it to be counted right.

That was the paper my mom took to my teacher. My math teacher, Mrs. Frederick, was a lovely young woman. When she looked at the page, she said, "I apologize, Mrs. DiCarlo, I don't know what happened. It appears that Elise had all the answers marked correctly." Well, this certainly truncated the conversation. From half wrong to none wrong happened in a swift moment. I was taught to be obedient and quiet when adults were talking. This meant I did not jump in and say, "Excuse me, those are the corrections that I made." What would Miss Love do? Smile at these two beautiful women. With that, nothing came out of my mouth.

The meeting simply ended, and I still did not know what those sideways Vs meant. This left such an impression on me that I wanted to be absolutely sure my kids understood the concept. I taught them that the big open side of the V is a shark's mouth that is hungry for the larger number. The point of the V is a little bird beak that wants to eat only a small amount, so it points to the lower number.

That experience in first grade solidified one of my core learning values that I use to this day. If I do not understand something, I ask questions. If I am not satisfied, I will check other resources until the concept is clear to me. Looking smart and being smart are two different things. I looked smart to Mom and Mrs. Frederick. It was ignorance that kept me from asking the questions I needed answered. I believe intelligent questions are far more an example of mental prowess than any other attempts for vain glory.

When my daughter was in first grade, she brought home some math papers with a few errors. I sat down with her to correct them so she could return the corrections to her teacher. Madison insisted, "We don't need to do that."

"Of course we do, you need to give this back to Mrs. Post."

The next day, I asked Mrs. Post about the situation. She said, "Oh no, she does not need to bring these back. She is fine."

With that knowledge, it took Madison exactly no minutes to decide that fixing errors was pointless. So, this summer we are doing our work and correcting it.

As for my children, I took every opportunity to say, "You are such a good boy" to my three little guys. As expected, they followed suit. Then someone told me, "Just wait till they are all teenagers. Three teenage boys will be rough. Enjoy them now." I thought, why would anyone say that? It was completely negative. That same day I resolved to tell my boys, "You will be such good teenagers. I know you will be wonderful teens." Then I made of point of recognizing the wonderful young people in our neighborhood. I would say, "Some people say teenagers are not nice. But you will be great young men." You can imagine the results this yielded. Words matter as they reflect what we believe."

Last week, my daughter, Madison, was throwing a fit about something that she wanted. There was no way we were leaving the house without the object of her desire. It was essential for her happiness, and she was devastated that she could not find it. Right during her bellyaching, I said, "You are such a good girl. I love how you listen." I called out not what was happening but what I wanted. She continued her tantrum, "That is not going to make me do anything different. I still need that toy right now." Then, no exaggeration, three minutes later she was pleasant and calm. She found another toy to take with her, and she was putting her shoes on to head out the door. All was well, and she was a good listener.

"Words are the most powerful thing in the universe... They contain faith, or fear, and they produce after their kind." Charles Capps

"If we understood the power of our thoughts, we would guard them more closely. If we understood the awesome power of our words, we would prefer silence to almost anything negative. In our thoughts and words, we create our own weaknesses and our own strengths. Our limitations and joys begin in our hearts. We can always replace negative with positive." Betty Eadie

"Do not let any unwholesome talk come out of your mouths, but only what is helpful for building others up according to their needs, that it may benefit those who listen." (Ephesians 4:29 NIV)

No Guarantees

MY GRANDMOTHER, Frances, had seen the invention of airplanes and was not about to ever get in a 'metal bird.' Her daughter and my mom, Marilee, only boarded planes with a tumbler of vodka. She would tell the flight attendants it contained 'medicine' that she dearly needed, and they would let her take it right to her seat. She used a plastic stadium cup filled with straight vodka and ice. Mom sometimes added an occasional splash of orange juice to feign innocence. She had good reason for her "clear companion in a cup." I didn't know it at the time.

I am the youngest of seven children, and I learned about their legacy of fear when we were journeying to San Francisco for my sister Bea's wedding. Different people in my family were taking various flights. When I questioned Dad about this, he said, "We can't all be on the same flight. If something happens to one flight, we must have some family members alive who can continue running the business." Wow, that was grim. Talk about seeing the glass half empty. We had not even departed, and our demise was already being thought through.

I learned that Dad had a solid reason for his multi-plane approach. He and Mom were flying at thirty-one thousand feet when one of the engines stopped working. Mom said there was a sudden plunge.

I asked, "Was everyone screaming?"

"No, not really. It got very quiet as we descended, and the other engine shut off. When that happened, your dad got out his rosary and instructed, 'We will be praying the rosary now.' You would be surprised how many people instantly turned Catholic and recited the rosary with your dad. All the while we were, of course, getting closer and closer to the ground. Everyone was praying, and one of the engines, without explanation, turned back on. We landed safely, but that gave us a scare."

We still traveled a great deal as a family and in my teen years, I flew regularly. To be more correct I was a passenger. We regularly traveled to New York, Canada, Mexico, and California. I went to college in Boston, and my family was in Kansas City. I managed my departures, connections, and arrivals in JFK, LaGuardia, Logan, MCI, etc. Any danger involved in the process was a fleeting thought.

On one occasion, I boarded a plane to LAX. I was sitting in a row directly opposite the emergency exit in the aft section of the airplane. The exit door was on one side of the aisle, with three seats directly across the aisle. I was sitting in the aisle seat, which made me closest to the emergency door.

At this time, I suffered from severe people-pleasing and low confidence. I took my seat and buckled in as instructed. I saw the flight attendants buzzing around, getting everything ready for take-off. The door across from my seat did not look completely closed, so I considered telling an attendant. Then I thought, "*Don't be an idiot. Of course, they will be sure the doors are locked before takeoff. There is probably some protocol that I am not aware of. Closing the doors must rank relatively high on their to-do list before takeoff. Just stay quiet and let them work.* Speaking up about the oversights of a professional person was out of the question."

I knew the doors on a plane pushed out and slid horizontally for passengers and loading in-flight drinks and snacks. I felt uneasy and knew intuitively that the door was not secure. However, I did not trust that feeling. *You are probably just panicking about nothing. Calm down,* I told myself. We were buckled in and set for takeoff.

The door, however, was introducing itself. It let us know it had yet to be securely closed about fifteen minutes into the flight. As the differential pressures on either side of the door changed, the door confirmed that it only looked closed but had not been locked. It popped out, and suddenly, the plane became a noisy wind tunnel. I instantly thought *I needed to move.* If it opened any further, I would be the first person sucked out. Today was not going to be my last day on the planet.

The pilot began talking over the speaker, "Everyone, stay in your seats. I repeat, stay in your seats with your seatbelts fastened securely. Do not move about the cabin. We will be making an emergency landing as soon as possible."

I became bold. I thought, *stay in my seat? Stay in my seat. No, thank you.* I decided I was done being the seatmate of the crazy door. I unbuckled and held onto the seat in front of me for dear life as I scooted around it. I let go only when I could grip the seat in front of that one. I moved away from my aisle in this fashion for three rows. I made the harrowing trip through the wind tunnel. Now, I buckled in for the emergency landing. This could have been prevented if I had just said, "Excuse me, I don't think that door is securely closed," about an hour earlier. For many years after that incident, I would always begin worrying about the next flight.

I was not the biggest fan of flying. I psyched myself up and would fly only when it was necessary. About seven years later, my boyfriend, Xavier, whose parents were diplomats in Bermuda, invited me to meet his family. We would be residing at their castle-like estate overlooking the ocean. The only way to get there was to fly over -- you guessed it -- the Bermuda Triangle. I told myself all the stories were complete rubbish, like ghost stories around a Halloween campfire.

It was easy to believe that as I boarded the plane; however, when we flew into the Triangle, I was convinced otherwise. Our small commuter plane was buffeted by winds, sending it up, down, and sideways as we searched for our tiny island target. I was terrified as I silently prayed for the impossible – a safe landing. It would not be a fairy tale if I were in a plane crash on the way to meet the prince and his family in the castle. In reality, things out of our control do happen. By the time we landed, I had never been more grateful to have my feet on solid ground. When I was on the island, I tried not to give the trip home even a thought. I knew it would ruin the glorious time I was enjoying. Although I made it my mission to stay in the present, it dogged me the entire time I was away.

Fear is a very real thing. It's a natural human emotion and is not in itself bad. However, fear is a beast to be examined. He's often dressed in disguise, standing in the shadows, waiting for his opportunity to hijack a perfectly rational mind. Other people can see this imposter for who he is and chime in, "You'll be fine. Planes are flying around safely every day." They can see through this irrational bully cruising around your brain, wreaking havoc. The well-wishers try to calm the rowdy intruder by handing out facts and figures based on reality. These may include, "You are safer in a plane than a car." Or "The creatures in the water are more afraid of you than you are of them." I am grateful for these do-gooder cheerleaders, but my fear quietly whispers, "It may be safe for them, but *you* are the exception." Reassurance disappears and silently drowns in the waves of my mind.

Is there a way out of such dire circumstances? I can simply avoid the activities where fear is winning. This makes my life shrink, and deep down, I resent that fear has bested me yet again. This might be the end of the story, but I have an aversion to losing, especially to the tyrant Fear. This is when I need to stop myself short and conquer this beast. I start telling myself that the dreaded activity is quite safe, maybe even fun. This works to a degree, but this adversary won't be shut down that easily. The pit is still in my stomach, and it will not relent until I take this situation to DEFCON 1. You guessed it. I need to actually *do* the thing I fear. I must accept terror, bewilderment, and disorientation as I look this adversary in the eye. But when I do, the most amazing thing happens; fear dissipates and reveals itself to be an insubstantial layer of fog that needed to be cleared from my vision.

Years later, when I had a family, I was nervous about boarding a flight home. We were at the airport, and a massive storm was brewing across the country. I spotted a pilot, boldly approached him, and said, "Will you fly if it's not safe?"

"No," he answered definitively. "We want to live, too, you know. I have a family and grandkids waiting for me in Atlanta. It's no different for me. I love my family and want to get there safely. We can usually manage the weather fairly well. We will probably delay here for ten or fifteen minutes."

That's when it dawned on me: I am not the only person who wants this flight to go well. Every single person I can see wants a safe flight. No one wants to enter a dangerous situation. All the people employed here are following directions and working as a team.

The bottom line is that we all want a guarantee. I want to know, for a fac,t that I will be safe in this car, this plane, this location, this hospital, at this event. I don't want anything unhappy to take place. Once I have a negative experience, my brain tells me it will always be that way. I don't want another plane I am riding in to make an emergency landing. I don't want to ever take a drink. For my friends, I don't want them to face another car wreck. I want my kids to always be well and safe.

Ultimately, I want a 100% assurance. Yet life's not like that. I can't control everything. As much as I don't like to admit it, there are very few things I can control. The fact is that I can only do my best for today. When it comes to alcohol, I don't drink today. I stay as healthy as I possibly can today. I plan today to the best of my ability and then try to let go of the results. Taking the action is my part. Determining the outcome is not. My sponsor, Diane, often tells me, "Either God is everything or nothing." There is no middle-of-the-road here. Choosing 'God is everything' brings me peace.

With this knowledge the healed part of my brain-voice kicks in, with, "Look at all the times it has gone *well.*" That's when I realize my brain wants me to focus on the unlikely possibilities and ignore the thousands of days all has gone well. Now I have new, real, and sunny evidence to go forward. I'm better for working my way through this. I have a road map for next time. I will swiftly stop the voice of fear. I will do this by talking back to the bully. I'll tell him how my life is getting better and better.

I have been through two near-death experiences, several 'incurable' illnesses, overwhelming odds, and unthinkable tragedy. Those experiences have changed the trajectory of my life. I needed each event to unfold exactly as it did for me to be right here, right now with you. For that, I am grateful. I fully believe that God works all things for good. God is the key to opening the door to freedom from fear. Pick up the key and use it.

I refuse to back down, not today, not ever.

"Let our voices be heard. I hope they will not be shrill voices, but I hope we shall speak with such conviction that those to whom we speak shall know of the strength of our feeling and the sincerity of our efforts." Gordon B. Hinckle

"So do not fear, for I am with you; do not be dismayed, for I am your God. I will strengthen you and help you; I will uphold you with my righteous right hand." (Isaiah 41:10 NIV)

"For God gave us a spirit not of fear but of power and love and self-control." (2 Timothy 1:7).

God And Only God

MOM AND I WERE EXHAUSTED. We were caring for Dad at home during the last months of his cancer. The days had turned into weeks. Night after night, a few hours of disjointed sleep had left me physically, mentally, and spiritually depleted. When I did crawl up the stairs and into bed, I let myself cry. For weeks, my nightly routine consisted of getting into bed, picking up my rosary, and beginning to pray and weep.

I quietly let tears roll down my face until my pillow was soaked. Mercifully, God would let me fall asleep for an hour or two before I needed to go down and check on Dad. His bed on the first floor was directly below mine. My hearing has always been excellent. I could always hear little snippets of conversations throughout the house. I would be able to hear Dad if he called for help from his first-floor chamber. That night, I fell into bed and began the light, hyper-aware rest of a full-time caretaker. It's like sleeping with one eye open, knowing you may need to jump up, fully alert, at any time. Recently, at the dinner table, my son, Nicholas, said, "Dolphins sleep in a state of partial awareness because they need to continue to surface for air when resting." In this nightmare with my dad, I would 'surface for air' only to be plunged downward by a ferocious wave, pummeled again by this hellish reality.

Dad's body was utterly wasting away. He was gaunt. His bones looked like they could pop out of his flesh at any time. His tumor was blocking his common bile duct. All the bile that would normally be processed by the coordination of the liver, pancreas, and kidneys was just spilling out inside his body. The toxic waste would make the whites of his eyes the color of Dijon mustard. Dad's skin also carried a sickly yellow hue. One night, I tearfully told mom, "I won't have a dad. I won't have a dad when I graduate this spring, get my job, get married."

"Don't you think it's devastating for him, too? He knows you are going to go on and accomplish amazing things. It breaks his heart. He knows he won't be here to see it."

I realized how truly selfish and stupid I was acting. I saw myself as the victim, like this was only happening to me. I was focused on myself and what I was losing. Well, what about my dad, who is going through the most horrific illness I have ever seen?

Cancer was a bully that stripped Dad of his many pleasures.

He loved to cook his famous spaghetti and meatballs for Sunday family dinner. But now, his ability to cook, eat, and drink wine was gone. Being ambulatory by himself was over. Walking outside, going outside, were things of the past. Trips upstairs to his bedroom, in the house he had built, were impossible. His disease held him captive on the first floor in one room with a hospital bed. He no longer traveled downstairs to watch a football game on the 'big screen.'

Nor could he work in his beloved shop. Dad could build, fix, or create anything down there. The huge area was filled with every imaginable tool, sawhorses, and large and small metal drawers packed to the brim with every conceivable nail, and fastener. On a

Saturday, Dad could be found at his workbench constructing things from nothing.

We had been building a dollhouse together through the years. It had hundreds of pieces made of balsa wood. We gently broke the pieces into their sections for the porch, first floor, and so on. We meticulously glued each piece in place. The house arose from the box as a phoenix from a fire. Before us stood a gorgeous home that might be found in the hills near San Francisco. I loved that project. It represented the time spent between a dad and his daughter. To me, it meant that anything is possible if you put your mind to it. Now, our building station was abandoned.

There are times when we can distract ourselves with entertainment, but it cannot sustain us in the most challenging circumstances. For that, there is God and only God. He alone can accompany us through the most difficult of life's journeys. Even those that contain only silence, constant pain, and the death of laughter. This is the precipice where we stood. There would be no cure for Dad. There was just one exasperating day followed by another. We navigated it moment by moment.

Out of desperation, Mom and I hired a helper to come in on some nights. I do not know how these people were willing to be employed as caregivers, especially for the dying. On the second night, Dad's caregiver was a man of about 6'3", Caucasian, overweight, with a scraggly orange beard and hair of the same color. As he strode in, I let myself be optimistic; at least this guy looked like he could lift Dad to get him safely to the bathroom.

I said my "goodnights" and "I love you's" to Dad and headed upstairs, but I did not sleep. I had made him cassette tapes with peaceful recordings. Dad loved the meditative nature of the pieces of music, including the chants of Taizé. Those chants also bolstered my faith and helped me feel close to Christ and the community of Taizé thousands of miles away. But what I heard instead was music that was neither gentle nor soothing

What in God's name is going on? I could hear it clearly in my room, so I knew it was blasting. Now fully alert, I could hear the faint voice of my father calling out for help. Why wasn't Chad answering? It was nearly 4:00 am. I jumped out of bed and ran downstairs. Dad had thrown up on his pajamas and was lying in bed, calling for help.

I said to Chad, "Can you please turn that down?" He set down his chocolate bar for just long enough to turn the radio dial down. Chad was not moving.

"Oh, Dad, it's okay. Let's get you cleaned up."

I walked Dad to the bathroom to take off his pajamas while I ran upstairs to get clean ones. I came back down, gave the pajamas to Dad, and started the laundry with no sign of Chad. I was frustrated beyond belief. He was ignoring the cries of a dying man! If I had been remotely in the right state of mind, I would have told him to leave.

Chad never came back. We had about three nights of equally unimpressive 'helpers,' to use the term loosely. We decided this was just not for us or for Dad. I went back to rotating nights with my sister, Jane. Mom was always there, but we also wanted to give her a chance to rest and sleep. We were exhausted, but we were not going to submit Dad to that kind of blatant neglect. We went back to taking it one day at a time, one moment at a time. This gave us the stamina we needed in the present moment. The Lord Himself knew what we needed, saw what we could not, and that the privilege of caring for Dad was finite.

Hospice workers had also been coming to see Dad regularly for a couple of months. They were outstanding, wonderful individuals who instructed us to let Dad know he could go and that we would be okay.

They said, "He has always taken care of all of you. He has been such an amazing provider. He may be holding on because he doesn't know how you will fare without him. Let him know everything will be alright. Give him permission to go."

This was a tall order for me, but I would do as I was told. It was now February 8, 1995. It was Jane's night to come over. She got to our house late that evening. Jane had a family to feed and get to bed first. I remember that at this point, hospice had given us a small vial of morphine to help Dad with his pain. We were instructed to draw up the medicine and place it in the corner of his mouth. We were told it was for pain and to give it liberally. I never heard anything further about the medication or its side effects. Now, I know it causes respiratory depression and, in high doses, breathing cessation.

I went to bed, but what seemed like only a few minutes later, Mom was at my bedside. "You may want to come down," her voice cracked. "He doesn't have much time." We raced downstairs. I took Dad's left hand into mine. I told him we would always take care of each other and would especially take care of Mom. I told him that he had done the best job taking care of us, and we would carry on from here. As I told him, "I love you," he took his last breath. One second, he was still residing in his body. Next, his life force was gone from us. Yet I knew that he still existed, just no longer here anymore.

In that moment, I realized I was unafraid of death. What was death, anyway? One single second of the journey that is us. I spent so much of my life fearing, avoiding, and pushing away the idea of death as something that ends our existence. But I realized in that mere second that death was actually an immediate transition. Is that really something to waste hours, days, or even years fearing? I felt peace, knowing that Dad was somewhere else. Lying before me was his body, but that was not my dad.

My mom's friends rushed in and started taking down all the charts I had made for tracking Dad's eating, sickness, medications, etc. It was as if quickly taking things away would mean they didn't happen. But records or no records, I knew this excruciating time could not be erased from my being. We called for his body to be taken away. Men arrived at our door with a shiny silver stretcher. Atop the stretcher was a body bag. They popped the wheels down as they entered, making a loud clang on the bright marble floor. It seemed rudely raucous as it clanked by me as I sat quietly on the front staircase. Ten minutes later, the stretcher rolled by our entire family. This time, the body bag was full. This was like someone grabbed the dagger already in my belly and twisted it hard.

The following days were a blur of planning and preparation for Dad's funeral. We would throw a last great party in his honor. This he would have liked. There was a coffin to select, readings, readers, priests to contact, and a cemetery plot to select. Although I had months to prepare for this, my denial had not let me purchase anything appropriate to wear. I borrowed a dress from a friend. That was the best I could do.

At the rosary service the night before the funeral, there was a line all the way down the aisle of the church. I was standing on the stairs up to the altar. A whole 'gaggle' of my friends from high school came. I can still see them: Ann, Amy, Nancy, and more filling the first few pews, sitting in solidarity with my pain. Dad had taught many of my friends to water ski. He had bought some of their winter coats and boots. He was the most fun Dad at the father-daughter dances. He would get out on the floor with the girls and ham it up. He was hilarious. The song *Tainted Love* rings a bell as one he particularly jammed.

As I was standing near the altar, a well-dressed man approached me.

"I am here because I want you to know that your dad gave me a chance. I was robbing him in his shop on Prospect Ave. Your dad was there (my dad often went to his office on Saturday mornings). He saw me robbing him and he said, 'What are you doing? Why are you stealing?'"

It turns out that was the perfect question and characteristic of Dad. If you were doing something wrong or if things were not going well, he would give you a chance to explain yourself. He gave people the benefit of the doubt.

"I told him I was stealing because I did not know what else to do. I didn't even have enough money to buy my family a loaf of bread."

"Your dad said, 'What if you didn't have to steal? Do you want to work?'

"I let your dad know that I was willing to work. He gave me a chance and a job. I came to work for him that Monday, and I have been there ever since. I just wanted you to know that about him."

At that moment, I didn't know this man's story would be engraved on my heart. It followed Dad's theme of thinking outside the box, finding solutions to problems, and giving anyone in need a fair chance. The most difficult times and beautiful moments of my life were ahead. I could not make sense of the world without my dad, but it turned out I didn't need to. I only needed to live in this moment, then the next and the next…

"The birth, death, and resurrection of Jesus means that one day everything sad will come untrue." J.R.R. Tolkien

"He will dwell with them, and they will be his people, and God himself will be with them as their God. He will wipe away every tear from their eyes, and death shall be no more, neither

shall there be mourning, nor crying, nor pain anymore, for the former things have passed away." (Revelation 21: 3-4, ESV)

"Do not let your hearts be troubled. Trust in God; trust also in me. In my Father's house are many rooms; if it were not so, I would have told you. I am going there to prepare a place for you. And if I go and prepare a place for you, I will come back and take you to be with me that you also may be where I am." (John 14: 1-3, NIV)

The Price Of Seeing The Stars

I WAS DEVASTATED by the loss of my father. For him, the sun rose and set on me. This meant that I was grieving not only my dad's incredible life, but also the feeling of being unconditionally loved by him. Following his death, I was flying back to New York, returning from a dear friend's wedding where I met Tom. We sat together on the return flight. While chatting, he said, "Just try not to hate your mom." I looked at him quizzically, yet simultaneously feeling like I understood.

"Your mom cannot love you in the way your father did. Everyone's love for you feels different. Your dad loved you in his way, and now he is gone. Your mom cannot love you like that. She can only love you in her way, so don't be mad about it."

I felt like Tom had just looked into my soul. How did he know all of that? This is likely because, as Tom shared, his mom died when he was a young man. He had done some deep internal work, which he passed on to me, and for which I was very grateful.

It didn't stop me from being angry. I was irate, at times, in my grief. I used to let God have it.

I would scream and cry, "I hate you, God, I hate you for taking my father! Could you not have taken someone else? Someone who was harming people? How about drug dealers who are killing young people? What about rapists or child sex offenders? What about one of those guys? Did you have to take my dad, a highly decorated war hero? He was a man who let Jews out of concentration camps at the end of World War II. He was a man who left college one semester before graduation to help his own father, and never got to go back. He had a wife, six children, and nine grandchildren, all of whom he loved and cared for. A man who lived the American dream, growing up in the ghetto and moving up and out by sheer grit. A man with hundreds of employees and friends, more than he could count, and who loved you, God, with all his heart."

"Why him? What is wrong with You? Why do you take the good people and leave so many venomous people to carry on? Why did you rip the very foundation out from under me? I'm only 24. I don't have a husband or family yet. Now, my dad will never meet them. And don't even get me started on my future children. He will never know them. And let's back it up further. I have no dad to give me away at my wedding. You know that moment girls dream of forever? That's just gone, shattered. Don't even get me started on how you let him suffer so gravely.

"What about the time he told me, 'If anything happens to me, don't call an ambulance or anyone to bring me back.' What kind of conversation is that for a man to have with his youngest child? You let his hemoglobin get so low that I was asked by his doctor, 'Can you get him to the hospital immediately? If not, he won't make it.' Only to have him get the stupid transfusion and go into uncontrollable shaking, chills, and fever. What the hell was that? I thought he was going to die right then. No, God, you suck. You absolutely suck. I don't even know if you are here anymore."

After my dad's funeral, all hell broke loose back at our house. My mom hosted a massive alcohol-fueled Catholic burial party complete with endless food and chaos. Just despondent, I went to my room. Such a mixture of emotions seethed through me. I was sad, angry, depressed, and exhausted, to name a few. Then I heard my dad's friend, Frank, asking my mom, "Do you think she will marry the guy who was at the funeral with her?"

"I don't know," Mom answered. They were talking about ME!

This was the last straw. I just buried my dad. Why are they talking about my marriage, which was totally imaginary at that point? It was my turn to scream, and I opened my door and said, "Stop talking about that. My dad is dead. Why would you even think about my wedding? I won't have my dad there. Don't say another word about it!"

I slammed my door and fell onto my bed, sobbing. That was just too much for my aching heart. I was still seeing the coffin being lowered as we threw handfuls of dirt on top. I so wished it were me going into the earth. I thought back to Father Freeman, Society of Jesus, at the funeral. He was standing next to me in the back of the church before they brought my dad's coffin inside. He said, "You know, I envy your dad. His problems are over. We are stuck here in this world, a world that is growing darker and more sinful every day. But your dad is free of it. Free of this world and all its encumbrances. Oh, I envy him."

Father Freeman, S.J., a Jesuit priest, was an incredibly brilliant man who taught at Rockhurst University well into his eighties. His "I envy him" speech was supposed to make me feel better. But for me, I wanted my suffering to be over, too. What on Earth was I going to do in this hellish state? All my brothers and sisters were married with children. I felt unbearably lonely. My soul felt completely hollow. All hope was being suffocated by my new reality.

I returned to New York and to the Pratt Institute to complete my Master of Fine Arts Degree. Dad died in February, and I was slated to graduate that May. One day, I saw a beer can knocked over on the pavement, soaking up its alcoholic contents. I thought, would it be better if I took a drink? I wish I could be that pavement, slowly being soaked through with alcohol. But I knew there was no relief for me there.

I was at the point that the Big Book of Alcoholics Anonymous refers to as 'the jumping off point.' It's a point where we can't live with or without alcohol. I was, in reality, wondering if I would live or die if I jumped from my fifth-floor window. It was a massive window with no screen. I stared out that window many times in contemplation. I did not fear death. I feared continuing to live. What if I didn't die? What if I were only gravely injured, maybe paralyzed, living in a wheelchair for the rest of my life? That would be even worse. What if I failed at dying? I knew I did not want to be in pain anymore. I knew the drink held nothing for me. I had no escape.

On Monday, in desperation, I called a free counseling clinic. The counselor I spoke with said, "We can see you in a week from Wednesday. How will that work for you?"

In a brash moment of honesty, I said, "That will be too late."

"Oh, okay. How about this, we can get you in this Wednesday at noon? Will that be too late?"

"No, Wednesday will be fine. Thank you."

I went to my first appointment with my counselor. I will call her Trish. A gifted therapist, she was also a wonderful human being. I shared my truth, and she loved me while I eventually learned to love myself.

Still battling incredibly negative feelings, the following Sunday night I was the resident assistant on duty at my dorm. I went into the resident director's office. There was a phone and a desk. I called one of my brothers, who had gone through a fantastic transformation a few years earlier in A.A. I told him that although I had not had a drink for a long time, it was crossing my mind. I knew drinking would not work for me anymore. He told me, "Maybe you ought to go see those people in Alcoholics Anonymous. They were too crazy for me, but maybe they can help you."

The second call I made was to a fellow resident assistant. I told her about my journey with alcohol and how I knew it wouldn't work for me now. She said, "You probably don't know this, but I am an alcoholic. I've been sober for 17 years. If you would like, I can take you to a meeting."

I knew the very meeting I wanted to go to. It was in a church in Park Slope. That was the area in Brooklyn where I lived before getting free room and board as an R.A. at Pratt. I lived directly across from a church with A.A. meetings on Tuesday and Thursday nights. I used to think, "Oh, those broken people are so lucky. They have each other." At that time, I did not think I qualified as an alcoholic because I had not had a drink in 3 years. Clearly, in my mind, I was not an alcoholic, although I had communion wine during those years and looked forward to it.

Mom, who did not want to see me in A.A., inadvertently helped me make it to my first meeting. She told me, "Mary Tyler Moore realized she was an alcoholic. She said in an interview that it was not how much she drank or how often. She could drink maybe once a month. It was not about the amount. It was how much she looked forward to it, how she romanced it, and was obsessed with it."

Thank you very much, Mom. Now I had my permission slip to enter A.A. Praying the night before that first meeting. I told God,

"I have been everywhere and tried many ways to get better. All I've got left is this A.A. meeting. God, this has got to work, or I don't know how I can go on. God, please help me."

I entered the doors of A.A. and recovery and have never looked back. I went to my first meeting with Gina in Park Slope. She took me to "coffee" before the meeting. I later learned that is code for how we 'kidnap' newcomers and brainwash them into the program, lol. I did tell Gina that I thought A.A. was maybe a cult and they were brainwashing me. She answered, "I think you should investigate what a cult is. And if they are brainwashing you, maybe your brain needs to be washed."

I learned that cults try to take all your money and separate you from your family and friends. Let's see. A.A. asks for $1 per meeting. This has stayed the same throughout the years despite inflation, etc. Gina told me, "Everyone puts a dollar in the basket. It's like an investment you put in your sobriety savings. You'd better put in two. You need a bigger policy." In A.A., you reconnect with family and friends through working the steps. This does not qualify as a cult.

Gina instructed, "Go to 90 meetings in 90 days, or if that seems too much, go to a meeting a day, and the 90 will take care of itself. If you want what we have, then do what we do. We work the steps and don't drink between meetings.

"Do five things every day, and you will not drink:

1. Get on your knees and ask God for another sober day.
2. Call another alcoholic.
3. Call your sponsor.
4. Go to a meeting.
5. Thank God for your sober day.

Do this every day, and I promise you will not drink."

I wanted that guarantee, so those five things became my practice.

One day, I was sick. I asked Gina, "What do I do if I don't feel well enough to attend a meeting?"

"It's okay if you miss today. Just go to two meetings tomorrow to make up for it."

I did as I was told. Gina told me, "Our Book says that we offer suggestions only, but for you, they are mandatory."

I believed her. I barely took a step without first running it by Gina.

When I went back to see Trish, I was nervous. I thought she would be mad that I went to A.A. I really liked meetings and my time with Trish, so I wanted to keep both. I opened with, "I went to A.A. this week. I loved it."

"That is fantastic. Tell me about it."

"You are not mad? I thought you would be mad at me for going somewhere else for help."

"That's not how it works. I'm not taking hostages. The way you know you are getting good help is that you are encouraged to seek out additional help. It's not all or nothing. That is distorted thinking."

I was free to go to A.A. and to see Trish. I continued to see her weekly in Brooklyn for a year. Then she moved to the Bronx, and I moved to Manhattan. Yet I kept going to meet with her weekly, even though she was three trains and at least forty-five minutes away. She taught me volumes about life and love. I kept telling her I wanted to break things off with my boyfriend, and yet I kept doing nothing. I felt terrible about myself for being so spineless. Trish came up with a genius plan. "Why don't you stop proclaiming what you are going to do? Why don't you just show what you want with actions, not words?"

I thought this was the best idea ever. By our next session, I had broken things off with my boyfriend. I was growing up for real. I proceeded to tell her about someone whom I believed was the love of my life. She replied, "You think that is love? That is abuse. You don't know what love is." This hard truth helped me surrender that area of my life to God as well. I let Him choose for me.

I continued to work the program with urgency. I did not think any part of it was optional, and I worked the steps to the best of my ability from Day One. Maybe there was an A.A. police officer, and I didn't want to get in trouble for messing up. This was a "life and death errand," as the Book says. My line in the sand needed to be drawn now. That would be for me, my family, and one day, my children.

My father's death was horrific. He had everything: family, homes, cars, boats, and people who loved him, but this disease wouldn't allow him to have another moment. I knew that alcohol was likely a factor in my dad's battle with pancreatic cancer. I decided to do everything I could to avoid a similar ending. I did not want to die that way. I did not want my future kids to see me that way. I did not want to ever go through that.

As bad as I was feeling, Alcoholics Anonymous gave me hope. In those rooms lived the possibility of freedom from addiction. I had to do only a few simple things, things I needed to get clear about, since I can complicate Rice Krispies. A man told me in one of my first meetings, "Glad you are here. Now, all you have to do is change everything about your life." We laughed, but he was right. A whole life of being self-centered cannot be turned around in a day. Yet, my self-centeredness was the main thing I could not stand. I begged for it to be lifted out of me. I begged God to take it away, and he did, one day at a time.

Now, I live to serve God and His kids. I am a generous giver. I love people for who and what they are. I use my darkest moments to lift others up. I am utterly transparent if it means someone will be helped. I do not care what you think of me. I know I am a good-hearted person. I know I do not need to keep up a false image of myself. I recall that earlier in my life, I was always trying to dress and look like women I admired. I wasn't even aware I was doing this. Finally, one day, I heard God say, "If you are so busy trying to be everyone else, who will be you?"

I realized the people I wanted to emulate were truthful, kind, loving, generous, and selfless. Their beauty came from being authentic in a world full of counterfeits. I live for my audience of One, and for me, that is God. I know He sees it all. God knows who and what I am. I do not need to defend myself. God fights my battles, and He never lets me down. I give God the credit for all my blessings. I could have died in my drinking days. The fact that I am alive and well is a miracle. My life is all icing. Taking the cup at communion is no longer something I participate in. That is not a part of my sobriety. I know who I am in Christ.

I now understand that God, in His infinite wisdom, allowed my father to die. He did not make Dad die or take him away. This was how life unfolded based on a million small facts. This was not to punish me, but so I might live. In exchange for losing one amazing person, I have rooms full of friends I have yet to meet. I have friends throughout the world in A.A., and I am grateful.

"My barn having burned down; I can now see the moon."
Mizuta Masahide (17th century Japanese poet and samurai)

"Sometimes even to live is an act of courage." Seneca

"For I am convinced that neither death nor life, neither angels nor demons, neither the present nor the future, nor any powers, neither height nor depth, nor anything else in all creation, will be able to separate us from the love of God that is in Christ Jesus our Lord."(Romans 8:38-39)

LAKE OF MY CHILDHOOD

MY FONDEST CHILDHOOD memories come from being with my family at Lake of the Ozarks.

We built the house as a family. My dad owned a construction company, and his professional experience helped immensely. We all went down during the final stages to paint the interior. Everyone had to pitch in, and at age 6, I was no exception. My job was to paint the main bedroom. I was given a pan of yellow paint and a roller too big to wield, because of its size compared to mine. I 'slooped' paint onto the roller and flung it onto the wall. Then I attempted to spread that glob of paint around with the roller. A dresser hid my foray into painting. Still, it was *my* yellow splotch, and I was proud of it.

Time at the lake equaled fun. Water skiing, tubing, fishing, sailing, and boat ride adventures. As I got older, my parents let me bring friends, and we had a blast. First, we stocked up at a lakeside store to get our favorite provisions. Then we headed down the dirt road, took a right at the T, and ascended the giant hill and around the corner to our massive metal gate. The gate opened to our property, all 350 acres. Prime waterfront real estate. The entire side of a cove, all the way to the end.

Dad planned to build a resort on the waterfront. We got as far as making our home. It was a prototype of the resort spaces. Each bedroom had a kitchenette, bathroom, and balcony for maximum exposure to the lake. We never built the resort. Instead, we settled into the peace and solitude of such a vast property. It was an oasis from the pressures of the city, and my dad did not part with any of it.

Once we passed the gate, it was three-quarters of a mile to the house. We stopped at the pump house to turn on the water. We worked before we played. One of my jobs was to sweep out the unfinished basement before we went boating. The basement had a sliding glass door, and people had a penchant for leaving it open on their way down to the dock. You might grab a few life jackets and forget about closing the door, inadvertently allowing some unsavory lake 'characters' through the door, such as winged bugs, crawling insects, and mice.

This sweep-out was like no other. The basement was damp and dark. I would pull the little string attached to the lightbulb to shed some light on the bug graveyard. I spread this red stuff around from a can before I swept. To this day, I am still trying to determine what that product was. It looked like red sawdust, only fluffier. I'd sprinkle it all over the basement and then sweep it into piles. Any lurking cobwebs and creatures were my responsibility. It was truly disgusting.

There were just enough chores to keep us busy and teach us the rewards of a diligent work ethic. I give my parents all the credit for instilling that in me. I have a friend whom I'll tell about a big project I am working on. He always sighs and says, "Well, we know you are not afraid of hard work." Thank you, Mom and Dad.

'Success comes before work only in the dictionary' was the lesson taught, along with fear not the night nor the darkness. Nature is our friend, as are its creatures. As a kid, I nightly trudged through the leafy forest to compost the dinner scraps. We needed to ensure this was far enough away from the house that the raccoons did not come trotting over. One night, I left some food scraps on the balcony, and adventurous raccoons came up to snack. They were adorable! However cute, their furry escapades were halted as Dad insisted that we take the food as far away from the house as possible.

I was around seven the first summer I attempted to water ski. My initial weekend of trying was fruitless. The skis we had for little kids were like wide planks of timber. Black with white checks covered the wood. There was a place for two feet, and that was it. How someone could stand on the back of those beams and hope to glide over the water was a mystery to me. But that was the deal. On my second weekend, Dad sent my brother, Frank, into the water to help me.

Frank was encouraging and said, "You got this; just stand up and hold onto the rope."

It sounded simple enough. I was up, I was down, I was up, I was down. This seemed to go on forever, and I marked my surrender by swimming back to the boat. As I approached, Dad said, "What are you doing?"

"I'm getting back in the boat," I announced.

"No, you're not."

"I'm not?"

"Not until you ski."

And that was the conversation—the end. I swam back out and put on the skis. I now knew what was required. This wasn't a negotiation. Getting up on these skis was a necessity. It took me two more tries, and I never looked back. I could ski all day if time allowed. It was effortless, and slaloming was even more ridiculously fun. I wanted to go out on our cove when the water was glass. Dad would get up with me at 6:30 am to get out on the water by 7:00 am on the weekend. No one else was skiing at that time in our quiet cove. The water was untouched, and the skiing was euphoric. I loved being on vacation with Dad because it was delightful when he relaxed. He worked harder than anyone I ever knew, but when he took a break, he let loose.

Mom is not much of an outdoorsy person. She never learned to swim, so the lake scared her, and the bouncing of any boat was not her favorite, either. Although we had many types of boats, Dad bought her a pontoon boat for a smooth ride. It had orange flooring and orange and white cushions. Mom seemed to like the pontoon better, but didn't love it.

Mom could see us on the dock from the kitchen window. There were strict rules about life jackets, and we obeyed. Mom would have delicious food waiting for us after a long day on the water. She was a selfless woman, and later, I learned she did not like being at the lake. These years of summers at the lake were for my dad and all of us kids. She cleaned, cooked, and made sure everyone had fun. She regularly served potatoes, salad, hot rolls, and barbequed chicken from the grill. Other times, we were greeted by a massive pot of spaghetti and meatballs.

Dad was fearless on and off the water. Having been a frequenter of the lake since his teens, he knew the waters well and could navigate the main channel or the small inlets with equal skill. We also had a sailboat. He would take it out with the confidence of an experienced mariner, although he wasn't really a trained sailor. Sometimes, we misjudged the weight on each side and took on too much water. There was a supply of empty coffee cans we used to bail out water, and we broke them out frequently. Whatever happened, we had a blast.

We also had a speedboat. Occasionally, we would run out of gas in the speedboat or get flooded and stop in the middle of the main channel. We met these problems with complete confidence. No cell phones, just complete trust that Dad's resourcefulness would triumph, and we would not be stuck out there forever.

We often took the fishing boat into the shallow water near our house. It would take hours to get a bite. For a real treat, Dad took me fishing at Troutdale, a little lake stocked with trout. There was no challenge here in catching our dinner. The workers at Troutdale would clean them for us on the spot. I can still remember the smell of the place as the fishmongers wielded their sharp knives.

Dad was the captain of our ski boat. He watched attentively as the skier dropped off the vessel's side, likely to receive the skis and rope via a perfectly aimed toss. Then, with the skier on the correct side of the boat, Dad would scan the horizon for other watercraft and athletes. Somehow looking forward and backward simultaneously, he would command the vessel to pull the skier up gracefully. Not so fast that the rope jerked from their hands, not so slowly that they wobbled and fell. It was a craft he had mastered. Skiers from novice level to expert appreciated his competence as our boat captain.

Two rules were mandatory: always wear a lifejacket for skiing and never go out with fewer than three people. A third person had to be in the boat to watch the skier constantly. In our years at the lake, there was not a single incident of a skier, swimmer, or boater getting hurt under Dad's watch. Dad managed to align safety and fun with precision.

After all the boating, water skiing, playing cards, swimming, and great meals, there was cleanup at the end of the weekend. Again, it was not an optional activity. After Mass and breakfast on Sunday, it was time to begin the cleaning ritual. All the bathrooms, bedrooms, and kitchen had to be cleaned. Taking out the trash was one of my duties. If there was time, we headed out for one last boat ride or just a trip down to the dock. Next, we would pack up the cars, head out to turn off the water at the pump house, drive out, and lock the gate. We left the property behind us but took our memories along.

It would be a massive understatement to say that my parents were generous with the lake house. That house was busy from the first wink of spring until the last leaves of fall. It seemed that anyone who asked would receive the keys to the house and the boat as well. That was another of his unspoken lessons -- we share our beautiful blessings.

Dad was no stranger to tenacity in all his endeavors. His intelligence propelled him to spearhead multiple companies. He was an entrepreneur before that was even a thing. Dad grew up in Kansas City in a neighborhood with low income and high crime. He worked his way up and out. His parents were immigrants from Italy who didn't speak English. Dad was living the American Dream, and being his youngest child, I lived it right along with him. He taught me to have street smarts and book smarts. He taught me to press into significant risks that would intimidate others. Dad trusted his instincts, which was a massive part of his success. He made his own formulas to attain his goals. He led us and gave us essential life skills, more by example than by word.

When Dad believed you were ready to do something, he challenged you. When I was thirteen, he taught me to drive and dock the boat. I was pulling skiers at 15. After all, someone needed to operate the boat while Dad skied, which he did well into his sixties. He gave me responsibilities beyond my age. He looked at my ability and saw potential. If Dad thought you could do something, it was 'game on.' The bar was held high for me, and he expected great things. He lowered the bar when he had to. I learned this one night at a cocktail party with my parents. I was sixteen and overheard Dad talking with the host's son. I heard him urging this teenager to aim for a C-minus in his D classes. He persuaded him to put in more time and effort to elevate himself out of the dreaded D range. I listened with shock and amazement.

When we returned to the car to drive home, I said, "Dad, what was that all about? I heard you asking Jack's son to get C minuses. C minuses? You always say I need straight A's."

"What you have to understand is that Tommy is struggling in school. Jack asked me to talk with him and encourage him to work harder. That's all I was doing. I must look at where his ability lies. I cannot just say, 'Go from Ds to As in the next month.' You are different, and getting all A's is possible, so I expect you to do it."

Kids will likely rise to the expectations of their parents. I was clear about his expectation of me.

When I was older, I read about a study done in a high school in California for gifted teens. Instructors chose the high schoolers for superior intelligence. The selected teens learned they belonged in a specific school for academic high achievers. The students in this school excelled in all academic areas, from mathematics to English and foreign languages. Their confidence in their abilities skyrocketed. At the conclusion of the study, the pupils learned that they were selected at random. There was no intellectual basis for their attendance, yet they excelled. The study solidified the power of suggestion, positive thinking, enthusiasm, expectation, and motivation. Our thoughts determine our experiences, and our experiences define our lives.

I enjoyed spending time with my parents, siblings, and friends at the lake. However, when I went to Boston College, I spent less and less time there. I heard from one of my family members that one of my relatives and some of his partying friends trashed the lake house. They made holes in the walls, and now mice ran freely throughout the hallways. They inflicted unconscionable damage to our beloved lake home.

My father cared for it so well, and I didn't go there for many years because I didn't want to see it trashed like that. I tried to remember it in its original glory. I savored my memories of the yellow bedroom and my role in painting it like a delicious bowl of soup. I reflected on the perfectly maintained house and grounds Dad worked to achieve. He never took the house or the land for granted. God shared all this beauty with Dad, who was a good steward, caring for it meticulously and, in turn, blessed others.

Twenty-eight years after my dad died, Mom told me, "He always felt bad that he didn't take you and your friends out on the water more often, so you could all play and have fun."

I told her in no uncertain terms, "That is ludicrous. Dad was a *blast* with me and all my friends. He always took us skiing and tubing, no matter what time of day we wanted to go. He also took us to the go-karts and water slides constantly. That is not something he needed to feel bad about at all. He was the best."

Fast-forward about 12 years from my college graduation. Jeff and I had two adorable baby boys, Jacob, two, and Will, one. We moved back to the greater Kansas City area, and it dawned on me that we should take our family to the lake. I knew Mom had just put over $80,000 worth of repairs, remodeling, and redecorating into the house she would never see. My brothers and their families were all enjoying it immensely. I began the conversation with my brother about when I could go down to the lake. He told me to let him know when I was thinking about going. The caveat was that I could not have the Fourth of July or Memorial Day weekends, ever. Those were alternated between two of my brothers and are unavailable for anyone else. So, I looked at the calendar and chose the least desirable weekends.

One of my brothers can get scattered. I cannot tell you how many times I would get double-booked on a weekend with someone else. Untangling those messes took work. I inquired about managing the calendar and was met with a firm "NO." I did not even have a set of keys to the house. Before we left town, we had to arrange to pick up keys from one of my brothers, and when we returned, the keys needed to appear in their hands immediately. Of course, I could have made a copy of the key if they had not said, "Do Not Duplicate." Then, one summer, a couple of years ago, they said I could have my own set of keys. Now, I was making progress. My kids were enjoying the lake home and starting to bring friends and celebrate birthdays at the lake.

I could feel my father's presence whenever I went to our lake property. No other place on Earth held that for me -- I could *feel* he was there. I experienced total peace. I would look out his bedroom window at the lake with the same admiration and appreciation he had. I imagined him busy outside, grilling, fixing, burning leaves. He was there in the trees, cutting down nuisance branches, clearing a car path on the gravel road, and identifying the endless varieties of flora and fauna. I saw the beauty through *his* eyes. Dad and I loved to watch the deer that freely traversed the property. One day I was running on the property and got a bit startled by a deer. It turned out to be a doe and her fawn. We both stood still for a moment, looking at each other as time stopped. After about a minute, the doe and the fawn pranced away as if concluding a meeting with an old friend. Dad would have loved this intimate exchange, too.

The following summer, I started talking to a builder about a house on the land for my immediate family. There were 350 acres down there, plenty of space for more than one house. The property stretched the entire lakefront on one side of the cove and all the land behind it. The builder I spoke with lived just a few houses away on the neighboring cove. "Oh, building a house there would be a piece of cake. Sure, our company could do it for you. It would not even cost that much, depending on how big you want to go."

I was elated. The wheels were turning now. Having a place of our own there would be a dream come true. Beaming, we returned home from another great weekend at the lake.

My brother called me the next day, "I just want you to know we just sold the lake property."

"What do you mean, 'sold it'?"

"It's under contract."

"All 350 acres, no. I was planning on building a house there. I don't even need an acre. I need to talk to the buyer. We can figure out a way for me to get a little piece to build on."

"No, I can't do that. We can't have this deal fall through."

I was sobbing, "Please just let me call him. Please! I promise I'll be very calm. I want to ask him."

"No, we can't allow you to do that."

I spoke to my brother again, and he asserted, "It's all said and done."

I did not know what to say. Have you ever fallen hard on your kneecap or slammed your elbow on a corner? It's so painful that it almost doesn't hurt for a few seconds. You're just in shock. Then it's excruciating. That is how I felt. I pleaded again, "Please let me call this man." Now I was hysterical, "I promise I will not ruin your precious deal. I want to ask him for a tiny piece of that land. Please let me call him. Please. Tell me who the buyer is."

"I cannot tell you his name. It's the guy who lives directly across the lake from us. He's been eyeing the property for years, and he and his friends are buying it. That is all the information I can give you."

Keep in mind that Frank was the listing agent for the property. The commission on the sale of three hundred and fifty acres of prime waterfront land in the Lake of the Ozarks, Missouri, is a staggering amount. The boats were also gone. When I inquired about them, I was told, "The boats, we sold them. They were not worth anything." A total of $0.00 for a sailboat, a speedboat, a fishing boat, and a pontoon boat?

When we hung up. I was screaming and in tears. *NO God, no, please don't let this be so. No, God.* I had just redeemed this lost part of my childhood, only to have it snatched away *again*. This was the unkindest cut of all. I could feel the panic of losing Dad all over again. The entire situation was beyond my control. It was taking place whether I liked it or not. Like a show where someone gets voted out, and they find out everyone was plotting against them. I was dumbfounded, sad, and angry. I felt lonely for the arms of my dad. I just found him there. It was the only place on Earth where that connection existed for me. I cherished it as nothing else. If he were alive, my life would look entirely different and better in many ways. Now, in an instant, it was all gone. The nausea and pain I felt are still palpable.

All the old wounds split open. I felt like a robbery just took place in my soul and the missing items: my childhood, my dad, my peace, and the joy of sharing a place I adored with my children. I was simultaneously grieving the past, present, and future. I felt gutted like a trout split down the middle. It seemed I was a fish furiously flipping around on the dry wooden dock. I longed for the safety of home yet was suffocated and denied the cool waters of survival. Hot tears filled my eyes and rolled down my cheeks. It was worse than death. When someone I love dies, I force myself to accept the brutal finality of it. There are no more cards to be played, and the game is over.

In this case, there were cards still on the table, cards that needed to be played for the game to end. But with my fingers outstretched, everything slipped from my grasp. It made me think of trying futilely to pull myself out of the water and into the boat when I was little. If my hands were greasy with sunscreen, I could hold on for a while, but I did not have the upper body strength to hold on and hoist myself up and into the hull. I absolutely needed help, and Dad's strong hand was quickly there.

This time, my hand closed around nothing but air. No, Dad was not coming, and this little girl was left in the water as the boat sped away. I felt alone and lonely as I drifted helplessly in the dark waters, knowing I had lost something I could never get back. No more bonfires for roasting marshmallows with my kids, no early morning glass skiing, no deer in the woods staring back at me with eyes of innocence, no more fishing off the dock, no more shooting fireworks into the clear night sky, no more hide and seek in the house, no more coolers, and rafts. The quiet place of peaceful meditation, looking out at the water, seemed to disappear. Looking out through my dad's eyes at his vision and his land would never come to pass again. Every fishing pole, boat, life jacket, bottle of sunscreen, and towel was gone as if they never existed. My brothers said, "You can still go rent a place to stay. Just do that." That's like telling someone, "You can never have real love, but hey, go watch a rom-com. It's pretty much the same." No. If you have ever had the luxury of a truly special and precious love, you know a rom com is a poor substitute that will only leave you more aware of what you do not have.

I did not have the heart to tell my children, especially my sweet daughter, Madison. Soon after the deal closed, she said, "I just want to make sure we are going to the lake for my birthday." I could not tell her. I could not make the words come out of my mouth that there was no lake house anymore.

Sometimes, life seems cruel. My dad died right in front of me when I was 24. I found him again at the lake house many years later. Then, suddenly, I lost our beloved location again. I carry Dad and his amazing lessons with me. Time spent together, wisdom, and love cannot be sold away to the highest bidder. They are not dependent on a signed contract or a commission. They are freely given and eternal. It's been two years since the sale, and it still hurts to know it's gone. It's like the death of a best friend, I know it happened, but I sure wish it didn't. Although sometimes it feels otherwise, I remind myself it's the property that's gone forever and not my heart.

Forgiveness does not require understanding what was done, and acceptance is not approval. It's been a couple years. I don't think I will ever understand denying me the opportunity to write into the contract one or two acres of my own. It would have meant absolutely nothing to the new owners and everything to me. And what did the new owners do with the property? They promptly turned around and sold the land to a developer who is building a resort. It's not as if they wanted to be stewards of the beauty like Mom and Dad. It's all so disappointing. I am required to forgive, so I do.

There are some things that are especially difficult to forgive. I sought out someone I believed to have forgiven magnanimously. I found Lucas, who was unfairly treated. He was convicted of a crime and sent to prison for thirty years. His case was exonerated after twenty-five, yes, twenty-five, years of living behind bars. He resided in a small cell from age twenty-two to forty-seven. The woman who picked him out of a lineup admitted that she did not recognize him. She only said he committed the crime because he was the only black person in the lineup.

But he forgave her, and I knew it, so I went to talk with him. I said, "Lucas, how did you forgive someone for sending you to prison for twenty-five years, losing twenty-five years of your life. How do you do that?"

"Well, it happened long before I left the walls of my cell. It happened as I read my Bible and learned about God. I realized the prison I was in was my own unforgiveness. I told God, 'I cannot forgive this person, but I know you can through me.' When I did that, I was free. I was free of the hate. I was still behind prison walls, but I was a free man. It was a few more years before I actually left that place, but I was already free long before. And that's what I still do. I ask Him to forgive *through me*. I cannot do it on my own strength. I know I can't, so I ask Him."

Many times, I call out to God, "I can't do it. Forgive through me."

The response of Saint Josephine Bakhita humbles me. As a young Sudanese girl, she was kidnapped and enslaved. The conditions and treatment she endured were despicable. She eventually became a Catholic Nun. She is quoted as saying, "If I were to meet those who kidnapped me, and even those who tortured me, I would kneel and kiss their hands. For if this had not happened, I would not be a Christian and a religious today," and "In God's will, there is great peace."

I'm not there but I am a student of those who forgive. I admire Lucas, St. Maximillian Kobe, Saint Josephine Bakhita, Saint John Paul II, and, of course, Christ himself whose final plea was, "Forgive them, Father. They know not what they do."

I deeply desire to be such a vessel of love. I humbly ask God, Thy will, not mine, be done."

"So then, each of us will give an account of ourselves to God."
(Romans 14:12)

"Everything can be taken from a man but one thing: the last of the human freedoms—to choose one's attitude in any given set of circumstances, to choose one's own way." Viktor E. Frankl, Man's Search for Meaning

"If your enemy is hungry, feed him; if he is thirsty, give him something to drink. In doing this, you will heap burning coals on his head. Do not be overcome by evil but overcome evil with good." (Romans 12:14-21)

A Thousand Words

HE HOUSE I grew up in was at 611 West 57th Street in Kansas City, Missouri. I lived there from when I was born until just after my dad died 24 years later. I was in Italy when Mom sold the house. She called and said, "Would you like anything from home?"

I was traumatized by Dad's death and found myself depressed and grieving. I could not think clearly when Mom asked me about all the items in the house. It seemed overwhelming to sort in my mind, so I replied, "No, I don't want anything."

I never returned to that home, as my mom had moved by Christmas. She built a condo in a beautiful building. It was stunning. I asked, "Where is the painting of the ballet dancer that was on the wall my whole life?"

"I didn't know you wanted it; we sold it."

"What about my ribbon collection and the things in my desk and closet? What about my photo albums and yearbooks?"

"That's all gone, too."

"What about our big family portrait that hung on the dining room wall?"

"Oh, your brother, John, picked it up, broke it over his knee, and threw it in the trash."

"I would have wanted that."

"Me, too, but you know how John is; throw it all away."

It all reminded me of the shows where they 'wipe' someone's memory. Only in this case, the 'wipe' was of the first 25 years of my life, and it was every item I ever owned. The memories were still with me as cruel reminders of all that was lost.

The family portrait was special; it was a moment in time with the six of us kids. I was about five years old and wearing a floor-length blue dress. I was wearing black patent leather and open-toed shoes with a small heel. My toes peeked out from under the fold of my dress and showed little white socks turned down at my ankle with white lace around the edges. My brother, Frank, could not find his good dress shoes that morning, so he had to wear 'waffle stompers.' My mom was stressed about those shoes, but they became iconic. Later, on a trip to our lake house, I did not feel well after the hilly roads. I leaned over. I didn't quite lean far enough and threw up on those 'waffle stompers' while they were still on my brother. They were never to be seen again. That photo held the only proof of their existence, and now it was gone. My sisters donned long floral dresses, seventies- and hippie-style. Both had long, wavy hair that accentuated their flower-child personas. It was fun to look at those old memories. But not for John. He constantly throws away everything. If you pick your head up from your pillow, John has thrown it into the fire. The minute the baby eats at the table for the first time, the highchair is thrown away. In his mind, those times are to be forgotten, buried, and done.

I came home that Christmas to find not only our house but all my memories—family photos, personal photos, yearbooks, gifts, clothing, shoes, and all my possessions—gone. I think some people get rid of things, thinking that if they don't see it, it didn't happen. But you can't erase that it really happened, and if it happened and you have photos, it's probably for a reason. It's likely that at some moment, those things, those people, and those places meant something to you. Maybe it hurts to see them. Maybe you can't make peace with them. However, you can't erase the past by discarding evidence of it. You might as well keep a photo or two. Later in life, you may want to look at them and tell your son or daughter a few stories. Maybe you will laugh at the old hairstyles. Maybe you will cry over the love you lost. Maybe you will smile and be grateful that everything that ever happened was for a reason, and it brought you where you are today.

When my mom was in her eighties, she would occasionally have a portrait taken of herself. We would get these for Christmas. She always looked beautiful. Age was no match for her beauty and elegance. I love looking at her photos. I even have her engagement photo in a frame. I like to look at it and wonder what she was like as a young woman. What was she thinking about? What were her concerns? Her joys? She looked happy and gorgeous.

I stare at it. I think I will never throw this away.

When there was going to be an estate sale of one of my mom's homes, I went by early in the morning. I looked through some stacks of framed photos. There was one of my brothers, John, likely in his early twenties. It was an expensive portrait framed in a thick, custom frame. He was wearing a dark navy suit and looked quite handsome. I remembered how he threw away all my things from 611; that's what we called our home on 57th Street. I still feel the sting of losing everything.

Because I'm human, I hurt and can see a situation as an opportunity to make someone else pay for the pain I believe they have inflicted. I am not responsible for that first thought. It may come from impulse, like a knee-jerk reaction. I don't need to judge myself for that, I have clay feet like everyone else. I am responsible for my second thought and my actions. For that, I have a moral compass. I do what is right, whether I feel like it or not. This is my spiritual practice.

I could hear my dad say, "Actions speak louder than words... The road to Hell is paved with good intentions... Treat others how you want to be treated... Take the high road... Kill with kindness." I picked up my cell phone and called John. "Hello, John. I am at Mom's house. The estate sale is about to start. On the lower level, there is a nice portrait of you. You may not want it, but your kids or grandkids would appreciate it. I can take it out of here for you and bring it by."

"Would you? That would be great. Maybe my daughter would want that."

"Sure, no problem."

I could see John's daughter smiling as she proudly displayed the handsome photo of her dad.

"If you don't think photos are important, wait until they are all you have left." Missy Mwac

"The right thing to do and the hard thing to do are usually the same thing," attributed to Steve Maraboli.

"The wound is the place where the Light enters you." Rumi

"For every time there is a season.. a time to search and a time to give up, a time to keep and a time to throw away..." (Ecclesiastes 3:6 NIV)

FAB FOUR IV

MEG AND MADISON

WE WERE a foster family licensed in the state of Kansas. One day, we got a call from our spectacular social worker, Jessie. She knew we would love to foster a baby girl, and she did not disappoint. As she said, "This is your girl. She's the one. It's my last day at work, and I'm moving to Nebraska. I will leave you in good hands. Do you want to go meet your sweet baby girl?"

Jessie proceeded to tell me the facts I would need about Baby Meg. I called a friend who worked in the NICU where Baby Meg was born. I told her we had the opportunity to foster little Meg, and she was all for it. My next call was to my husband, Jeff. I needed to get his blessing. On February 11, 2015, he agreed that we could foster Meg, a selfless decision on his part. Fostering was not in Jeff's heart as it was in mine. I was very grateful when Jeff agreed we could foster this baby, and on his birthday, no less.

When I say NO ONE wanted this baby girl, I mean NO ONE. Not a soul was available to take her home from the hospital. Zip, zero, nada. No interest whatsoever. Baby Meg was born addicted to heroin from her biological mother. Helping anyone detox from that kind of addiction is a massive undertaking of epic proportions. It was no different for Baby Meg. She could rarely settle and rest. She would shake uncontrollably and cry. Lights were kept low in her room in the NICU, and the sound was kept to a minimum. She was beautiful, and all the nurses loved her and held her as much as they could. Her grandparents told me, "She is yours; we don't want her. We can't take care of her. You can keep her. We are both busy with our lives. I run my own business, and my wife is busy teaching full-time with no sign of retirement in sight."

Without a foster family, Baby Meg was slated to live in the NICU for at least the first three months of her life. No one wanted to take on a baby who would require 24/7 care as she detoxed from drug addiction. Meg was the innocent victim of her mother›s addiction. I started visiting Meg in the NICU in my every free moment. I began meeting with the doctors and nurses daily to review the plan for Meg's care. Soon, we had a plan to bring her home. I believe the only reason her medical team considered this was because my husband and I are doctors. Still, they grilled me with detailed instructions on caring for Meg.

First, there was the methadone that needed to be dealt with under lock and key. It was measured in increments of .01 ml doses and required to be the precise dose given at the exact time multiple times a day. We were instructed, "She can't be taken places like normal babies. She can't go to the store or a shopping venue. She needs to be kept at home. The lights need to be low, and the noise must be at a complete minimum."

Keep in mind that at this point, we already had three boys, ages 12, 11, and 8, and our dog, Aslan. My children were very involved in school and sports, so we had commitments all over the place. I could not just drop my life and stay in a quiet, dark room with this baby for a few months. I did not see how this could work out, but I trusted that God did.

It was a huge responsibility; no one would fault us for not taking it on. I spent a good chunk of time in prayer over this, as I knew it would impact the entire family. One day, I pulled over in a Target parking lot to pray.

God, this is too big for me to know what to do. I can get 10 people to tell me, 'You don't have to do that. It would be insane. How would that ever work?' I can also get a bunch to say 'go for it' as well. Ultimately, I know this is between You and me. I let You down once before on something significant and life changing. I have told You how sorry I am for it. So, although others may tell me I can say no, I know I cannot. I promised that I would do whatever You asked of me. You can make a way where there appears to be no way. You make streams in the desert. I love You.

I left the parking lot with a sense that the decision had been made. Still, I wanted some outward confirmation from God. I was on the way to volunteer at Sunday School at my church. Usually, there were two adults for each classroom of kids. I thought of this sweet lady who usually volunteered with me.

I know, I thought, I will ask her opinion. I prayed, *please, God, please use someone here to speak wisdom and discernment into our situation. Please let the answer be clear.* I resolved to ask my classroom partner for advice and really listen for God's wisdom through her.

I bounded up the stairs to the classroom. I was excited to see who God would use to give me a word regarding this life-altering decision. I flung open the door, ready to listen. You can imagine my disappointment when I found a thirteen-year-old boy setting up the room.

"Hi, I'm Elisemarie."

"I'm Joe."

"Will you be in this classroom tonight?"

"Yes, Ms. Tina could not come, so I'm here to help."

"Okay, great."

God, this is not funny, I told You I would really be attentive to the very person you brought me to tonight. I at least expected a legal adult. What can this kid possibly have to say about fostering a baby who is withdrawing from heroin? I know I said I would ask the person who was here tonight, but really, a kid. Okay, I hope You know what You're doing on this one.

As the evening progressed, there was some free time for the kids to work on their projects. I took the opportunity to inform Joe of our family's fostering option and ask him what he thought about the experience.

He answered promptly, "I don't really see a downside. The baby would get the help she needs. Your family would get the opportunity to serve. It would be a good experience for your boys. When would they ever have the chance to do something like that? I would say, do it.'"

Well, from the mouths of babes! I loved how Joe didn't try to figure out HOW it would work. Just that it would work. I felt peace in the way he saw things. It was innocent wisdom. It made sense.

Then there was the issue of quiet. We had an awesome dog, Aslan, who was a yellow Lab. He was such a good boy. However, he liked to bark at things he saw passing by in the front or back yard, and he had a low, deep, sonorous bark. I thought about the possibility of finding him a temporary home. I asked everyone I encountered if they wanted to care for Aslan for a while. I was met with many *I'll think about it, and I'll get back to you responses.*

Finally, I was at a swim practice with my boys. They had a young and darling coach who was also super responsible. I asked her about taking Aslan. She said, "Oh, my brother has dogs, and I take care of them pretty often. I dog-sit them or take them to the park. If I took Aslan, he could have fun and run around with my brother's dogs. I think it would work." The next thing I knew, we packed up Aslan for a little sabbatical with Tracy. All seemed well.

In the coming seven to ten days, I was extensively trained to care for Meg. I bought her clothing, toys, bottles, formula, and special sanitizing bags for her bottles. It was a weekend night, and we were driving home from a swim meet when I received a call from the hospital.

"Meg will need distilled water to mix in with her formula. You will need to go to the infant section and find it. Buy that. You can't just use regular tap water."

It was late at night, and we were picking her up the next day. I wanted to be the perfect foster mom for Meg. I would 'dot' every i and 'cross' every t. I would do as I was instructed. If they wanted water from a particular spring in the middle of Kansas, I would have walked to find it. They wanted her bottles to be sterilized each time in these special bags used in the NICU. I went out and bought those. This little lamb had suffered enough. I was determined that there would be no more suffering on my watch, only love.

I spent the day in the hospital with Meg before we left for home. That day, we were no longer in the NICU; we were in a private room. I was there to have a little time with Meg and handle all her needs. This was done in the safety of the hospital, where, at any time, I could call for help. I loved how super-concerned the staff were for this baby. They wanted to be sure that I could give her the level of care that the full-time NICU nurses provided. Meg was delightful that day. She was super sweet, and we got along swimmingly. I didn't need to call for help.

We were visited by several doctors and nurses throughout the day to see if all was well. The staff began giving credibility to my four years of medical school and my three actual babies. I held Meg almost the entire day. I know this because I would feed her, change her, rock her to sleep, and lay her in her bassinet. I watched the clock, and not more than 10 minutes elapsed before this baby was awake again, crying. That is what the withdrawal was like for her. She had no lasting peace. I was concerned about how I would only sleep for 5-7 minutes at a time on an ongoing basis.

This led me to Sister Lourdes of the Sisters of Mercy. The beautiful work of her Order is to provide respite during the night so that other caregivers can have a break. She was able to come three nights a week. She could leave the convent at 9 pm and had to return by 5 am The convent was in Kansas City, Kansas, 35 minutes from our house, and in a less-than-desirable part of the city, but the convent grounds were safe.

KVC, the Kansas fostering organization, told me that they would cover her fares to and from our house. I called many cab companies and found one that would give me a flat rate for her round trip.

A couple of weeks into care, KVC informed me that they had made a mistake and could not cover the cost of her rides. This added to my ever-burgeoning plate, organizing six weekly rides to a part of town that was, at a minimum, inconvenient. To this day, I am thankful for my nieces and nephews, who helped with rides, along with many others. That meant I got 30 additional minutes with my boys at bedtime or 30 extra minutes to sleep.

Jeff took on some of the 9 pm drives, and I took the 4:20 am stretch. I was grateful for Sister Lourdes and the way she loved and cared for us. I received 5-6 hours of sleep on three nights. I kept extensive notes about Meg's sleeping, eating, shaking, and crying. I wanted to monitor her progress. Sister Lourdes perfectly followed suit, keeping equally meticulous notes on her nights with Baby Meg.

We lived to give Meg a total team effort every day. Since she needed to be held constantly, we made that happen. My three sons would get home from school and begin rotations of holding Meg for 30 minutes each. We were glad to do that for her. This allowed me to prepare dinner, fold laundry, go through their schoolwork, and clean the house. The boys were terrific with Meg. She was delighted with them and beamed in a way that only a 5-week-old baby can. I will always be proud of them for helping to care for Meg. They selflessly loved her.

Yet this sweet baby would still shake and cry. I was upset by Meg's needless suffering. The judge assigned to our case was Judge Thompson. She was known for caring about the kids whose cases came through her courtroom. In our first court appearance with Judge Thompson, I wanted to let her know how Meg suffered. I was beyond nervous to do this, but I needed to push through for Meg. With a shaking voice and having exactly zero experience in the courtroom, I began.

"Elisemarie DiCarlo, Meg's foster mom. If it pleases the court, may I say something?" Judge Thompson gave me permission, and I explained, "Meg is precious. We are blessed to have her. I want to inform the court that she cries when we are not holding her. She shakes. She cannot settle to rest for more than fifteen minutes, and the withdrawal is a daily battle for her."

That was all Judge Thompson needed to simply explode.

She turned to Meg's biological mother. "Did you hear that? Really, did you hear how that innocent baby is suffering? Crying. Shaking. Do you really understand what she is going through?" Meg's bio mom nodded.

Judge Thompson continued, "Good, because you caused all of it. Maybe you need to think about that."

I took Meg to a pediatric hospital weekly, where they would weigh, measure, and assess her progress. Then, the doctor would write a prescription for her methadone. I would drive across town to another hospital, go downstairs, follow several corridors, find the pharmacy, and hand the prescription to one of the pharmacists. The room was usually packed with patients getting their medications before leaving the hospital. There were commonly 20 people waiting for medications. I would wait for my turn. Usually, this took about an hour.

When it was time for Meg's medication, they would carefully titrate the liquid to the exact amount she needed for the week and not one drop more. The concoction was placed in a small vial so I could draw it up through a dropper that measured to the tenth of a milliliter. I would rush home as the medicine had to be kept cold. Then, I would set alarms on my watch to remind me to give Meg her doses. The amount and the timing of administering the medication changed weekly and needed to be exact. Then, we would use that medication for a week, go back to the hospital, and see a neonatologist to begin the process all over again. This went on for about ten weeks.

We were also constantly visited by KVC case workers. They would walk through our house. Ask about every person, everything about little Meg. All the while, the caseworker did not tell me any of the requirements for family visitation. I was left on my own to wing that. I knew the grandparents wanted to see Meg. I thought, of course, they do; it's their grandbaby. I proceeded to give them every possible opportunity to see Meg. We had a schedule where they would pick Meg up on Saturday mornings and bring her home on Sunday night. Why did I allow this? I just thought it's their grandchild; of course, they want to spend time with her.

I also sent them emails daily about Meg's progress. Again, I wanted them to know that Meg was safe and thriving. I gave them all my information so they could reach out anytime to learn about Meg and her progress. I took them in as a family. If Meg was going to stay with us, as they had made perfectly clear from Day One, I wanted us all to have good relationships. I did this for Meg, but mainly for the grandparents. I remember staying up extra late with my eyes burning to ensure they got their nightly email. I needed sleep, but I thought it was essential to give them updates regularly.

Meg's case worker was brand new. I am pretty sure she was winging this whole thing from day to day. I do not mean this harshly. She was just fresh out of college. This was her first day on her first job. She did not have answers to most of my questions. No problem. Everyone is going to be new sometime, and that's a tough spot to be in. She was doing the best that she could. It's just that this involved me not being informed as to my rights as a foster mom.

This would have all been just fine. We could have learned the ropes together. However, this baby girl's fate was in the balance, and the social workers' missteps were life-altering. In any case, no one told me what the rules were for family visitation. I knew that the grandparents could see her. I thought if I were a grandparent of this beautiful baby girl, I would want to know everything I could about her, and I would want to see her often. The Golden Rule came into play. Treat others as I would like to be treated. I texted and emailed them throughout the week. I let them take her to their house every weekend for an overnight. I worked with their schedule and what was convenient for them. I supported them in seeing Meg as much as possible.

I knew we were willing and wanted to adopt this baby girl. I heard, "We don't want her; she is yours." I took these people at their word. I also told myself that she might be put back with her biological family. That is just what the State of Kansas does. It's insignificant to the state that her biological mom had been to treatment 27 times without any lengthy time sober and clean. If a bio parent has a car to sleep in and any money at all, they get their kid back. It's reunification, above all. I firmly believe cases need to be looked at individually to determine what is suitable for the whole child. But as my dad would say, "When they made the rules, they never asked me."

I knew that it was a possibility – be it a very remote one- that the State would find a better situation for Meg. I told my kids, "We need to love Meg as our own. Hold nothing back. If she stays, we will be happy that we treated her as family. If she goes, well, then she needs our love even more on her journey away from us."

As the weeks passed, Meg was thriving. We finally completed weaning her off the methadone. She became regulated in her body and spirit. She rested for ten hours at night. The Health Department from the State of Kansas came out to check on Meg's development continuously. One day, they said, "Meg is just perfect. She is exactly on target developmentally. You have done a beautiful job. We won't be coming out to check on Meg anymore. We know she is in good hands and thriving." Meg was doing everything a two and ½-month-old baby was expected to do. She had turned into a calm, happy, and always adorable baby girl. She loved to have fun, giggle, and squeal with delight at the mobile above her.

It was Monday, after a weekend visit with her grandparents, when I received a call from her case worker. "We are going to come take Meg on Thursday."

Holy God, the floor opened beneath me. Thursday. Thursday, no way, no, no, no! Immediately, I was weeping. Amy explained that they could take her anytime since we had Meg in our care for less than three months.

I said to Amy, "Take her, take her where?"

"The grandparents want her now."

"Yes, now that she sleeps 12 hours a night. Now that she is developmentally perfectly and on track," I hurtfully replied.

Did they not have the decency to talk with me about this? The person who had bent over backward to ensure they saw that sweet baby whenever they wanted? This was a blindside. Well played. I take care of her, demonstrate that the baby you were willing to throw away is actually perfect, and then you take her. I just believed better of people. I don't expect selfishness. I don't expect people to do inconsiderate, selfish, and illogical things. Maybe this is illogical of me. I expect them to think of others rather than what they want at that moment. I've been like this since I was a little kid. In our home, you had to think of others; anything else was unacceptable.

I thought to myself, that was cruel. I wish I had a recording of when they said, "We don't want her; you can have her." Of course, they want her now that she is easy. Now that she has been weaned through round-the-clock shaking, crying, loose stools, chills, and all the traumas. Now that someone else had held her as she shook and cried from three to five am. Well, that must have been convenient, my mind railed. Have someone else make everything right, and just take Meg when she is the way you want her.

Meg got well because we loved her. We loved her when no one else did. We loved her enough to put aside our wants and needs for her good. We knew she was a gift from God and that she deserved our best. Meg did not heal because we followed the protocol for getting her free of it, although we did do that. She got better because of *how* we did it. It was done with unconditional love.

She was an "at-risk, addicted baby." We saw her as perfect the way she was, with intrinsic value. We saw her as a risk worth taking, although we just met her. We accepted her with open arms from day one. Now she is whole, happy, and healthy enough for them, and they are going to "take her."

Like she was a doll, a plant, or a sack of groceries, they forgot at the store. I was told by more seasoned foster parents that the grandparents say they will take the baby only to give it back to the biological mother. In this case, bio mom was not making progress and was still using. Meg was going back to her birth mother, who had been the cause of the entire tragedy. The grandparents were the funnel to getting Meg to her drug-addicted birth mother. This was a cruel twist I did not see coming. It was one I could do absolutely nothing about.

Why? Because the system is the system. The system is set on reunification at all costs. If there is a family member with any money, say $10, and has a place to live, even if it's in a car, they can get their child back. A sweet friend of mine, Jennifer, was fostering a set of twin boys. They were 2 years old and adorable. I asked, "What do you think will happen to them?"

"Well, we will give them everything we can. We will fill them up with love and care. Then they will be returned to the very same unacceptable situation they came from."

Jennifer said this as if it were a fact that she was rattling off on her grocery list. That is just the way it was. Accept it. The thing for me was I did not know this at the outset. I thought they would look at what was in the child's best interest. I thought they would consider the environmental, physical, spiritual, and emotional factors involved. No, the system says, "Your DNA matches, so you have the right to be a complete mess. We will happily uproot your baby from a place where they are thriving and loved. We will give them back to you to keep making grave mistakes that will shape the person they will become. We will ruthlessly rip out the hearts of their caretakers with no regard for them. We will leave those who have truly sacrificed with nothing. For those who have sacrificed nothing, you get everything. Sounds good to us. Thank you for playing."

I cried my heart out as the days ticked by. I called everyone I knew who could possibly help with this crisis, to no avail. Meg would be picked up on Thursday at 12:30 pm. And that is all there was to it. When it comes to love and the safety of a child, I would do anything. I considered leaving the state and then leaving the country. No, I could not flee forever. I was losing it. I had been on time and early for every appointment, meeting, conference, court hearing, and doctor visit for Meg for the last 3 months. I had done everything asked of me by everyone involved. I had done it how they wanted it, when they wanted it, and with whom they wanted it. Why? Because I saw this baby as an incredible gift from God. As one who was suffering the consequences of actions she did not take. Most of all, because all I had in my heart for her was love.

When that dreaded Thursday came, I was at swim practice with my boys and Meg. Practice ended at noon and was close to home, giving me ample time to get there by 12:30 pm. But 12:30 pm came and went, and I was nowhere near home. My mom, who was 89 years old at the time, was at my house. She said, "I am not going to have you there on your own when they come to take this baby." My mom understood the pain of losing a child, especially a very young baby. It was my mom who called my cell phone.

"Where are you?"

"I'm at the pool with my kids."

"Well, the social worker is here to get Meg. She says you were supposed to be here at 12:30. Are you coming?"

"Yes."

With that, we loaded up the car and headed home. To this day, I look at my delay as peculiar. I think I just wanted to say I'm done. I am done following every single little command to the T. If this is how it will go down in the end, then I am done. I am done being on time and catering to your every single whim. I will not be on time today, as it gives me one little thing to have control over. You have left me powerless and impotent. Yet, I will not be on time. For once you will wait, the hours I have waited when you are late.

For once, for the countless hours I have prayed and wondered, you will wonder. For once, you may feel a tinge of nervousness for the endless anxiety I have endured. Yes, you will go through ten little minutes of discomfort for the 43,278 minutes I have pressed through. I know this is not kind and not the person I ideally want to be. It was the best I could do at the time.

We arrived home to say our goodbyes to Meg. I can still see the old black car seat we placed her in. It had some grey fabric that was ripped, pilled, and old with stains. It was a piece of junk.

I reluctantly buckled her in, my tears dripping off my face and onto her little pink blanket. I then lifted the car seat into an equally dilapidated vehicle. I watched as the doors closed, and my heart drove away. I love you, Meg.

I had received a message on my cell phone two days prior. It said, "This is Joanne from the NICU, where Meg was. I have gotten a call about a baby. They want me to take her because I have her half-sister. I just cannot take another child from the state. I have my boy, my daughter with severe developmental difficulties, and my other daughter, whom I have adopted from the state. I also have my own three kids. As a single mom, I cannot do this. I'm sure this sounds crazy, but would you consider taking her? You did an awesome job with Meg when I saw you with her here in the NICU. Our girls could know each other; we could make sure of that."

It turns out that this baby girl was already slated to go to another foster family. Joanne called KVC and said, "I saw Elisemarie taking care of that other critically ill baby. She's great. We can keep the girls in touch as half-sisters. I will do that if she takes her."

Now, KVC was required to have a 'best case hearing.' This is where they look at all the positives and negatives of each family and choose the 'best case' scenario for the baby. This was held the next day. I was stressed beyond belief.

My phone rang at 11:30 am.

James, our family case worker, told me, "We had our meeting, and the decision was that your family is the best case for Madison."

"Oh, my goodness! Thank you so much, this is wonderful."

"Before you get your hopes up, I need to tell you that they are saying the baby may not make it. She was born prematurely; she weighs less than five pounds, and they don't know if she can survive. We will let you know how things are going in a few days."

Meg left our house at 1:03 pm on June 11, 2015. My phone rang at 1:17 pm on the same day. Again, it was James.

"Would you like to go to the hospital to meet Madison?"

"When?"

"Any time. Now, if you want, head over to the NICU at the med center whenever you like."

I was in shock. This was all like a whirlwind. The boys and I got ready to go to the hospital. I called the NICU ahead and spoke with a nurse, "I am wondering what time Madison's next feeding will be?"

"It's in twenty minutes."

"Okay, can I give her a bottle then?

"She doesn't take bottles. She is fed through a feeding tube."

"Oh, I see. Could I try to give her a bottle? I don't want you to hold her feeding or anything. It would just be nice."

"It's not a problem; you can try. It's just that she's not able to feed that way. Don't get your feelings hurt if it doesn't work out."

"Of course, I really thank you for letting me have a chance, we will see you soon."

Jacob, Will, Nick, and I hopped in the car and sped to the medical center. We entered the NICU, which was quiet as a mouse at this time of day. The nurse took us to meet Madison. She was precious and tiny. The nurse set down her little bottle of formula and left us in the quiet. The boys met and held Madison, then went to get a snack. I picked up sweet Madison and her bottle. I put the bottle in her mouth. She drank the entire thing down without hesitation. Her nurse was amazed. There would be no tube feeding for that hour, nor ever again. The nurses began giving her bottles, and the tube was removed.

You never know what can be done with the power of God and love. He makes all things possible. All things, especially the impossible. I felt the hand of the Lord in our time there with Madison. She seemed to take to us and us to her. I felt terrible leaving her there in that NICU all alone. No one was holding her. Most babies in the NICU have Mom, Dad, Grandma, or Grandpa there around the clock. No one had been there holding Madison for the thirty-three days of her life. That was on a Friday. On Monday morning, I got a call, and the nurse said, "When are you going to come get your baby?"

"When can I?"

"Any time; she has been discharged already this morning."

I was so excited I didn't know what to do. I grabbed my purse and ran to the car to get to the hospital as soon as possible. I ran up the stairs to the elevator and to her hospital room. The nurses had packed up a few things to send home with Madison, like formula and a couple of diapers the size of postage stamps.

She said, "Did you bring something for her to wear?"

"No, I just ran out of the house."

I forgot that foster children leave the hospital with absolutely nothing. They own nothing. With Meg, I had time. I shopped for a perfect little outfit for her. I even bought clothes for her while she was still in the NICU. That morning I just ran out the door as fast as I could for Madison.

"Don't worry, we will find a onesie for you."

Madison was dressed in her onesie, the only piece of clothing she now owned. I had her car seat and blanket ready in the car. The nurse knew about what happened with Meg.

She said, "Don't worry. She's your baby. No one is going to come after her."

That was kind of her, but I had been too badly burned. I knew anything could happen in this crazy system. I would take it one day at a time. Once again, I loved her and cared for her as if she were ours. That was the best way; either way, it went. Madison was a delight. She was a perfect baby and adorable. She was super tiny, as she had to get to exactly 5 lbs. for us to take her home. I held her in one hand. She was tiny but she already held a light inside of her that shines to this day.

We were elated with the sweetness that Madison brought to our home. Still, I was grieving the loss of Meg. I would try hiding my crying spells by going into a bathroom or a closet. One day, by my bathroom sink, my nine-year-old son, Nick, heard me softly crying and came over to give me a hug. He asked what was wrong. He knew I was missing Meg. Our eyes met, and he understood my tears immediately. Nick said, "Remember, we gave her the foundation. The foundation to love that all her other relationships will be based on. Without the foundation, you can't build a house or anything lasting. We gave her the foundation."

I had shared an article with him about the first bonding a baby makes. It is crucial to develop all bonds for life. It's imperative that the baby forms a strong attachment with her caregivers and learns the safety of being taken care of, heard, and loved. I hope we gave Meg an excellent foundation. I know she will likely never remember ever being with us or who we are. That's okay; the love is still there, planted in her. Nothing can take that away.

The first Christmas after Meg left, I was still struggling with the loss of her. It just felt like someone was missing because she was not there. By the grace of God, her grandfather brought Meg by on Christmas Eve. It was so bittersweet to have her close. She went over to the steps and appeared to want to go up them. Her room was at the top of the stairs. She cried when they picked her up to go. I felt she knew how much we loved her and that, as a baby, she just intuitively wanted to stay. As the years passed, I asked if we could get our girls together to play. There was always a reason they said they were unable to meet up with us. As I understand, Meg lives with her grandparents during the week and sees her mom on the weekends. I hear she does well in school. I will always, always love her.

Now I know that Meg left us so we would have a place for Madison. That was God's plan for all of us. Although I didn't see it at the time. I accept now that Meg was meant to go. What I will never say is that it brought her a better life than she would have had with us. I just can't say that. It got her a different life. I hope it is a very good one in its own way. But better? I cannot say that. I will always think of Meg as my child that was taken away. I get tears in my eyes when I think of her or hear her name. I don't think that will ever change.

Our journey with Madison would be complicated and twisting through the child welfare system. One day, our social worker said,

"Let's meet with Madison's family member at the KVC office near their home."

With Madison secured in the car, I drove to the most dangerous neighborhood I have ever seen. I was lost, and, luckily, a police car pulled up next to me. I had my window down and called out to the officer. He answered me curtly, "Go to the next light and take a right." Quickly, he rolled up his window and sped off as if to say, "Listen, lady, I have bigger fish to fry than 'you're lost in the big city' questions." Upon finding the office, I bolted in with Madison. The woman at the front desk was visiting with the social worker. She said, "We haven't even had one murder yet on this block this year." We waited for over thirty minutes. The family member never showed. I asked the social worker if we could follow her out of this downtown neighborhood. From what I know of the circumstances, I genuinely believe Madison would have been emotionally, spiritually, and physically damaged there. My friend, Diane, always says, "You saved her life. Look at what a difference you have made in her life. She is so lucky to have you."

"No, Diane, she saved me, no question."

"Well, you are both lucky, let's just say that."

Fostering Madison would take two long and stressful years. Finally, on May 24, 2017, we had our 'Gotcha Day,' and Madison was finally, officially, ours, just as we believed all along.

I know all things are in Divine Order and that my good and loving Creator is watching over us all. There are no mistakes in God's world. I trust that. Even when it hurts, especially when it hurts. Good night, my sweet Meg, wherever you are. May you always know you are deeply loved, and Madison, may you know you are the love of our lives. We cannot imagine even a day without you. I love you endlessly. God chose us for you, and you for us. We are blessed beyond comprehension. Thank you for being precious! As I always tell you, "Being adopted means we CHOSE YOU, and that is very special." Sometimes when we are visiting with a new friend, I will say, "Madison, do you want to share what is special about you?" With a huge smile, she declares, "I am adopted."

> "Jesus said, 'Let the little children come to me, and do not hinder them, for the kingdom of heaven belongs to such as these.' When he had placed his hands on them, he went on from there." (Matthew 19: 14-15, NIV)

> "The Lord bless you and keep you; the Lord make his face shine on you and be gracious to you; the Lord turn his face toward you and give you peace." (Numbers 6:24, NIV)

> "Religion that God our Father accepts as pure and faultless is this: to look after orphans and widows in their distress and to keep oneself from being polluted by the world." (James 1:27)

It's Not That Bad

A S A PARENT, I like to prepare upstream for possible rapids. One area in which I am adamant about this is addiction. I have witnessed too many loved ones swallowed up by that tyrant. My husband and I are both sober. We were sober when we met. Our children have never seen us take a drink or a drug. I knew they would be genetically susceptible to addiction, as our family trees are filled with alcoholics and addicts. Intelligent, attractive, high-functioning, charming, accomplished addicts.

I was keenly focused on anyone I met who worked in recovery with young alcoholics. So, when I met Dan and Mary, I filed those names away. First, because I love them, and second, because they work in a very successful recovery program for young addicts and alcoholics. When our boys were looking for high schools, I asked Dan and Mary for input. I hoped private schools would be less susceptible to drugs and alcohol. Mary quickly said, "No, those schools can be worse because those kids have so much money at their disposal. They have nice cars and the money for drugs for themselves and their friends."

I had to admit that was true for me as a teen. I had every material benefit I could imagine. In my wallet were credit cards and cash. My purse held car keys and condo keys. My closet was a haven of designer jeans, t-shirts, and shoes. My tennis coach was the best in the city. I traveled to New York, California, Canada, and Mexico, all in my teens. None of this filled me up. This was the most confusing part for me. If all this stuff could not fill the hole I felt in my soul, what would work? I was in pain, and I just wanted to escape my awkward discomfort with myself. I wanted out of those feelings, and alcohol gave me a quick, unearned, and false sense of escape. My bonfire of pain seemed to be squelched by alcohol, at least temporarily. But I always woke up, and my problems were worse. My shame grew exponentially, and I felt remorseful. Another chink was taken from the armor of my self-esteem. My solution to the torment was to pick up more of the poison that was killing me. Alcohol drowned out the stinging and throbbing of my dying heart, and the downward spiral continued. By God's grace, I hit bottom before I died of the deadly disease of alcoholism. I can still see the face that stared back at me when I looked in the mirror one fateful night. I saw the emptiness in my eyes. The light was growing dim within me. I considered the pathetic shell of a person I was becoming and the oxymoron of having everything and nothing at all. Ironically, I was standing in a bathroom in a basement of a bar. My only way out was to take the steps. It was those steps and those of alcoholics anonymous that truly saved my life. I see those same empty eyes in many young people who come to my practice as a therapist. I do not sugarcoat their use of alcohol, drugs, cutting, eating, vaping, or anything else they are doing to escape their pain. Just today, I told a patient who is doing drugs, "Just remember you are an addict. You are addicted. This is not safe for you." I always remember my sponsor saying to me, "I love you enough to tell you the truth." It's loving to shoot straight with these teens. I could not live with myself if I pat them on the head and said, "Oh, poor you,

you are a victim." Why? Because you can't be a victim and a victor at the same time, and I can't let them stay small and sick.

Sadly, many young people come into my practice who have become addicts under their own roofs at the hands of their parents. I know parents who provide alcohol and pot for their teens. They think they are 'cool' parents and 'friends' with their kids. This is not for me. It takes courage to provide discipline and boundaries for my children. I am not their best friend; I strive to be the best parent. I don't need to win a popularity contest with them. I have heard it said that if you are willing to be their parent for at least twenty-one years, then you can earn the privilege of being their friend. They won't always like the rules, but that's okay. I'm not required to change the rules so they can do 'what everyone else is doing.' I tell them, "We are not everyone else. You are in this family; this is how we do things." They don't have to love or even like me. I am required to act in their best interest. I love my children unconditionally and would do anything for them. Even the Bible says, "Those He loves He disciplines." Consequences give them boundaries, and boundaries help people feel safe. Sometimes I receive a bad attitude, the silent treatment, or a roll of the eyes. It is then that I know my children are feeling upset that they don't always get their way. But this is about building character, not comfort.

When they follow the rules, the rewards are high. If they break them, the consequences are real. For example, I asked my boys, "What do you want as a reward for going through high school without drugs or alcohol? I know it's a big deal, so I am willing to pay you $250 a year for doing this, a total of $1000. We can do this or something else if you like." Two of our boys jumped on that opportunity. For Will, I put a sign with a K on it in his room and taped it to the wall so he could see it each morning and before he went to bed at night. A thousand dollars is a chunk of change, and Will was determined to get it.

My kids don't win popularity contests because they do not do what popular kids do on weekends. I know from my own experience what those entail. One Saturday night one of the boys headed out to a party at a friend's house. I require the family's last name and have called the parents to see if they know the party is occurring. Will gave me the name, and I got busy and did not call. The party was about thirty minutes from our house. Will returned in one hour and fifteen minutes. He barely had time to get there and turn around. I asked him, "What happened? You could have only been there about ten minutes?"

"Well, it was pretty much over when I got there."

"It was over?" I asked quizzically.

"Yeah," Will responded as he headed downstairs to his room.

I thought those guys were cruel to invite Will when the party ended. Why did they do that? Did they want to make Will feel bad? The mama bear in me knew something was off. The K was on the wall, and I knew that was motivation enough for Will. A couple of years later, Will told me, "So many of my friends in high school got wasted all the time." I thought back to a particular night. Maybe that party was a teen drunk fest, and Will knew he had to get out of there, and fast. He had decided to go for the money, and once he decides something, you can be sure he will see it through.

I asked Will during the first year of high school, "Has anyone ever offered you drugs?"

"Yes."

"Well, what did you do?" I panicked

"I said no."

"Was that the end of it? Did they pressure you? Who was it?"

"Mom, I'm not saying that. They could get in trouble. There is a code among boys that you don't rat anyone out."

We tell our teens, "If you are at a party and there is drinking, drugs, or anything that makes you uncomfortable, you can call us, and we will come get you. No consequences and no questions asked unless we believe lives are in danger." While the reward is high for staying clean, we have also told our kids, "If you use drugs or alcohol, you can't live here. We don't allow it in our home."

One time, I caught one our boys vaping, and tears rolled down his cheeks as he softly said, "I am not the person you think I am. I am not the good kid you think I am." People with an addiction are not bad people getting good; they are sick people getting well. This is where we get it all wrong. People are not innately bad, yet people do choose wrong actions. It is these ill-intended actions left unchecked that can poison our very souls and turn us into something we are not.

Later, we found one of our boys smoking pot; I did not softly say "let's talk about this." No, I asked him, "What are you doing and why does your room smell like this and don't give me some bogus answer because you are busted."

Then I made him walk downstairs, where I threw the contraption on our driveway, and it shattered into a thousand pieces. I informed him, "It's time to start cleaning up your mess. You will meet with Dan, my friend who runs a rehab for young people, at his soonest available time."

Some call this generation the snowflake generation. We are so afraid to parent that we just let teens softly drift, and they drift all the way down to the ground like a wayward snowflake. This was not a snowflake moment at our house. That one instance of being caught smoking weed landed this kid a meeting with the director of a rehab program. I left the whole situation in Dan's hands to evaluate.

No one wants to see that they have a problem or that their kids have a severe issue with drugs or alcohol. I have made plenty of missteps as a parent. That is just the way it goes. I am human and will not nail all the correct answers as I walk the steep mountain of parenting. I knew I would be too easy on my son. I wanted to excuse his behavior and give him another chance. I wanted it to be just 'not that bad.' But is 'not that bad' the ideal I strive for? Is 'not that bad' the excellence I promote every day? I knew that my instincts would be to protect my son, to not make a 'scene' about this, and to say everything was "just fine." However, kids can be protected to death, and my sponsor told me F.I.N.E. meant I was Fearful, Insecure, Neurotic, and Excitable. She also explained that F.E.A.R. meant False, Evidence, Appearing, Real, but in recovery, we Face, Everything, And Recover.

I knew we needed to face everything at this point in our journey together. I needed a professional evaluation, and Dan was the one. I believed he would say, "It's not that bad. He's not addicted to the stuff." We arrived at Dan's workplace. I was sad that this was where my brilliant, athletic, fun, fantastic kid landed. The 6 x 4 waiting room contained a rundown couch and an even less desirable rug. My son and I silently sat there, and I started bawling as I thought, 'This is where it all ends up? "

I threw my personal pity party, and no one came—poor me with the kid who is smoking pot. I started to think about how this would look. My son is leaving his prestigious boys' school for rehab. What would I tell other parents, and what would they think, and worse, what would they say? This is where I stopped myself short. I knew what other people thought of me was none of my business. This was about saving my son's life at any cost. I thought of my very first sponsor in recovery. she was known for saying, "You can't save your face and your ass at the same time. You're going to have to pick one. Make a good choice."

This was a grit moment for me. If others judged, then so be it. I decided it was a done deal if he needed to leave school to get sober then that was the plan. Getting well is a process. I was willing to take him out of school. I was willing to be the center of some chatty gossip.

I prayed, God, let me not care what others think. This is not about looking good. It is about recovery, the most important thing my son may ever need. Help me live for my audience of One. Give me the courage to do what is right for my son.

The two talked in that office for what felt like an eternity. They exited together, and their mood seemed lighter. I was ready for Dan to say, "You can take him home now. He does not belong here."

Much to my surprise, he told me, "Your son has an addiction. Have we seen much worse? Yes. Have we seen people with an addiction do less? Yes. What I can tell you is that he qualifies for our program."

His recommendation was to pull him from school to start an immediate, full-time, outpatient drug rehab program. The other option was school during the day and rehab in the evenings. Either way, at sixteen years old, this boy was entering treatment.

Parents tell me that they can't get their kids to stop smoking or drinking. I didn't try to make our son stop. I gave him the opportunity to stop killing himself. By getting experts involved, I relinquished my right to enable him. I gave him a different way of life based on spirituality and service to others. I was willing to do this even if it had material and social costs for him. Whatever he lost materially, he gained a hundredfold spiritually and emotionally. I could never give him the quality or speed with which he received so many tools for staying sober and living the most beautiful life possible.

Just because something is legal does not mean it's good for you. Smoking is legal and yet it causes sixteen different kinds of cancer, and 1,300 deaths per day. Alcohol, opioids, painkillers, Xanax, sugar, gambling, sex, overeating, aspartame, saccharine, and even water can be toxic if left unchecked. Being aware of a genetic predisposition to addiction is something to respect.

This was the correct path for our family and our son. In the moment I caught my son smoking, all the pieces fit together for me. All the lies now made sense. Keeping his window open in the dead of winter, the candles, the air fresheners, the 'sick days,' the snacking, the isolation, the irritability, the poor athletic season, the lethargy, and the falling grades. All of it merged into a perfect picture of addiction. It was looking at a disturbing work of art that I wish I could unsee. It was as if I were sleeping peacefully, and someone threw a bucket of ice-cold water on me. Once seen, I could not deny it.

My son had a problem.

I hated myself for not seeing it sooner. I knew something was wrong, but I listened to my friends, who said, "He is just a normal teenage boy. This is what they do." I wish I had followed my gut feeling, which was telling me, "Maybe boys act like this, but this is not my boy. Something is wrong." However, punishing myself would not help anyone.

Now I had seen it with my own eyes. I knew my son felt the horrible loneliness that lives in the heart of every addict. It's an isolation so deep that anyone would want to escape it and stop feeling that pain, even for a moment. When we find food, alcohol, drugs, people, possessions, stealing, pornography, shopping, video games, or anything else that provides a good rush of dopamine, we ring that bell time and again. Lab experiments have found that *if* a rat gets cocaine every time it presses a button, it will press that button continually. The consequences are irrelevant, and the rat will die pressing that button one last time. But with people, there is hope. We can miraculously stop destroying ourselves. We can courageously address our addictions. We can summon the strength required to live in this present life, no matter how difficult the challenges may be.

I learned that I can be extremely uncomfortable, and that is okay. I now have comfort in the discomfort that life sometimes brings. Whatever I am feeling I let that feeling just be. I let it pass. If I feel nervous, so what? If I worry that I can't do it, so what? If I try and fail, at least I tried; many do not have the courage to do so. Everything I do, I *get* to do. I get to go to the store. I get to clean the bathroom. I get to fold the laundry. I get to scrub the floor. Before sobriety, I didn't have a floor to clean or a bathroom to wash. I didn't have the money to buy whatever I wanted at the store, and I didn't have my own bathroom to clean.

These are the things I absolutely needed to learn. I needed the support of people, and a God I could wholly depend on. I gained both of those in the rooms of recovery. I found friends beyond what I had ever experienced. I found love and acceptance of myself and others, which means more to me with each passing day. I have given myself permission to be the person I always wished I would be.

As a dedicated counselor, I give my time and energy to working with struggling people. I transparently share my struggles with them. I will uproot any part of my past and talk about it if it will help someone else. My heart truly goes out to anyone who is trying to get free of an addiction. I recently told a patient, "The elevator you are on is going down. You can get off any time you choose. I can't want this for you more than you want it for yourself. This can be your miracle opportunity to get sober or nothing. It's up to you."

When my beautiful son was a couple weeks sober, he was on the phone with a friend. I heard a sound wafting down from his room. It was something that I realized I had not heard in years. It was the sound of laughter, his silly, fun, adorable, infectious laugh. God, I had missed that laugh. I missed you, my son, happy you are back. On the best days I am blessed hearing that laugh. It's pure sunshine.

"The only person you are destined to become is the person you decide to be." Ralph Waldo Emerson

"When you become a parent, remember, don't allow anything in your life that you don't want reproduced in your children." Unknown

"Being a mother is learning about strengths you did not know you had and dealing with fears you did not know existed." Nishan Panwa

"And I am convinced of this, that he who began a good work in you will carry it on to completion until the day of Jesus Christ." (Philippians 1:6, NIV)

IN THE CAGE

THERE WAS a time when I was stuck with such physical pain I did not scream or cry. I was suddenly nauseous. My world was spinning, and my involuntary response was to waste no energy reacting to the pain. All my energy was in a fight to suppress the pain and move myself to safety. It was six years ago, my son, Will, was in eighth grade and decided to become a baseball player.

That's a tough challenge for even a talented athlete because most boys have been conditioning for that since they were three years old. I took him seriously and found a fantastic coach to work with him on his hitting. He became a gifted hitter in no time. He even went a few months later to try out for a top-ranked local baseball team. Coach filled me in. "He can hit the crap out of the ball. He's just not there yet with his whole game, but no one's gonna argue that he can't hit that baseball," he proclaimed.

I also took him to the batting cage at least twice a week during this time. On Wednesday night, our usual batting cage adventure evening, our son, Nick, also needed a ride to soccer practice. My husband wanted me to take our three-year-old, Madison, with me.

I wanted to give Will my complete attention, so a conflict arose. Jeff and I usually work our family schedules with ease. We figure out who's going where and when and decide how to orchestrate the evenings. On this night, Jeff really wanted me to take Madison along, and I dug my heels in that I was only going with Will.

I'd won the battle, and soon we were walking inside to get Will's tokens for the cage. When we walked back, I noticed the cages were empty, so I walked into the cage next to Will to get a closer look at his swing. He was hitting the ball particularly well, and I started encouraging him, "Nice cut…I liked that one." It's important to note that what stood between Will and me was a thin net. On the next hit, the ball launched foul and back into the net, smashing exactly into my left eye. It launched into my eye at nearly seventy-five miles per hour, and from three feet away.

Instantly, the pain I experienced was unexplainable. It was worse than the pain of childbirth and far more traumatic. I crumbled to the ground, then crawled blindly out of the cage. I quietly said, "I'm not okay." Will was still batting and oblivious to what was going on. It was loud in there, and he was focusing on that ball-feeding machine like an eagle getting ready to swoop down on its prey. Everything was fading to black, so I knew I needed to get my head down before I fainted and hit the ground too hard. Like a blind person, I felt for the bench and laid down.

A man was immediately standing over me. He yelled for Will to stop hitting and asked, "Are you hurt?"

"I've been better," I gasped.

"I think we'd better call for help…Hey, we need some help over here!" He yelled to the people standing in another area of the facility.

A man came running over. he was a paramedic who happened to be there with his child. He looked at me and said, "We're going to call an ambulance, we think you should just get checked out, let's make sure you're okay. Are you fine with that?"

"Yes, that's fine."

The first person who came over was now looking closely at my eye.

"How bad is it? Is it bleeding?" I inquired faintly.

"There is some blood, and we need to get you some ice…Can we get some ice over here? You just lie still. Help is coming. How old is your son?" he asked.

He seemed to be asking me a constant stream of questions. I know from my medical background that this is common when you are trying to keep someone oriented and conscious. Quickly, the EMTs arrived and came running over to me.

One said, "We need to take you to the hospital."

These people are trained for emergencies and know what needs to be done. They don't need to explain the injury; they just want to be sure you get help. They did not give me details about my eye; they just strapped me to the gurney to wheel me out.

I said, "My son can ride in the back with me," loud enough that Will heard and was right by my side. Will tried to get in after me, but they directed him to the front.

He objected, "My mom wants me in the back with her."

"No, you need to ride in front, young man," they firmly insisted.

That's when I knew this was serious. They think I'm going to die or code or something and they don't want him to witness that, so they put him in front.

The sirens were blaring, and the EMT asked, "What hospital do you want to go to?"

"Menorah," I whispered.

He radioed ahead, "We have a female with a blown pupil…"

A blown pupil! Now the sirens were both internal and external.

I was suddenly back in medical school in my overnight call room at the hospital. I was exhausted and tucked in under the provided hospital blanket. It barely qualified as a covering; it was more of a glorified towel. I had just closed my eyes when I got the page to come to the ICU. When I arrived, I located two residents who were bright-eyed and bushy-tailed. They said, "We want you to go examine this patient. Especially look at her eyes and come tell us what you think."

I proceeded slowly to the patient's side. It was a young woman in an obviously serious medical condition. When someone has been in an accident, it's just like on TV, you flash the light in their eyes to see if their pupils respond. This is called the pupillary response. This describes the physiological changes in pupil size when exposed to light. If the pupil reacts appropriately, it closes when light is flashed, indicating the optic nerve is intact. The optic nerve is the only part of the brain that is visible to the human eye. If it's damaged, it typically indicates something more serious.

The woman I examined had one pupil that did not close when bright light hit it. It stayed large or 'blown.' This is also known as a Marcus Gun pupil, named for an ophthalmologist who made outstanding contributions in his field. It's a death knell-type sign pointing to brain bleeding.

When I heard the EMT say I had a blown pupil, I was terrified. "Wait a sec, I have a blown pupil?" I queried.

"Yes."

Why didn't anybody tell me that? Why did you not tell me that I am on death's door? That's a sign of a brain bleed!

I began quietly crying, almost in a whimper and I felt hot tears streaming down from my eyes and into my hairline. I was also shaking uncontrollably. A surge of adrenaline pulsed through my body, and I could not stop trembling.

"You know, it's worse for your eyes right now if you are crying. You need to not do that. Try to stop crying and calm down," Paul, the EMT, instructed.

If you are anything like me, having someone tell you to calm down only makes it impossible to do so. If I could calm down, I would have already done that.

"I want you to try some yoga breathing or something right now. You need to try to calm yourself."

"Can't you do something to make the shaking go away?" I begged.

"It's from within your own body. It's adrenaline. There is a lot going on."

I tried to take deep breaths while my mind repeatedly chanted, "You have a blown pupil."

Next, Paul received a call on the ambulance phone and informed me, "We can't go to Menorah. We need a level 1 trauma center."

We zipped to a different hospital and blew past a waiting room full of people. An upbeat dude with long wavy hair arrived, saying, "Hi, I'll be taking you to your CT scan."

I did not have time to address any fears, as the next thing I knew, I was sliding into that machine for a brain scan. I was whisked back to a room and was informed that the surgeon had been called and was made aware of my situation.

I have seen people go into 'simple' surgeries that do not survive. Most people think surgery is straightforward, but so many things can and do go wrong all the time.

You know the truth about these things. This is an emergency surgery. Don't get into some fantasy that it's 'routine;' you may not make it out so talk to your son for real. You don't want him to hate baseball and ruin the joy of his life, so say something.

"Will, I want you to go on playing baseball, even if I don't make it. Especially if I don't make it, I want you to go all the way to the majors," I said through my tears.

Then a medical resident came in to examine me. I knew he looked familiar, and I said, "Is that you, Nick?"

"Yes, hi. It's my first night on call on this service."

"What are the chances? I'm so happy you are here," I said, taking a deep breath.

Nick is married to my cousin's daughter. I asked him to pray with us, and we joined hands to plead with the Lord. I instantly felt the peace of God. There is simply no way that I ended up in this hospital on Nick's first night on call, in his service in the ER, by accident. After we prayed, he told us, "I'll be back in a few moments with the attending physician."

While I was begging God to save me from going to surgery, the attending came in. He instructed, "Please cover your right eye."

I did as I was told.

Then he said, "Tell me what you see."

"Nothing."

"I mean, you can see me over here, right?"

"No."

"How about my scrubs? What color are my scrubs?"

"I don't know. All I see is white," I explained.

It was at this moment that I realized I could no longer see out of my left eye. My brain and right eye were compensating for my injury. Shock kept me from realizing I had lost vision in my left eye entirely.

God, now I am very scared. I can't see anything out of this eye at all. Please help me. Please let me see. This is worse than I imagined.

The doctor left the room, and when he returned, I learned the results of my CT scan. Although it seemed impossible from my presenting symptoms, my CT showed no signs of a brain bleed. The ocular surgeon was not coming in. This was a miracle. I was one of the few cases of a Marcus Gun pupil without a hemorrhagic event pressing on my optic nerve.

I was not down to my final moments of life. I was lavished with the gift of more time. I wanted the pain to stop, and I wanted to see, but living was Job One, and that incredible gift was in hand. I was going home. I celebrated with Will and Nick and thanked God for my excellent fortune.

I left with several eye drops to put in every two hours. Jeff did this for me since I could not see. Each time, I felt anxious because I still could not see. My ophthalmologist agreed to see me first thing in the morning before he started seeing patients for the day. When I arrived at my appointment in the morning, I was beginning to see something other than a total whiteout, but my vision was far from restored.

My pupil remained quite large and unable to react by closing when exposed to bright light. For this, I needed to wear sunglasses continuously. When I was in a well-lit room, it felt like I was looking at the blazing sun. My eye was also swollen and bruised with all the colors of a smashed bunch of grapes. I continued the drops and learned over the following weeks that the damage to my eye might be permanent. My pupil looked crazy, and my vision was weak. But having something wrong with your eyes is a personal experience that can't be seen or readily experienced by others. I wanted to wear a sign that said, "I was in an accident. My vision is very strange. I can't see you very well, and if you try to show me something, I've got a 50/50 chance of seeing it. I might ask you for help to read."

That is precisely what I did. I asked people in stores to read labels to me. If my kids wanted something in a particular flavor, I asked other shoppers what variety was in my hand. It was strange to literally rely on the kindness and sight of others. I was on a strange new journey with my vision. The most uncomfortable part is that I did not know the destination. Over the next couple of years, my eye continued to heal. My vision was permanently changed; it's now my new normal.

Do I trust that God meant this for good? Absolutely. Just last week a friend was downhearted about the results of her eye surgery. I could share with her that although it seemed to take an inordinate amount of time for my eye to heal, it did get much better, and so would hers.

I am more convinced than ever that our pain is twofold.

First, pain serves me in my own spiritual growth. I needed to rely entirely on the goodness of God to see me through. I reached a place of total personal powerlessness. Many times, I thought about how determined I was to go with Will. If Madison was there, we would have never been standing that close to Will and this entire incident would not have occurred. I thought back to how insistent Jeff was that I take her. God uses other people to keep me out of harm's way. Sometimes, I am so stubborn about my own way that I step out from under God's umbrella of protection. I have free will; the harm came to me. Still, God does not say, "Too bad, you made the wrong choice, and I abandon you." No, He is a totally loving and completely forgiving Father. He showed his power and grace to bring me through. God used the experience to grow His relationship with me.

Second, I firmly believe ALL my pain is to be used to help others. All my victories are for your benefit. I am not supposed to hide the messy parts of my life. The purpose is to present them with unwavering belief and hope for others. Was this a terrible experience? Yes. Was it wonderful? Also, yes.

I often think of how responsible and caring my husband was as he sacrificed his night of sleep to faithfully place those drops in my eyes. My son, Will, was deeply remorseful for what I went through. I understood I was experiencing the consequences of standing too close to a foul ball in a batting cage. I have never done that again, and I hope you don't have to, either.

God demonstrates His intimate proximity to me in my times of pain, trial, and darkness. He lives in my son, who was holding my hand and never left my side in the hospital. He breathed through my relative Nick, who was the first person on the medical team to enter my room. His determination was in the presence of Paul, the EMT, who refused to let panic take hold of me. In the days that followed, my cousin Mary reached out to me. She is a nurse and revealed, "The first man who saw you get hit in the batting cages and came over was the doctor I work for. He is an ophthalmologist."

What are the chances that the first person who came to my aid was an ophthalmologist and the second was an emergency responder? God works through people, and although it felt like everything was out of control, it could not have been orchestrated more perfectly for my safety. That's the God we all have. He is right here with me. I love it when I keep this in the front of my mind because I feel blessed to tears, just like I do now. It overwhelms me that I am carried like that every second, yet I know it's true. The omnipresent love of God always was, is, and will be. God is the anchor for my soul, the rudder for my ship, and my true north. Trials, rather than challenge this belief, only affirm it.

This is something I can see with my eyes closed.

"The Spirit of the Lord is on me, because he has anointed me to proclaim good news to the poor. He has sent me to proclaim freedom for the prisoners and recovery of sight for the blind, to set the oppressed free, and to proclaim the year of the Lord's favor." (Luke 4: 18-21)

"As he went along, he saw a man blind from birth. His disciples asked him, 'Rabbi, who sinned, this man or his parents, that he was born blind? Neither this man nor his parents sinned,' said Jesus, "but this happened so that the works of God might be displayed in him." (John 9:1-3)

"A Chinese farmer gets a horse, which soon runs away. A neighbor says, 'That's bad news.' The farmer replies, 'Good news, bad news, who can say?' The horse comes back and brings another horse with him. Good news, you might say. The farmer gives the second horse to his son, who rides it. Then, the son is thrown and badly breaks his leg. 'So sorry for your bad news,' says the concerned neighbor. 'Good news, bad news, who can say?' the farmer replies. In a week or so, the emperor's men take every able-bodied young man to fight in a war. The farmer's son is spared. Good news, of course." Chinese Parable

PLEASE STOP

WHEN I FIRST STARTED DATING MY husband, Jeff, he had just completed medical school. We both moved to Los Angeles from New York City. Whenever a roadside emergency occurred, I would urge, "Jeff, stop the car. Go over and help."

He responded, " EMTs are on the scene. They really don't need me there," and kept driving. I was upset that Jeff would not stop. He finally convinced me that adding more people to the equation was not helpful. He insisted, "There is nothing I can do."

I tended to think, "You are a doctor. You need to do something." There is a common belief that doctors can save the day. One case that stands out to me is when we were entering an upscale restaurant in Los Angeles, and an older man was having a seizure. At my urging, Jeff went over to the couple's table. I don't know what medical intervention I expected him to perform, but at that moment, I understood that the situation was beyond anyone's control. It was not until completing my own medical school training that I realized the folly of my Doctor Superhero ideas. Many doctors are trained to treat particular disease processes, and their areas of expertise are relatively specialized.

I reached a point where I no longer asked Jeff to jump in and help. I don't know which was worse: thinking he could do something and believing he was unwilling to help or realizing that there was nothing he could do. Both felt equally helpless.

As an M.D., I needed to acquiesce to the validity of Jeff's choices. The trained professionals at an accident scene follow protocols and specific algorithms. Interruptions from outsiders are frequently viewed as an extraneous nuisance. Sure, I carry a kit with general remedies to stop bleeding and for cleaning and dressing wounds. Epi-pens and Narcan can also be lifesaving remedies. But I don't have a little red bag with a cross on it to address the myriad problems in existence.

It's still surprising to me how often God wants to use me to help people mentally, physically, and spiritually. I feel confident that there are plenty of other people more qualified to handle these situations, but for whatever reason, God puts me there. It's usually not something too dramatic. One time, I was involved in pulling a kid out of the water who had fainted at the pool's edge during swim practice. Those situations always seem urgent, as passing out in the water is a real danger of drowning. There have been many other fainting cases, mostly at church or swim meets. Both of which I attend regularly.

One notable case was a teenager who fainted at a sweltering hot Kansas swim meet. The meet officials had hired a medical service, not trained EMTs or doctors, to oversee the meet. The professionals working for the service carried the girl into an air-conditioned room, in my opinion, that is where their helpful decision-making ended. The girl was unconscious. They placed her on a couch, propped up her head, and back to an almost seated position. The girl's skin was turning all shades of bluish-purple, and I thought they might lose her, so I inserted myself in the situation.

I said, "I'm a doctor. Her head needs to be down. We need to increase blood flow to her head. Do not prop her up."

This is a common mistake. Think about it. Fainting is your body's way of instinctively surviving. Your body knows you need blood flow to your brain for survival, so it takes matters into its own hands. It sends your head to the ground on a plane with your heart so your body does not have to work so hard to get blood to your brain so you can continue to live. I have lost consciousness more times than I would like to think about, mostly in my twenties. I know now my body was trying to keep me on the planet. It was trying to save me. When someone tells me they feel faint, I get them flat on the ground to help restore blood flow to the brain. Also, if it's safe for them to consume something, I get them Gatorade or a drink with sugar. Water will not help when your body needs electrolytes to stay in the game.

Most days, I get a free pass. I don't have to think too much about being or needing a doctor's care, and for that, I am blessed. There was a Sunday afternoon about two years ago when physical health was not on my mind. It was a gorgeous day, and I was determined to look at a fantastic property. It was not far from our home, only about twenty minutes southeast.

There were two ways to get my eyes on this fantastic acreage. One was the highway, which would prove shorter and faster. The other way was through back roads, which was more scenic. I chose the latter. Few people find looking at land as heart-racing as I do, so it was a push to get Jeff and Madison to go along for the ride. However, they acquiesced. I also really wanted our son, Nicholas, to go with us. Nick was fourteen and giving us a little of the typical teenage pushback. I remember I was just insistent that he go. He bested my insistence by saying, "Mom, no. I will not drive all the way out there to see a piece of land. Besides, I have things to do and don't want to go."

I remember it like yesterday; he was determined not to go with us. It was even to the point of seeming weird and out of character for him. Regardless of where it came from, he won that argument cleanly. It did cause a delay. Then Jeff, Madison, and I set out, letting Nick know we would return in an hour. As anticipated, we took the back way. Jeff was anxious to wrap up our little land tour, but I met a neighbor and asked many questions. We were about to leave at one point, and the owner offered, "If you want to make your way down to the water, there is a path just behind the house." I could not resist this, much to the chagrin of Jeff and Madison, who were now chomping at the bit to head out. Finally, I was satisfied that I covered all the area's highlights, and we got back in our car and on the road. We exited onto Holmes Road, a major one-lane street running north and south. I looked down at my phone, scanning the area for my next land conquest, when Jeff exclaimed, "Man, that dude is flying!"

I looked up just before Jeff said, "And now he's not."

Never before or after have I seen Jeff so rapidly stop the car, pull over, and flip back around as I did at that moment. We went from northbound to southbound in an instant. The motorcycle had t-boned a tiny red convertible that was entering, taking a left onto Holmes Road. It was a motorcycle vs. vehicle collision. The bike, flying well over 90 mph, slammed directly into the little red car. The bike stopped suddenly. The biker did not. He was catapulted sixty feet forward, flying and landing far from the car and motorcycle collision site. I only caught a glimpse of the motorcycle and saw three other motorcycles following the first bike.

Now, everyone stopped. Suddenly, we were running up Holmes Road. We came upon the convertible and bike first. I glanced over long enough to assess that the driver and passenger were both alive and bleeding. But like any triage scene, the most endangered must be attended to first. I remember thinking, they look like they will live. But, God, what is up ahead?

I saw the biker lying on the pavement. Pieces of the bike were strewn along the sides of the road. The pavement was blood-stained. A man was doing chest compressions, and Jeff and I ran over. Madison was now screaming and crying, terrified to continue with us or stay behind. She had seen the bloodied bodies in the open convertible, and now the sight of the carnage was too much for her.

I told her, "Just go stand on the side of the road in the grass. You will be okay there. We need to go to him."

This was not acceptable to her. We were going to be too far away from the site of the man lying on the road. Other people were getting out of their vehicles and walking toward us, asking how they could help. I started telling people to pray. Jeff went to call 911, as I stayed with the man doing the chest compressions. One woman appeared from out of nowhere as if an angel. I asked, "Would you stand by the side of the road with my daughter?" She immediately swooped over with the kindness of a good Samaritan. I can still see her getting down to look Madison in the eye and talk with her. She took her hand, led her into the grass on the roadside, and faced her away from the accident. I was so thankful for that woman. I never saw her before that moment, and I never saw her again in all the confusion and flurry of people.

If she does end up, by some fantastic chance, reading this, I want to say, "Thank you. Thank you for keeping my baby from the worst of what was to come. Thank you for facing her towards the soft grass blowing in the gentle breeze. Thank you for making her feel safe in the most unsafe situation. Thank you for talking to her about goodness and heaven. Thank you for being a calming presence. Thank you for playing with her. Thank you for shielding her from this trauma. Because God knows, I felt so torn. I wanted to protect her, but I also knew I needed to be right where I was with this man. I did not want him to die alone.

Even now, I hope I did the right thing. I know it was traumatic for Madison, and it was for all of us. It was all happening so fast. I could hear Jeff talking to the 911 dispatcher. He was describing the accident and asking for help.

I was sitting with the man on the pavement, desperately feeling for a pulse. The first man on the scene, who arrived maybe twenty seconds before us, was doing chest compressions. I started telling the man, "Just stay with us, hang on, help is on the way. Just stay right here."

Wanting to say his name, I asked, "What's his name?"

"I have no idea."

"I thought you were with him."

Still pressing, "No, I was in the group of three motorcycles behind him. We don't know him."

I still could not feel a pulse.

I started to berate myself for this, thinking, *I know his pulse might be thready, but do I suck so badly at this that I can't even feel a pulse?. Am I that far out of practice doing this? Why can't I feel it?*

So, I asked the guy, "Were you able to get a pulse?"

"If I was able to get a pulse, would I be doing chest compressions?" he jeered sarcastically.

I have no judgment for this individual. He came upon a profoundly upsetting circumstance, as we all did. However, it was all happening so fast that I could not read the sarcasm. Did he mean, "Listen, you stupid woman, of course, there was no pulse?" Or "What is wrong with you? Of course, there is a pulse."

I knew his quip meant one of the two was true—I did not know which one.

I desperately searched for a pulse. I placed my index and middle finger precisely on the brachial artery. With each moment that ticked by, I hated myself more for being unable to find it.

I stopped bashing myself to return to prayer:

God, please help him. Please wrap Your arms around this man. Let Your comfort, healing, and love enfold him in his darkest hour. Let Your presence be known to him. Flood him with Your peace. Stay with him. Never leave his side. Please, Father, help him.

I begged the onlookers, «Please pray.» Some obliged.

I was sitting by his outstretched wrist and was so focused on his wrist that I had failed to take much of an overall assessment of this man. I did see his mouth, and that blood was dripping out of it. Slowly, my eyes drifted down toward his yellow t-shirt. It had writing on it. Then, I saw something that made my heart skip a beat. It was the crest from St. Teresa's Academy, my high school *alma mater*. Next, I asked myself the only logical question. What man would wear a t-shirt with a high school crest from an all-girls high school? The answer that came made me nauseous with pain. The man must be the father or brother of a girl attending that school. The sudden loss of a father is something I know all too well, and I could only imagine the devastation of losing my dad this way.

Jeff's loud cadence was bursting through my thoughts, counting chest compressions, "One, two, three.." If you have ever taken CPR, you have a glimpse of how absolute the exhaustion is of continuing chest compressions for five, ten, fifteen, or twenty minutes. It seemed an eternity slipped by before we heard the welcome cry of approaching sirens.

A police car was the first to arrive. I thought the emergency personnel would come running and quickly relieve the guys giving chest compressions and me on 'pulse duty.' But nothing could be farther from the truth.

The police officer approached at a normal pace. He started asking questions and told everyone to continue with compressions until the EMTs arrived. He looked over the injured man and removed a gun from his pocket. I had not even noticed that. He started talking to the EMTs arriving at the scene. NO ONE ran. One bent down and said, "The helmet is cracked in half. All of his teeth are gone."

I had not noticed any of that. How could this man be gone? When I looked him over, I realized there was barely a scrape on his body. He looked intact externally, and I had underestimated his internal wounds. The blunt force trauma to his brain and other internal organs likely caused internal tearing and hemorrhaging upon contact. High-speed impact can cause internal lacerations, hemorrhagic injury, and catastrophic loss of blood flow to critical organs. Brain trauma is the number one killer in most motorcycle accidents. Today was no exception.

The EMTs did not run over to the scene, either. It seemed everyone was taking their own sweet time. They finally removed the helmet and heard them say, "It's cracked in half." I understood that upon impact, the helmet cracked on the pavement. They lifted his body from the ground onto a board and into the back of the ambulance. We still did not know his name.

I asked one of the EMTs, "Is he gone?"

"They won't officially pronounce him dead until we get to the hospital."

"What hospital are you going to?"

"Patrician Woods."

"What's his name, how will we know for sure?"

"We can't release any of that. Just watch the news."

Hours went by before we returned home. When we arrived home, I was very shaken up. I went to my room and crawled into my bed with my computer. I told Madison, "You can sit beside me and rest. I need to write and process things. I will feel better."

Madison said, "I want to draw."

Madison processes her feelings through art. I don't have her drawings anymore, but I remember that she used colored pencils to draw several scenes. In the first, a nurse pushed a man in a wheelchair. I wanted to be as honest with her as possible without further traumatizing her, so I said, "Tell me about your drawing."

"It's him, he's in the hospital and getting better."

Deflated, I said, "He may not actually get better. He may have been gone already the whole time we were with him."

She did another drawing. In this one, the man stood surrounded by bright yellow light. He was walking toward another figure who appeared to welcome him with open arms.

That drawing felt true. It seemed to satisfy both of us. Many days, we still talk about it. Madison will take the side that helmets make motorcycles safe. I will argue that they are not. She says, "Well, it's safer than without." She has a point. Still, it's a deadly game, not worth playing.

Our man was likely the father of a graduate from Saint Teresa's Academy. He lost more than his life that day. His daughter did not get the chance to say goodbye to her dad. My husband was the last person to see him alive.

For us to be there that day, everything needed to be timed to the exact second. If I hadn't taken a quick peek at the lake, we would have passed the scene before it happened. If we had stayed longer, gone a different way home, stopped to use the restroom, or taken another turn, we would have missed this entirely.

But we didn't. I often ask God, not "Why?" but "What now? What did You want me to learn, see, do, or hear? What am I to do with this going forward?"

First, I want to share it with you. It could be a literal cautionary tale that saves a life, or it could be a figurative call to slow down. Either way, I need to know that today is precious. Nothing, and I mean nothing, is promised. I've known this lesson for years. So, what do I do about it? Before I lose sight of anyone I love, I let them know how much I care for them. They may be leaving for school, work, a retreat, a trip, or for life. I don't know how long, and if we are honest, neither do you. So, I look into the eyes of my sons, daughter, husband, mother, nieces, and dear friends and say, "I love you." I want that to be the final note in the symphony playing before intermission.

Yes, by the grace of God, the orchestra usually picks right up where it left off at 3:00 pm, in the carpool line, at 5:30 pm, next Tuesday, or during spring break or summer recess. But I know the heartbreaking silence of the notes that stop playing, the instruments that no longer call out their sweet notes, and the loss of the oboe, flute, or piano that makes the entire piece feel empty and incomplete.

For today, I lavish the sounds of the instruments still singing out their tunes, the warm strum of the guitar, the gentle dance of the clarinet, the deep tones of the cello, the playful fiddle, and the moody and confident saxophone. I thank God for the notes that still ring out loud, pure, and true.

"Say not in grief that he is no more but live in thankfulness that he was." Hebrew Proverb

"I believe in Christianity as I believe that the sun has risen: not only because I see it, but because by it I see everything else." C.S. Lewis

"The Lord himself goes before you and will be with you; he will never leave you nor forsake you. Do not be afraid; do not be discouraged." (Deuteronomy 31:8)

WATCHING MY SON
FADE AWAY

IT WAS SO exciting that my oldest son, Jacob, wanted to check out Creighton University in Omaha, Nebraska, a school he was seriously considering. For me, it was surreal. I had not seen the campus in over a decade. It was gorgeous, and new buildings, landscaping, and dorms evidenced progress. On our tour, we stopped by one of the dining halls where the chef was making some food for the President's Cocktail Party for donors. He let us taste some of the delicious creations. I just remember it was some homemade bread, cheese, and cherry concoction. We were all just famished and exhausted from driving the three-plus hours, walking to Creighton from our hotel, and canvassing the entire campus. I don't know which factors made it seem like the most delectable treats we ever tasted.

Jacob was now super excited about this school as an option for college. When we went back to our hotel, hot, exhausted, and hungry, we called my dear friend Chris to work out the logistics of meeting up with her for dinner. My children, Madison, six, and Nick, fourteen, wanted to go play in the indoor pool before dinner. I had precisely zero energy left to go to the pool. I told them they could go to the pool for about thirty minutes. No longer than forty. Time was ticking by, and Will, my 16-year-old, was downstairs playing a game in the lobby, just across from the pool.

About thirty minutes elapsed when Will called and said, "You better get down here. Something weird is going on." I ran down the stairwell. As I arrived, Nicholas and Madison were just getting on the elevator to come up to the rooms. I heard them coughing profusely, and just as the elevator doors were closing, I yelled, "Meet you up top." I ran back up the stairs. The elevator had just opened. Madison was throwing up, and Nick was just coughing and saying, "It's the chlorine. Way too much chlorine."

"Oh my God!" I screamed.

I instructed Jacob and Will, "Boys, turn on the shower and get Nicky in, we've got to get the chlorine off."

I ran to our room with Madison and immediately got her in the shower. She was still coughing to the point of gagging. I took some of the body gel from the dispenser, hoping I could wash the chlorine off. I wished I could wash her lungs.

"Mom, you have got to get to Nick!" Will said as he burst through the bathroom door, where I was tending to Madison.

"What do you mean? What's going on?"

"It's just bad, really bad, you have to go!"

"Ok, you stay here with Madison, I'll head over. Just stay with Madison. Call if you need me."

With that, I ran back to the boy's room. Nick was lying on the bed. I looked at him and was terrified. He was ashen, pale, and looked only half alive.

"Nicky, what's wrong, what is going on? Nicky, what do you want me to do?"

He said factually, "I need to go to the emergency room. I don't know if it's panic or the chlorine, I can't breathe. Call an ambulance."

Nick is one tough kid. He could pretty much cut through a limb and just say, "I'm okay. Let's keep playing." I knew that for him to make such a request, it was serious. My mind was spinning. I went to medical school at the nearest hospital. I know that place like the back of my hand. Do I call an ambulance? Do I just take him myself? Which would be faster? What about Madison? Is she okay? Is this a panic attack? Is this chlorine poisoning? Do they…My thoughts were suddenly interrupted with, "Mom, now. I need help." Nick's light grey skin tone now looked like someone had added just a touch of lavender paint. My denial was killed. I knew the situation was dire.

My fingers pressed 911, "My kids were in a pool. It's an indoor pool at IMG in downtown Omaha. They have chlorine poisoning; we need help now."

Thankfully, the fire station was two blocks away. Will reported that Madison was wrapped in a towel outside the shower, and Jacob was with her. She was still coughing but okay. Three firemen entered the hotel room, with two more trailing.

There was my son, Nicky, fading from existence in front of my eyes. Fix it, help him I thought as they did seemingly trivial things like take his blood pressure and ask him to very slowly inhale and exhale. Nick did not seem to be improving. The firemen kept working diligently with Nicky. They kept him conscious by talking with him.

I knew his life hung in the balance, and I prayed with the urgency of a desperate mother, *Please God, let him be okay. Please, God help us.*

Nicholas was still coughing and gagging. His color was tragic, and his chest heaved for air. The fireman told me that the pool had been tested, and the chlorine level was twenty times what would be considered safe. The hotel staff had been alerted. Someone was working in maintenance who did not know how to read the chlorine levels in the pool.

The fire chief looked at me and with a dire voice said, "A few more minutes in there and we could be looking at an entirely different situation. You are fortunate that your kids got out of there when they did. The chlorine levels are toxic."

Nick was now breathing more regularly. Jacob had gone to get Gatorade and some salty crackers for Nick for when he was ready to try to eat and drink.

An hour later, when I went downstairs to investigate the crime scene where my children were silently poisoned, there were emergency personnel with masks and oxygen tanks walking around the pool. It was a hazmat team!

The door to the outside was open and propped wide. Massive fans were in the lobby, adjacent to the pool, and at the far side of the pool to blow out all the chlorine-laden air.

When I asked to speak with the manager, I was told he was not there. The staff assured me they had closed the pool. They stated, "Because of the inconvenience of the pool not being available for you and your children, you will not be charged for your one-night stay."

The inconvenience of not having a POOL FOR US TO SWIM IN? Was that what they thought was the inconvenience?? How about my two children gasping for air? My Nicky is just stepping this side of eternity. My Madison was vomiting, coughing, and crying in the shower. What about the fleet of emergency personnel that needed to be summoned to handle the toxic air and the fading children? The terror of their mother and their two brothers frantically trying to assist the two younger children?

Nicky endured the most traumatic and terrifying event of his life. Two of my children are beyond scarred by the experience, and you think this is about NOT HAVING A POOL FOR US TO SWIM IN? Are you daft? Your compensation is that I'm not paying for this hellhole? I would not think of giving them a dime. I was disgusted by their insensitivity.

They said, "We don't know anything about the chlorine levels being high." They denied that the incident happened and took no responsibility. They denied it while the massive fans were droning on in the background for the next ten hours. If nothing happened, why are all the doors propped open? Why is the pool closed?

This was maddening at the least. I was determined that they would own up to their crime. The fire department was still there a full hour and a half after I had called. I asked how I could get a report on the incident. I was given a phone number to call and an incident number.

I found the number for the company's upper-level management. I told him what happened, and he hung up on me. Can they do that? Would they want to do that? This is insane. When we arrived back in Kansas City, I called an attorney friend of mine. He ended up saying, "Your kids lived, and they are okay." When that is the outcome, you won't win in court.

Is that okay? Is this what we hope for our children? Are they just okay? My son, Nicholas, has used this experience as fodder in every single school essay assignment about trauma. All my children have been avid swimmers since age one or two. They are on competitive swim teams year-round. Now Nicholas has an extreme fear of water. He panics if he is in a lane by himself. Open water is even worse, and his phobias of water have only grown. He did not swim on his high school swim team as a freshman. Instead, he did cross country and lacrosse, two sports he had not played before. However, they were acceptable as they were on land. He is an excellent swimmer. Nick can swim thousands of yards of distance in a one-hour practice. Now, he is afraid of the water.

This is what trauma can do to people. It makes them deathly afraid of a situation, even if they had mastery over it. It strips their sense of safety away. It cripples and shrinks down their world, and even if their fear is faced, the activity has gone from joyful to stressful.

Would I conclude that my children are unharmed by what happened? Never. Did the company ever acknowledge, apologize, or make recompense in any way? No.

Why? Because they are a huge corporate player, and I am an individual who makes my living helping suffering people. My pleas for recompense have been ignored and unanswered. I called many times only to be transferred, put on hold, and ultimately disconnected. This is what big corporations can get away with if we let them. I bet there is someone out there who finds this injustice infuriating. If that is you, would you be willing to help? Please let me know.

I am eternally grateful that my children had the amazing, good sense to get out of the toxic air before it was too late. I am blessed beyond words. I cannot imagine my world without their beautiful faces. Thanks to God, I do not have to.

"Injustice anywhere is a threat to justice everywhere." Martin Luther King Jr.

"If you are neutral in situations of injustice, you have chosen the side of the oppressor." Desmond Tutu.

"Jesus said, 'Father, forgive them, for they do not know what they are doing.'" (Luke 23:34 NIV)

No Tears

My FRIENDS TRIED to prepare me for dropping off Jacob, our eldest, at college. Kate told me, "Prepare to bawl!"

Our doctor warned, "That first one is tough, real tough. There will likely be tears all around."

I knew that I could not really prepare for this strange new part of life where one of my babies lived so far from home, so I decided to try to stay present and feel whatever arose. We all drove down as a family to Tuscaloosa and the University of Alabama. We arrived on a Saturday evening and attended mass together. The church was lovely and friendly. After communion, Jacob excused himself and came back about five to ten minutes later.

When I inquired about his time, he told me, "I went to look for a quiet place to pray. There is a nice little chapel to the side by the front entrance."

I felt so blessed that my eighteen-year-old son was looking for a place to meet with God. I'm so proud of the man he is becoming right before my eyes. We talked about his feelings regarding this new chapter of his life.

"I am not worried. I don't need to impress anyone. If I want to join swimming or running, or chess club for that matter, I could do any of those and not worry about what it looks like to anyone."

I love that about Jacob. He is so grounded in his own person. He puts others at ease, and they like him, not because he is trying to impress them, but because he is authentic, genuine, and real to talk with. Everyone seems to want to be his friend. He is respected and looked up to by his peers, siblings, and instructors. By his friends and family, he is deeply loved and appreciated.

I ran in the morning to take care of myself and mentally prepare to say goodbye to Jacob for a while. When we dropped him off at his dorm that Sunday morning, I did not cry. I wasn't fighting back tears; I did not feel sad. I felt proud of Jacob. He worked hard to attain a full-ride scholarship and earned his place. He made this happen, and it was a glorious accomplishment to witness. I was in no hurry to say goodbye because I completely enjoyed his company. When we parted, I felt joy and a sense of peace.

Upon returning home, I felt the loss of Jacob in our daily lives. That was more difficult than I imagined. I missed the silliness of his laugh, the softness of his 'goodnight, Mama,' the warmth of his smile, and the sparkle in his eyes. I missed the sharpness of his mind, the kindness of his manner, the purity of his spirit, and the depth of his soul. I longed for all the intangible and tangible things that are Jacob.

I disliked walking by his empty bedroom only because he was not there. I once heard a teaching from a mother. She said, "When we walk by our kids' rooms, let's make sure we stop, smile, and say, 'Hi.' Just so they know we care, and we are so happy to see them." I do this often. When my children were young, I told them, "If I could sit across from God and ask him for everything I ever wanted in a child, I would have sold myself short. You are much more than I ever expected or dreamed you would be." That's still true.

In one of our recent conversations, it was illuminating to talk about all the 'crazy' things he thought in high school. He talked about the teenage brain, "So many things seem to make sense that later just don't." The mama bear in me thanked God we made it through all the high school trap doors. I also relish hearing about his anatomy, chemistry, psychology, and genetics classes. He uses his time at school to learn and improve himself daily. My respect and admiration for him have only grown.

I am counting down the days until spring break, when we will meet up with Jacob on his drive home from Alabama. Having everyone together is my greatest joy, and I am reminding myself right now to care more about being and less about accomplishing.

The road with Jacob and all my kids has been far from perfect. Hard times come with the territory of growing up, and each of my children faced different challenges. Right now, all is well. I know what the opposite feels like. If you are in a challenging time, I want to encourage you to hang on and know that there is always hope. There are lessons in the obstacles that are priceless. Look for the silver lining.

My children are incredible blessings to me. The tears I cry now are of joy.

"There are only two lasting bequests we can hope to give our children. One of these is roots; the other, wings." Attributed to Hodding Carter

"But Jesus called the children to him and said, 'Let the little children come to me, and do not hinder them, for the kingdom of God belongs to such as these.'" (Luke 18:16, NIV).

"Whoever welcomes one of these little children in my name welcomes me; and whoever welcomes me does not welcome me but the one who sent me." (Mark 9:37, NIV).

GET HELP

I KNOW THAT many parents send their first born off to college only to find that child is partying way too hard, eating too much, cussing like crazy, possibly experimenting with pot or other drugs, grades are failing, pounds are put on, brain cells are diminishing, muscles are wasting, fat is increasing, laziness is overriding.

I feel very fortunate that my experience looks nothing like this. I am so blessed to have my college freshman, Jacob, home for winter break. We were blessed with the news last Tuesday that Jacob was staying home another week. "Thank you, Lord," I said. When Jacob gets home, he walks in the door and directly into my bedroom. He awakens me and tells me all sorts of details about his evening out, and always ends with "I love you."

Last night was particularly fun; Jacob was telling me about trying sushi with his friend, Max. He told me, "I was invited to dinner with the counselors. We had sushi. I have never had sushi before."

"That's so nice of them to invite you. What did you have?"

"We tried so many things. We ate a lot, and I am so full. I did not like the raw tuna, not at all. Eel was great. I really liked that. We got a bowl of raw fish. I did not care for the octopus. Oh, and I had scallops for the first time. Those were pretty good." Then, as always, Jacob gave me a little hug and, on his way out the door, said, "I love you, Mama."

Do you know how blessed I am? My boy, Jacob, has been sober since he was 15 years old. He is in recovery and living proof that there is hope for anyone with addiction or mental health issues. Yesterday, Jacob and I recorded a podcast. I was so fortunate to interview my own son about his journey with mental health and how his emptiness led to addiction. What a brave kid. Before we started, he asked if he could talk about addiction. I said, "Sure, I am fine with it. You know this is going to be available to the public on a podcast. I just want to make sure you don't have a problem with it, knowing that."

"No, it's cool with me."

This led to one amazing discussion with Jacob. It's amazing to hear what happened from his perspective vs. mine. I was almost brought to tears when he talked about how desperately lonely he was. Drugs gave him an instant result, an escape from those feelings as he said, "…with no real work on my part."

I so respected that Jacob talked about how someone with depression may feel guilty. He went on the explain, "You may even feel guilty for feeling bad. I know that I did not have any real reason to feel so bad. My life was good so I couldn't figure out why I felt this way. There was no true reason I could point to in my life. But it's okay to have problems and normal to have struggles; it's just important how you address them. You don't need to feel guilty for your feelings. Talking to someone is key. I hope people will reach out for the help they need."

We ended the podcast with Jacob's words. I felt a sense of fulfillment in hearing my son carry the message that I strive to constantly share. The butterfly effect left me blissful. I basked in the joy of it.

"Always remember you are braver than you believe, stronger than you seem, and smarter than you think." Christopher Robin, Winnie the Pooh, A. A. Milne

"Help will always be given at Hogwarts to those who ask for it." Albus Dumbledore, Harry Potter and the Chamber of Secrets, J.K. Rowling

"Ask, and it will be given to you; seek, and you will find; knock, and the door will be opened to you. For everyone who asks receives; the one who seeks finds; and to the one who knocks, the door will be opened." (Matthew 7:7-8 NIV)

Christmas In October

WHEN I AWAKENED on a cool October morning in 2023, no part of me wanted to go out and serve. It had gotten colder in the mornings, and so a bit less exciting to run outside. But showing up is an area I have done so much work in over the years. If I say I am going to be somewhere, then I will be there. That's it. Keeping my word, keeping my commitments is entirely essential to me. This eliminates some of that inside chatter about not wanting to do something. The debate was over when I signed up, so suck it up and go. I just really was not looking forward to going to the inner city yesterday. I had my 8-year-old, Madison, with me, and I just was not sure how this would all pan out.

Don't get me wrong! I love serving in the urban core. I did a year of service work where I lived in a convent, of all places. I served with kids in the inner city every day. I have continued this as an adult. I'm just saying that sometimes I don't want to do it. Sometimes I just want to be like a toddler and say I don't want to! But I have a brain that says, "I'm going, I'm going." That is something I appreciate now.

So, I am driving down I-70, and my daughter and I are both saying how we just dislike the inner city. I'm sorry, I love wide-open spaces. I have done my city time living in Boston, New York, Milan, and Los Angeles. Don't get me wrong, there are wonderful cities that offer amazing opportunities. However, right now I am in for space and quiet as I find God there in the stillness. I find peace.

We arrived at the house downtown, and I saw lots of cars, trucks, and young men walking throughout the area. This was Christmas in October. Folks who need help can apply to Christmas in October to get help with major home projects that they cannot do and/or cannot afford.

When we got there, I wanted to find my son, Nick. There were two houses, and I just picked one address. We parked nearby. I didn't see Nick, so I asked another Rockhurst student where the other house was. He said, "Right there," and pointed to the house behind the first one. "They are right next to each other."

"Do you know where Nick is?" I enquired.

"Yes, Nick is at the other house."

He pointed me in the direction. Then I walked through the backyard where so many moms and boys were doing yard work. Madison and I jumped right in, stuffing leaves and branches into leaf bags. Now I am furiously surveying the land to find Nick. I finally stopped gathering yard waste.

I told Madison, "We need to go find Nick."

She resisted, "No, Mom, let's stay here."

"I need to find my son."

Now I was getting nervous, as he wasn't at either house.

"We are going," I tell Madison with total firmness.

As we walked to the side of the house, I saw strong, adult men with power tools demolishing the old deck. I saw Nick working right alongside them. They were decimating the old lumber, and we began carrying the pieces to the dumpster. There were many trips up and down the sidewalk to the overflowing dumpster. Madison was an absolute trooper. She carried small and large pieces of lumber covered with chipping paint and bent nails up the street. I was so proud of both Nick and Madison.

After a while my eyes scanned a white stone wall with a little door tucked in the side. There is a woman standing with her arms folded, just staring out. Looking not sad, but not happy, either. I don't know what the look was, I just felt moved to go talk with her. What was it like to have all these people coming to help with this project? She was trusting high school boys and adults with her home.

I introduced myself and said, "Is this your home?"

"Yes, it is," she replied.

"Well, we are so blessed to be here working on it for you"

"Oh, my it's such a blessing. You know I am sight impaired, and I can only see about this far in front of me," she marked out about 10 inches with her hand and continued, "You know, I call to get repairs, and I get taken advantage of. Someone came out to fix my ceiling that had fallen in. They said it would be eight hundred dollars. I gave them four hundred and never saw him again. Then I had to hire a big company to come out and pay them all over again. So, my friend and I both applied for Christmas in October. I was so happy when they called and told me I made the list. This is a blessing. Thank you so much for coming out."

"I want the boys to know this story. Can I film you explaining it?"

"Sure."

As she explained what happened again, she started to cry.

I stopped the impromptu interview to give her a hug. We chatted a bit more.

Before I walked away, she said, "May I have another hug?"

What a brave ask! In a world so full of texts, technology, and distance, she had the courage to request a hug.

"Of course," I said as I embraced her. I knew in that moment that was why I was there. That was what God called me down here for. Not to do yardwork, dispose of trash, or paint the exterior of the house. Those were all things I did, but I knew I was here to hug Faye. That was my divine appointment.

After that, I cleared and cleaned her yard as no other. I thought about how she could not see all this mess. She did not know how overgrown it was, nor how much trash was back there. But I did. I am healthy enough to do this. When the lawn and leaf bags arrived, I cleared with fervor. I started asking the boys to help me. We filled bag after bag and carried them to the curb. Faye was a good person. She deserved this more than anyone. I would not ever attack my own yard work with such energy. This was for Faye. This was to make her life a little bit better, even if our paths only intersected for the five hours I was there.

She used to be a teacher in the urban core. Now she suffers from Lupus and other ailments. There must have been forty guys working on the two houses. This was important work that needed to be done for Faye's safety. Her porch was falling in and was a real danger. After that, I thought I had to get everything out of this yard. I've got to deal with all the trash because I can see it, and she can't. I want to make this the best possible front porch and back porch that's ever happened. This yard cleanup needs to be the best that has ever gone down because she deserves it. Faye knew she needed help, and she did the most important thing, which was to ask for it. I'm not even saying I was some over-the- top job foreman. There were guys just putting there all into these projects from dawn until dusk for two days.

Leaving, I felt amazing. My daughter had a blast, too. I've got to remember never to give in to that voice that is saying, "You don't need to go. You don't feel great. Just stay here and rest. Someone else will do the work." While some of that may be true, this woman needed real contact with people. She needed to be heard and cared for. She needed a hug, and not from someone else. If I let the negative voices win, I miss those moments, and they cannot be rescheduled.

That was my divine appointment.

"And he lifted up his eyes on his disciples and said: 'Blessed are you who are poor, for yours is the kingdom of God.'" (Luke 6:20).

"Blessed is she who has believed that the Lord would fulfill his promises to her!" (Luke 1:45, NIV)

"What good is it, my brothers, if someone says he has faith but does not have works? Can that faith save him? If a brother or sister is poorly clothed and lacking in daily food, and one of you says to them, "Go in peace, be warmed and filled," without giving them the things needed for the body, what good is that? So also, faith by itself, if it does not have works, is dead." (James 2: 14-17, NIV)

KANSAS CITY
INTERNATIONAL AIRPORT

SINCE MY SON, Jacob, has left home for college, I enjoy the rides to take him to the airport. This Sunday was no different. Unlike my other children, Jacob sits in the front passenger seat next to me as I drive. We dive into the many topics we have not thoroughly explored. At one point, Jacob said, "Money is important. It just is. I am not saying it will make you happy, because it won't. I am just saying it's important for basically everything."

"I totally agree. Money can't make you happy, but it sure solves a lot of problems along the way. I also want to say I'm sorry if I messed up in teaching you about money. I am sorry if I said things like, 'we can't afford that' because that is simply not true. I just recently learned that I should have told you something like, 'I choose not to buy that cheap toy that will stop working five minutes after we get home because I value where I spend my money. That is not the kind of quality I look for when spending my money.

I worked hard for my money, and I choose to spend it wisely. That does not feel like a smart choice to me. So I choose not to spend it on that item.'"

I told Jacob, "You need to start saying, 'I am wealthy' every day.'"

"Okay, but I'm not wealthy. I have $600 to my name. Well, that's not entirely true. I did make a lot of money over the summer, and I used that to buy a car. So that is where my money is."

I told him, "It's not about the money. Are you not rich by the world's standards? You have more than most in the world. You are receiving an education worth hundreds of thousands. You have your scholarship to an amazing school. You need to start with gratitude. You have clothing, food, and shelter. That right there makes you rich. On top of that, you have an incredible mind. Nothing hinders you like a lack of sight or vision. Your assets may not be in cash as they are invested at this time in your education, in your car. You have money; it's just in different places than your checking account."

"Yes, I am wealthy in that sense. I mean, I am receiving hundreds of thousands of dollars of education. I did buy a nice car. All the other things are true. I have assets and about $600 cash, too."

Jacob continued, "What about debt? I know everyone hates debt, but couldn't it be a good thing sometimes? I mean doesn't it depend on what you go into debt for?" he queried.

"Absolutely. Most go into debt to pay for medical school, but once they graduate, they will be able to pay it off in a second. So, it's okay to go into debt if you have good reason to believe it's an investment in your future. Many people go into debt to start businesses or go to school. In that case debt is not the enemy. Debt is something you can choose to go into and get out of with ease," I explained.

In another conversation, I asked Jacob his thoughts on medical school.

"Alabama has a really good nursing school."

"Does it have a medical school?"

"No, but Birmingham does. It has a very good medical school."

"Do you think you want to go to medical school near 'Bama or come home to KU Med?"

"Probably come home to KU. That would be less expensive anyway."

"Agree."

My little heart was doing cartwheels of joy as I offered, "I'll do your laundry."

As Jacob exited the car, he said his trademark, "Love you, Mama." He called me Mama as a baby and returned to that name for me only about four years ago. I love it. Jacob is the only of my children to call me by that name. It just feels so special. He stepped out of the car into the sounds of planes taking off and landing, and I tried to impart some last lessons.

"You really are wealthy. I love you."

"It's pretty noisy, so I can't really hear you, but I love you very much, Mama."

As I watched him walk away from the car and disappear into the bustling airport I flashed back to Jacob walking into kindergarten on the first day. He just said, 'Bye, Mom,' and walked away. Didn't look back to wave or say see you later or anything. This boy had places to go, and he was laser-focused on kindergarten. Today, when I watched as Jacob entered the sliding glass doors. I thought, there it is. He is my heart walking around outside of my body. That is something my best friend, Magdelin, told me when I was a new mom.

"It's like your heart is out there in the world. Outside of your body, and it feels so vulnerable."

That is as true now as it was at the moment Jacob was born. Magdelin and I have talked countless times as our kids have transitioned to toddlers, children, teens, and adults. Each stage has its challenges and joys. Each stage must be walked courageously by parents who just want their kids to stay, but also want them to live their lives out in the world. The conflict must be held in a mother's heart. It's the waters we learn to navigate for the rest of our lives. I rejoice that Jacob is enjoying his full ride to Alabama. He deserves it. He worked for it and earned it fair and square. He is sending himself to undergrad. It's like we all won the lottery.

Still, my heart aches to hear his joyful laugh, look into his kind eyes, and do a crossword puzzle together. This is part of the journey of motherhood. Like all other parts, it has its joys and heartbreaks. I love you, Jacob.

"Learning and teaching should not stand on opposite banks and just watch the river flow by; instead, they should embark together on a journey down the water. Through an active, reciprocal exchange, teaching can strengthen learning and how to learn." Reggio Emilia

"Education is the kindling of a flame, not the filling of a vessel." Socrates

"I will instruct you and teach you in the way you should go; I will counsel you with my loving eye on you." (Psalm 32:8 NIV)

WEDNESDAYS

ON WEDNESDAYS, my son, Will, has the day off. I love that Will does not try to run around and exhaust himself with his to-do list. He honestly sets out to enjoy his day. Yesterday was a Wednesday. Will has been asking me to do all sorts of cool things with him on Wednesdays.

Last week, he was going to the WWI Memorial and Museum in Kansas City. He asked me to go, but I had pressing work to complete. Will asked me to watch a movie with him, again, but I declined as I was working. Yesterday, Will asked if I would like to watch *Schindler's List* with him, not a light film for a midday break. I started to say that I needed to get work done.

I had an intense and sudden God moment.

You do not have time to watch a movie with your 19-year-old son? How many moms have the privilege of their teenage boys asking them to do anything, let alone watch a movie together? Your son is asking you to do things together. Do you even see how blessed you are? Will is such a wonderful young man. He doesn't drink or use drugs. You don't have to spend your time taking him to rehab or worse. He works one full-time job, one part-time job, and carries a full load of college classes. Get your thoughts straight. All this amazing kid wants is to share this movie with you. Get your ass downstairs.

At that moment, I told myself I am not wealthy if I cannot take an hour break with my son. This was something I did not like to hear in my brain. Wealth means many different things to different people. As a child, I knew we were wealthy. I could see it all over, in the homes we owned, vacation properties, cars, and complete freedom with money. If we were not going to do something, we were not going to do it, but it was not because we could not afford it. We could afford anything, or at least this was my perception. However, this was house money. This was the evidence of my parents' tenacity and determination. This spoke to Dad's never-give-up mentality and Mom's total faith in abundance and generosity.

I have considered myself to be wealthy for at least the last 25 years. I once heard that if you have one pair of pants, one shirt, and another to change into, and 1 dollar in your pocket, you are among the top 1% of wealth in the world. In the United States, even the poor are rich by these standards. I once heard Amanda Frances recall her friend telling her, "A million dollars a month is nothing. I know people who could not live on a million a month."

This may sound ridiculous, but it's just their experience and perception that counts. Likewise, in this situation, I was convinced that I was not a rich woman if I could not take the time to sit on the couch with my son and watch this movie. I just heard in my mind, "You are not rich if you can't stop work for an hour and do this." I truly disliked that thought. I know I am wealthy, so I needed to act like it, instead of being full of fear that it would all evaporate if I took this time out from working.

Also, Will has sophisticated taste, especially when it comes to the arts. He is intrigued by the music and films of the forties, fifties, and sixties. He rarely watches a modern film as he sees through the cheap glitz and false glamour. It was no surprise that Will chose *Schindler's List*, as he wants to be intellectually challenged by the films he watches. He likes depth. The movie, directed by Steven Spielberg, came out in 1993. I saw it in the theater within that year. I have heard that Spielberg considers this the best film of his career, and for good reason. The cinematography is beautiful. The camera stares into faces, picking up the nuances in expressions. It is rare to see cameras linger over facial expressions as much currently.

Modern films pack as many dollars into every minute as possible. They keep it short because our attention spans have become depleted by instant everything. The 75-minute film has become the ideal for box office success. The perfect expenditure of time maximizing profit. But this not like that. This film tells a story, a true and tragic story. Filmed in black and white, the bloody gore of today is absent. When an individual bleeds in the snow, it turns black, not red. The stark black and whites bring the viewer shockingly into the harsh reality of the subject matter. There is no distraction of color, only hate crimes committed at point-blank range.

If I cannot stop and take a few minutes to be with my boy that I love to watch a cinematic masterpiece, then I am not wealthy. This is a thought I cannot entertain. Why do I make this money anyway? For me, it's to have freedom regarding how I spend my time. Freedom to be with the people I love the most. At that moment, I decided that to fulfill my definition of wealth, I needed to drop everything and spend time with Will. The time spent was priceless. Our discussion of sheer brutality and maniacal power was intense.

I realized I didn't want to watch this sort of movie over the lunch hour. It's heavy, I would get invested. I am extremely selective about what I will allow in my mind. I keep my channel clear and positive. I thought this would bring me down. I also know that when you love someone, you invest in what they are interested in, not what you prefer. Believe me, I have studied more Pokémon cards than I ever knew existed. I have been to hundreds of kid's soccer games. I have listened attentively to Spider-Man vs. the Spider-verse. This is not news to those of you who love. This is what we do. So, this would be the film; there was no arguing this. It contains essential material, and Will wants to watch it. Now I'm in. Far from damaging my soul and its work, I was immediately sucked in by the heartbreaking beauty of this film. Simultaneously, I felt good about the time spent with Will. As he walked out the door, I said, "Thank you for letting me watch the film with you. Have a great day."

Will replied, "Thank you for watching."

Our exchange was warm, and my heart was full. I know true wealth. I am grateful.

"Wealth consists not in having great possessions, but in having few wants." Epictetus

"Health is the greatest gift, contentment the greatest wealth, faithfulness the best relationship." Buddhist Teaching

"But my God shall supply all your needs according to his riches in glory by Christ Jesus."(Philippians 4:19 KJV)

SATURATED

THE FIRST SPORT I introduce my children to is a matter of survival. I have spent countless hours in the pool with each of them before they are one year old, and this continues until they can swim safely on their own. The swimming pool is my happy place; I also teach swimming and coach a premier swim team in Kansas City.

As a child, we frequently spent time at the Lake of the Ozarks. It was one of the best parts of my childhood. It was also a well-known fact that my mom never learned to swim and was terrified of the water. She was plagued constantly by fears that any of us would drown. Life jackets were essential for her peace of mind. I cannot imagine how terrifying it was for her to see all her kids popping into that dark lake water, knowing she had no way to help them. Lake water is not known for its cleanliness, either. In fact, one year, there was an outbreak of a severe bacterial infection contracted from the lake.

The infection spread to pools and lakes throughout the area. Notices were posted at every private and public pool requiring each person to shower before entering the water and to abstain from entering if they had any signs of the infection. I was determined to be fearless about the water. I did not want this pesky infection to keep us out of the water in the summer. Of course, the signs were posted, but I tried not to let them get in the way of living life.

This was taking place as my kids were in elementary school, excelling in swimming competitions, and spending countless hours in the water. When Jacob entered the third grade, I knew something was off with him. We tried changing his diet to no avail. He was already a skinny kid, but whatever he ate seemed to fly through him. We visited his doctor multiple times. It was heartbreaking that whatever we did, this sickness was the mountain Jacob carried with him. He was also a fantastic soccer player. When he attended the tryout for the next-level team, it was 103 degrees in the shade. He did not have his usual stamina and was not offered a spot on the team.

This illness plagued him for the entire fall of his third-grade year. In caring for Jacob, I came in close contact with him and his illness. I was vigilant about my handwashing, but I was not perfect. Even if you wash your hands, some of the hardier germs can survive. By early fall, I was suffering from the same illness as Jacob. Now I was on a relentless search to find the cause and cure. My doctors also made all changes to my diet, and nothing helped. I was down to only being able to drink clear liquids. Even then, they ran right through me, and I would need to stop and use the restroom once or twice on the ten-minute drive to my children's school.

I also learned that kids who are chronically ill are susceptible to depression and other mental health struggles. Sweet Jacob was no exception, and soon he was battling the demon of depression on top of his physical illness. It's a parent's worst nightmare to watch your child suffering, search for answers, and come up empty-handed. I was also feeling downhearted about my illness and my daily weakness. My life shrunk down to only short trips outside the house. The disease gradually took its toll on me, grinding me down.

Finally, someone recommended Dr. Watkins, a GI specialist. He seemed quite intelligent and thorough. He prescribed some medication for me. It had horrible side effects, but he warned, "No matter what, do not stop taking this." He prescribed two large doses twice a day. The uncomfortable side effects set in quickly. I was not getting any better, and I wanted to stop the medication, but I was willing to do whatever was required. After several days had passed, Dr. Watkins' nurse called.

She opened with grave concern, "Are you okay?"

"As okay as I can be, why?"

"You have a terrible infection. You need to stop taking the medicine immediately. It's completely wrong. And how are you doing? Do you need to be hospitalized? Most people with this are hospitalized for some time."

I didn't feel the luxury of a hospital stay, away from my three young boys, was possible. "No, I'm managing here," I responded feebly.

The good news was that I could stop taking that terrible medicine. The bad news was that there was no medicine available for me or my Jacob. Still, I could not give up for either of us; there had to be something out there. I was able to arrange for Jacob to see another GI specialist in a well-regarded children's hospital.

I can still see the yellow walls of the exam room, the tissue paper on the patient table, and a doctor lacking in bedside manner. She knew I also contracted the illness, so she was talking to both of us. About midway through the appointment, I asked, "When will we get better?"

"Oh, I don't know that answer. Maybe in a few months, maybe a year, maybe never," she bluntly blurted.

Astonished, I asked, "You mean it could stay like this forever?"

I wanted to rewind that moment and cover my son's ears. Please don't tell a suffering child he may never get better. We left empty-handed and devastated.

I was reminded of a time I felt terrible. My whole body felt entirely fatigued, and my muscles ached. I was feverish and clammy. It was a Sunday afternoon, and I was powering through weekend activities with my kids when I came to a screeching halt.

With my husband in charge, I announced, "I'm going to the doctor now."

My doctor was not in, and I was seen by a brand-new doctor, straight out of residency and green like spring grass. I give her credit for testing me for the influenza, which came back positive in two seconds. This was before Tamiflu, so there was no treatment. I felt so horrible that I said, "I feel awful. Am I going to die?"

To which she responded, "The flu is a deadly disease, and thousands of people die from it every year. It's a serious illness. You could die from it." After dropping that bomb, she went on to tell me to go home and rest. There was no way to *rest*. A thousand sirens were now blaring in my head, telling me I could die.

As doctors, we are taught to tell patients the truth, especially about the severity of their illnesses. While I understand this, it discounts the power of the mind to heal. I read about one physician who constantly told her patients they were getting better. Her patients healed wholly and rapidly. She credits her healthy patient population to her consistent positive messages. She believes in them; she sees the results consistently.

Yes, some people may die of an illness, but many more will survive. What about flipping the facts to how many have a positive outcome? My brilliant O.B., Dr. Kandalavala, once told me, "There is a .05% chance that your baby may be born with a defect. However, that means there is a 99.95% chance he will be absolutely fine. Don't stare at that .05. Every time it crosses your mind, remind yourself that the 99.95% is much more likely." My son was born in perfect health.

Previously, I thought it was logical for doctors to have cures for all illnesses. A trip through any four-year medical school smashes that fantasy. Now I know they are making educated choices about what will likely work. Of course, those guesses are backed up by research, studies, and experience. But people are more than numbers and likely outcomes. You are not your diagnosis. You are a person with a soul, a spirit, a mind, a body, a voice, and countless other untapped sources of strength. You can make contact at any moment with God, who is all-powerful and all-loving. He hears your cries of distress. He wants to help you. He hands out free gifts like miracles, healings, and answers to prayers. If God had a refrigerator, I believe your picture would be taped to the front. All your awards and accomplishments would be hanging prominently on the walls of his house. He would have a sign in His yard that reads, "I love _____."

Doctors are not gods or magicians. We don't know what is going to happen to anyone. They are 'practicing' medicine. It's right there in the job description – 'practicing.' That means something that is not mastered. It's a practice. It's ever changing. They told our medical school graduating class, "Most everything you have learned in the last four years will soon be obsolete. Especially when it comes to medications and treatments. This is why you must commit to being a lifelong learner. More important than *what* you learned is *how* you learned. That's a skill you will need to take forward every single day as you *practice.*"

When that doctor told my son he would never get better, I wanted to say, "You don't know that. He's a kid. A new treatment could be discovered next week, or next month. Even if there is no treatment, God can heal." I knew this. I had my own experience of being cured from an incurable illness. I know to throw away the negative rhetoric that often pervades traditional medicine. I am a firm believer in miracles, but my third grader did not yet understand the power of the Universe.

At any age, being told, "You may never get better," is a challenge for the mind. It was difficult for me to flip that to "I may get better," then to "I will get better." I told Jacob with certainty, "You will get better. I don't know when, but you will." I prayed every day for both of us to heal. Gradually, we were able to add one or two foods to our diets. It was a process that went on for years. We didn't discuss it often. I just noticed that foods entered and exited Jacob's diet. Things he used to love, like milk, were gone forever. He is twenty-one now and I have not seen him touch a glass of milk since that time. Jacob fully regained his strength and health. He went on to swim four years on his high school swim team and was chosen as captain in his senior year.

The struggle to regain strength after such an illness is monumental and painstakingly slow. I am a dedicated runner, but weakness prevented me from stepping out of my door. Suddenly, a memory crashed through my mind of my dad. He was ill with cancer, gaunt, and frail. He loved to be outside in the fall. I asked him, "Want to go for a walk?" I thought it would be good for him to go outside and get fresh air. We walked down our driveway and one house farther to the corner. We turned south and walked up to the next corner. That was it. Dad was exhausted and needed to return home. That was our last walk outside. He could not go far, but he took the steps he was able to take.

I started to do the same. I didn't make it one entire block, but going out was the victory. Each day, I pushed myself to go just one step more than the day before. Soon, I was walking two and three blocks at a time. As I worked up to six blocks, I started to jog one.

Twelve years later, I use the same process. I was training for a half marathon, and I needed to go for a run. It was 8:15 am when I got home from dropping my daughter off at school. The forecast said that rain was to start at 9 am. I could have easily said, "Forty-five minutes won't be enough time." Instead, I told myself, it's not raining now, I'll just start and see how far I get before the rain comes down. Turns out it started raining at mile three. I took the next three miles in the cold rain. I was already wet, exactly how much wetter could I get? My shoes and clothes were saturated by the time I returned home.

My soul was saturated with something much more important: Gratitude and a deep sense of personal well-being.

"Above all, do not lose your desire to walk. Every day, I walk myself into a state of well-being and walk away from every illness. I have walked myself into my best thoughts, and I know of no thought so burdensome that one cannot walk away from it. But by sitting still, and the more one sits still, the closer one comes to feeling ill. Thus, if one just keeps on walking, everything will be all right." Soren Kierkegaard

"The mouths of fools are their undoing, and their lips are a snare to their very lives. The tongue has the power of life and death, and those who love it will eat its fruit." (Proverbs 18:7 and Proverbs 18:21, NIV)

"For I will restore health to you, and your wounds I will heal, declares the LORD, because they have called you an outcast: 'It is Zion, for whom no one cares!'"(Jeremiah 30:17)

BELOVEDS V

HE'S IN THE DETAILS

FEW PEOPLE HAVE IMPRESSED me more than Kate. When we first met, I was an overwhelmed parent of a freshman on the swim team at Richmond High School. We were at the mandatory swim, dive, and manager parent meeting held in late August. My oldest son, Jacob, was the first of our three boys to attend this Catholic college preparatory school. I was nervous, excited, and anxious, and Kate matched me with the opposite of those emotions. Her energy was calm, reassuring, and secure. She was kind and unassuming, freeing me to ask her all the random questions floating around in my brain.

Kate either provided me with answers or suggested where I could find the information. Every time I saw her, she was wearing a lovely dress, not in any way flashy, but conservative, classic, and floral. Our sons were on the same team; that was all she needed to know to be my friend. This type of person, who is kind to everyone and never condescending, is striking. These are qualities that defined my mom, Marilee; I strive for them and recognize their authenticity as a lighthouse bursting through a dark night at sea.

My first meeting with Kate was over seven years ago, and her consistency of character is noteworthy. She carries an inner peace and simply radiates with beauty, light, and humility. Kate and I intersected at our son's high school. I saw her at swim meets, back-to-school nights, and graduations, all with poise and a glowing smile.

Fast-forward five years, and the swim and dive teams needed a home pool. The Southbridge YMCA, lovingly called 'the tomb,' where the team practiced for over a decade, was closing. The swim and dive teams were now homeless. But leave it to the tenacious and resourceful swim-and-dive parents to figure out a solution. They came up with enough money to buy the dilapidated complex for the high school. The swimmers, divers, and managers now had a pool to call home.

We received a letter in the mail detailing how to donate for the privilege of naming certain parts of the complex, such as $200,000 to name the boys' locker room and $500,000 to name the weight room. Donations covered the repair and restoration of the facility, and name plaques were engraved accordingly.

On the inside of the building, the pool area was named The Pamela Wilson Natatorium. This year, my son Nicholas was returning to the team as a junior. The annual parent meeting was held in August. I coach swimming on many weeknights, so I arrived late for the parent meeting with my daughter, Madison. We rushed from her swim practice to Richmond High School for the meeting. The only problem was that there was no one at this location. Richmond has a vast campus, and I did not even know where to begin looking for the meeting we were now late to attend.

Who could I reach to find out where to go? A low level of panic stirred within me as I went down the list of possible helpers. This was one time I was grateful for that team group chat. I pressed on with today's meeting and got to the Cooper Plex location. What exactly was a Cooper Plex, and more importantly, where was it? I scanned the school's interior in my mind, looking for anything that seemed like a Cooper Plex. After a couple of deep breaths, I realized that Cooper Plex was the new moniker of the Southside YMCA. With this revelation, Madison and I jumped back in the car and headed over, but it was now very late. When we entered the side door, it was completely quiet except for the unmistakable voice of Coach Meyers talking to all the parents.

Towards the end of the meeting, a man walked in and announced the passing of Pamela Wilson. The only place I knew of this name was the building I was standing in: The Pamela Wilson Natatorium. Coach Meyers went on to discuss this tragic occurrence, an avid supporter of the team, and a significant loss to our community. In the coming week, I learned that the swim and dive team, along with the managers and coaches, were going to attend her memorial service. Parents were also included, and I thought it was quite considerate that the boys were going to attend and were sorry to miss it.

I later learned that Pamela Wilson was the mother of my dear friend, Kate. Then, I felt awful that I did not attend the funeral or at least reach out to Kate. My mother taught me it's never too late to reach out to someone to offer sympathy for their loss. I wanted to do this in person, and Kate was having a gathering for all the swim and dive parents the following week. I wanted to do something special for her, so I made these lovely cupcakes to share at the party. They turned out wonderfully and looked perfect, all assembled on a sweet plate that would be a gift to Kate.

With that task completed, I went to my room to get dressed and ready to go to her house. When I returned to the kitchen, I discovered only four of my ten cupcakes remained on the plate. I found crumbs and frosting nearby on the floor, and my very guilty-looking dog with a vanilla-frosted nose. I am sure I said a few firm words to Miss Chloe that I will not mention here as I headed out the door with the now embarrassing four remaining cupcakes. Upon arriving at Kate's house, rows of cars lined the street and driveway. One was nicer than the other: Tesla, Porsche, Mercedes, and the like.

I walked up to the castle-like estate with my crumby little plate of cupcakes, rang the doorbell, and proceeded to enter. I found Kate, and she greeted me as warmly as ever. She received my so-called cupcakes gracefully, and I placed them next to the plates of perfectly decorated cookies and cakes in the dining room. At this point, I just wanted to quietly shove them down the garbage disposal. I told Kate the truth about the cupcake heist, and she endearingly related a similar tale of dog chicanery. The home was perfect for Kate and her family, and she was the consummate host, always smiling and perfectly at ease with sixty other adults in her home. My own parents had many wealthy friends growing up, and we often frequented their gorgeous homes. This house was by far the most beautiful of any estate I have ever entered. All the decor was perfect to the last detail, without feeling like it was a museum where an alarm would sound if you touched something.

The colors resonated with me, as I love blue, and Kate's first floor has walls covered with the most beautiful shade of blue grass cloth. If it were edible, I would have eaten it. Instead, I devoured it with my eyes. It felt like walking through a beautiful cloud. Next, I opened the door to the back door to the outside and discovered an entire oasis complete with multiple patio tables and chairs, exquisite lighting, a spotless pool, and a whole additional house with glass walls behind the pool. The transparent walls displayed incredible works of art. I imagined swimming right next to your private art gallery while enjoying the shade of the perfectly placed trees and pots overflowing with luxuriant blossoms. Partygoers were laughing and talking with one another on what seemed like a page out of Architectural Digest.

I know pain is beyond the comfort of even the most beautiful home with the most perfectly placed silver picture frames and Waterford Crystal. Pain and loss cut across all lines of social class, skin color, education, and myriads of other superficial things that tend to separate people. Also, there are grieving people constantly among us. Why don't we talk about it? I know that sometimes I don't want to address the pain or bring up the agony they may be experiencing. However, grief is generally not over just because a few days or weeks have passed.

I remember walking into my high school graduation mass with my mom. As we crossed the parking lot to the entrance of the building, one of my teachers approached, also going to the mass.

After saying hello, Mom said, "James, I am truly sorry for the loss of your son; I know that must be incredibly difficult for you. We are keeping you and our family in our prayers."

"Yes, it's unimaginable. We are grateful for your prayers. Thank you," he responded.

I was so embarrassed, and in my teenage mindset, I said, "Mom, why would you bring that up? We are walking into graduation. Why did you have to bring that up to Mr. Akins and have him think about all that now?"

"Elisemarie, do you not think that it's on his mind constantly? He is thinking about the loss of his son every second, whether we say something or not. It's kind to let him know we care. We know he's in pain, and saying something about it is the right thing to do," Mom instructed.

I didn't quite understand her rationale, yet with the losses that quickly unraveled before me, I soon appreciated her wisdom. So, when I saw Kate, I said, "I am sorry about your mom. I didn't even know she donated the pool for the boys. I am so sorry I missed the service."

(This also speaks to Kate's humility. She doesn't run around saying, "My mom paid for the pool." I really think I would be tempted to at least *mention* that to people. Kate has me beat in lack of vanity, for sure.

"Oh no, don't worry about it," Kate graciously replied. "She was older and not really well."

"Sometimes that does not make it any easier."

"True, it was still unexpected, and I miss her," she elaborated.

Weeks later, on Friday, October 31st, there was a ceremony at the Cooper Plex. This ceremony was to dedicate a Mary statue at the entrance to the swimming building to Pamela Wilson, Kate's mom.

It was a gorgeous sunny day outside as we stood and prayed, thanking God for Pamela's generosity and asking for comfort for her family. Something prompted me to capture the time in a video. It might be nice for Kate to have, so I took a few photos of her near the statue, too. I have always enjoyed photography, and I ran my own photography business at one point. Now, I love to share moments I capture as my special gift to those I care about.

I usually avoid taking photos when people have the Sun shining directly in their faces, as it can be less flattering. However, the statue of Mary was facing west, so Kate was looking in the direction of the sunset, too. Kate looks perfectly radiant in the photos, and I texted them to her, thinking I would send the video later.

Time and the business of life allowed that task to fall off my radar. However, in the last week, I began thinking, "I need to find that video for Kate and send it to her." The thought traipsed across my brain several times in the last few days. Yesterday, I awoke to my usual talk with God. It was early, and everyone else was still asleep.

I take this time to invest in my relationship with God and ask for His discernment over my day. I said, "God, I love you.

I love you so much. I love you, God. I love you, Jesus. And I love you, Mary."

Sometimes I question if God is present with me every second because I don't pray for as long or as formally as I used to. I enjoyed constantly poring through my Bible and writing down every single scripture that stood out to me. That is such a rewarding process, and I still love doing that.

However, when I am not in a season to do that, I need to trust that God is not mad at me. Am I mad at my son for not being by my side constantly? No, He's in college. He's doing his work in the world. I don't love him any less. In fact, I love him more. The time we spend together is precious. I am a firm believer that recovery, prayer, and God are a bridge *to* life. My sweet sponsor used to say, "Recovery is a bridge back to life. Don't get stuck on the bridge." After I receive, I am called to live and give.

I believe that those eternal words are printed within me. I can access them at any time, with or without the actual book in front of me. God is guiding me and with me every second, and He shows up every day.

I say simple prayers such as, "God help me find my hammer," and it shows up immediately. I'm not saying there is a parking space finder God, but it's worth trying. When these things happen, I sweetly sense His presence and remember I'm not alone. I used to search for evidence of God in my life. Now I know that life itself is evidence of God

Yesterday, after my prayers, I found myself scrolling through photos on my phone. I don't recall what I was looking for. I came across the beautiful pictures of Kate and thought, "She looks absolutely radiant there with Mary." Then I saw the video and said, "I am sending this now," and I completed the task.

Why had it taken me so long to get that to her?

The next moment, I was getting ready to take Madison to a swim meet north of the river, so we had to hustle. I received a text from Kate. It read, "December fifteenth was my mom's birthday!" I looked at my watch and could not see the tiny date, so I pressed a button to illuminate the face. It read, "Sun. Dec. 15th."

Later, I was speaking to a patient. As part of her therapy, I asked her to write a letter to a very important person in her life who had died tragically in a car wreck.

"Did you write your letter to Betsy?" I inquired.

"Yes, I wrote it on Sunday, the fifteenth. That was her birthday," She explained.

"Coincidence is God's way of remaining anonymous," Albert Einstein

"We pray, we wait, we hope, we believe, and in God's perfect time we see his plan unfold." Anita Abraham

"For my thoughts are not your thoughts, neither are your ways my ways, declares the Lord. For as the heavens are higher than the earth, so are my ways higher than your ways and my thoughts than your thoughts." (Isaiah 55: 8-9)

"Kairos refers to the right, critical, or opportune moment. It is qualitative rather than quantitative, focusing on the significance and the rightness of a particular moment for action, decision, or event. Kairos is often understood as 'God's time', a moment of indeterminate time in which something special happens. It's seen as the perfect moment when God acts or when a decision must be made to align with God's will."

Stronger Together

I HAVE BEEN LISTENING to David Goggins' book, *Never Finished*.

I asked Jacob, "Have you heard of David Goggins?"

"Yeah, isn't he the guy that didn't train for a one-hundred-mile run, broke both his legs, had kidney failure, and still finished the race?"

"I think it's something like that." I smiled as I knew this scenario was medically impossible.

But if you know Goggins, it doesn't seem out of the question, so I was just waiting for that chapter. I told my son, "I am so Goggins."

He smiled and said, "You think? Of course you are, you don't need to tell me."

This is not to say I have anywhere near David Goggins's physical acumen; I simply resonate with his mental and physical approach. As I was listening to Goggins 'life-changing transformations, I flashed back to my own moment of clarity. I was twenty-four when I witnessed my dad's death.

I prayed, "God help me remember this moment. Help me remember that life is here one second and gone the next. Please keep my soul alive to this fact. Don't let me fall asleep into a world where I believe I have endless time. Keep me awake to the urgency of life, Your precious gift to me. Don't let me waste time like it's trash to be thrown away. Help live well for the time I have."

I shared this with a counselor, and she said, "No one can do that. We can't live at that intensity all the time. It's too deep. We need to live on the surface most of the time." Clearly, she did not know me well. If you tell me I can't do something, I will be sure to prove you wrong time and time again.

Life became urgent for me that cold day in February of 1995. I am not messing around. I am in this life to be the absolute best I can be. I had decided to complete my Master of Fine Arts Degree from Pratt Institute in New York. I finished that MFA degree at the top of my class. During my dad's illness, I had felt a calling to a healing profession, specifically medicine. So, as crazy and opposite as it seemed, I set my sights on medical school. I didn't take the necessary math, physics, biology, chemistry, or science labs when I attended Boston College, so that meant two more years of study, including summers.

I packed my bags and headed to Los Angeles, California, where I attended UCLA for my premedical requirements. I established residency and started with night classes, which made this task surprisingly affordable. I did not go there to just attend; I knew I had to dominate these classes. You can't just stroll into medical school. There is nothing average about the required grade point, test scores, and endless resume-building items. I studied with fervor. I devoured my textbooks. I completed the corresponding workbooks. I wanted to excel, and I knew tutoring was offered. I just didn't know who it was for, so I was hesitant to attend. I don't know who I thought they were for. Then I talked to a few friends and decided to go *one* time only. That is the moment I learned that all the smart kids go to tutoring. It wasn't a room full of failing kids. These were the academic killers, competitive to the bone, who went after every point on a test as if their lives counted on it. From that day on, I attended every possible tutoring session offered. I would go to class on Monday morning and to tutoring on Monday night. There was no time to waste. I needed to perform, and I had the gumption to do it.

Some of my classes were early in the morning and others were from 6:00 pm -10:00 pm. It did not matter to me what time; I would be there. I would not miss a single class. In between classes I ran or swam in one of the gorgeous pools on campus. Then I would hit the library for hours.

I usually sat in the front row of this huge lecture hall. When the professor asked for questions, I never shied away from the opportunity for clarity. I went to my professor's office hours if I needed further explanation. If I didn't have questions, I went to listen to the discussion. I knew my entrance to medical school would depend on the tiny decisions I made each day. There might be candidates more genius than me, but I would not be outworked. I could be accepted or rejected for any number of reasons, but it would not be for lack of effort.

One day, I was not feeling well. I didn't think I could make it to class. I called my accountability partner, and she said, "Can you just go and sit there? Sit in the back and don't even take notes."

What was this insanity she spouted? Who would go to a class and sit in the back? Who would have the audacity to just listen and not jot down a single concept?

I sat silent for a moment, so she added, "Just show up, that's all. Can you do that?"

That seemed a low bar to jump over, so I went to that class and did as I was told. I learned the value of showing up well or sick. I have harvested this lesson many times in the years that followed. I don't need to feel perfect physically, mentally, or spiritually to do what's right. Imperfect is perfect.

I lived close to UCLA, so the parties raged on weekends and most weeknights. Helicopters flew overhead and sirens blared. All the while I was tucked in my apartment making note cards and doing my work. I made some incredible friends in those two years. I had an organic chemistry class with my friend Sophia. She was on the UCLA women's soccer team on a scholarship. That right there tells you about her talent and drive. We were discussing our Organic Chem class, and I asked her, "You don't really think we need to do all those workbook problems he assigns, do you?"

Without a moment's hesitation, she replied, "Of course you do. You've got to do all of them."

Right then, I knew she was not messing around, and I liked that. Sophia and I became fast friends. I was her lab partner for our three-hour stints with beakers, test tubes, and all sorts of concoctions to weigh and measure. One day, she arrived at our lab class with a huge duffle bag and announced, "I'm leaving with the team right after lab." This was when I learned about her travel schedule. She had to constantly miss classes for away games. Sophia explained, "I need to start traveling for soccer, so I won't be able to go to class. Can we review what I missed when I get back?"

"Of course!" I replied.

It was now my personal mission to see that Sophia and I passed this class with flying colors. I covered for her by taking detailed notes during class. I went to tutoring to make sure I could explain it all to Sophia. Her goal was nursing school, and I was determined to help her get there. She would hustle into our lab class with her huge pack for soccer, only to leave for an away game right after class. One day, in addition to her pack, she was on crutches. After we talked about her injury, I added optimistically, "Well, at least you get a break from soccer." However, she still had to dress out for all the home games.

We would talk about our weekend plans during our Friday labs and other chemistry classes. Sophia was so pretty, and we were friendly with the guys in our classes. They asked us to go out with them one weekend. I heard their offer and promptly replied, "I don't drink." The truth just spilled out for everyone to know. I explained to Sophia that I was sober and that my drinking days were over. As an elite athlete, she was leading a clean life as well. Partying was not the priority. I had made that mistake already and thrown away a few years of college, so no judgment, it just was not for me.

Sophia quickly rejoined the travel team and returned to her soccer schedule. I saw it as my responsibility to keep Sophia current on our classwork and labs. She had my word on this, so I took it seriously. I had to know the material well enough to teach it to her. As the final neared, Sophia and I met for study sessions where we went over that thick workbook full of problems. Now we taught each other from the book I originally hoped to blow off entirely. That Organic Chem final was a beast. When it was handed out, it felt like a tome. It was fifteen or so pages of problems, short answers, multiple choice, and 'write out the solution'. I remember the satisfaction of acing that test. It was challenging, but I decimated it. I was able to do this thanks to my commitment to help someone else. Sophia would graduate days later, also having cleanly passed the class.

A few days passed and I found a note tacked to my front door. It was two full pages long, handwritten on notebook paper. It read:

"Dear Elisemarie,

"Thank you for helping me get through my classes this year. I could not have gotten through O. Chem without your help. Congrats on crushing the exam. I am also thankful for our friendship. First, because of how we cracked up through those boring and endless labs, weighing, measuring, and usually spilling things. I lost count of how many test tubes we shattered, either by letting them roll off the table or by not securing them properly. Luckily, we had Denny for our T.A. Thank God he looked the other way during our shenanigans and multiple trips to the supply drawers.

"I also admire your sobriety and everything you are working for. I want to let you know that my dad is an alcoholic, but he never stops drinking for good. He gets sober and makes lots of promises. My mom and I get super happy and hopeful. Then he starts back drinking time and time again. He just cannot put together any length of sober time. I started to believe that recovery was just impossible.

"Then you told us you did not drink, and you go to meetings. I admire that you have been able to stay sober for years. You don't just talk the talk; you walk that walk. I know you work hard at that, and I respect you for it... Thank you for being a wonderful friend to me. Thank you for giving me hope that a sober and meaningful life is possible for my family, too.

"All the best, Sophia."

In the entire year that we sat next to each other daily, I never knew Sophia's dad was a practicing alcoholic. I wish I had known; I would have been happy to be there for her.. After the delivery of the note, I never saw or heard from Sophia. I know her plans were to return to Colorado to her boyfriend and family, whom she loved. I imagine that she is a very successful nurse and is taking great care of her family. I see her dad as sober, and her family healed. I thank God for her and her sweet friendship.

With Sophia's help, I solidified several of my core values. First, never give up. Second, push through the seemingly impossible. More importantly, the only way to be sure I really understand something is to be able to teach it to someone else. Friends are necessary. I would continue to need friends in the year I took to take the MCAT and applied to medical school

I asked a medical school advisor, "Would it be okay if I applied with an arts background?"

"Actually, that would be quite the trick, if you could make your left brain and your right brain work like that. If you could do that, it would be a feat."

Right then, I knew the 'if' was out of the question. I told myself that I needed to study twice as hard as every single other person I saw in class. I had to double down and nail these tests and classes because I was going to get into an American medical school.

How hard is that to do? The acceptance rate when I applied for the class of 2005 was roughly 37 percent. The required GPA was a 3.60, and the average MCAT was 29 (it was graded differently then). Not to mention the laundry list of shadowing across several specialty areas, researching a disease process with direct patient interactions, volunteering for hundreds of hours in at UCLA Santa Monica Medical Center, attending as many surgeries as possible, keeping an A average, working full time at the birthing center at UCLA, and being a published author. All of this had to be accomplished by my first medical school interview.

I had an interview over Christmas break, set up in Omaha, Nebraska at Creighton Medical School. I arrived the night before, and it was incredibly cold. We stayed at a nearby hotel, and I wanted to be rested and prepared to shine for my interview. However, the hotel we were staying in had a fire. Everyone had to evacuate outside the stairwells on the street in the subzero temperatures for about an hour from 2:15 -3:15 am. This was a perfect opportunity for me to start sucking up the discomfort that lay ahead. I was accepted at Creighton and could not have been happier. I loved the school and the Midwest location.

In August 2001, a very exciting moment arrived. I started medical school in America. I moved to Omaha and acclimated myself to the sobriety groups there. I was introduced to a sober fourth-year student. We met in the medical school research library.

He instructed, "If you want to get through medical school, you need to do a few things:

1. Find a partner to get through the classes with. Study together and keep each other accountable.
2. Never cram. You can't cram medical school; there is simply too much information every day to cram it all in at the end. You must make a study schedule that includes where and what time you will put in the hours required every day. Stick to your damn schedule no matter what.
3. Keep showing up and don't leave until one of two things happen: they either tell you to leave, or you graduate."

The first two years are learning and memorizing at a pace like you have never seen. Third year, they throw you in the hospital and try to destroy you with inordinate amounts of work. Fourth year, they build you up a little so you can get out the door and graduate. It's going to suck but you can do it."

I thought, "Sounds familiar. Thanks for the training, Sophia."

"If you have knowledge, let others light their candles in it."
Margaret Fuller

"And no one can live happily who has regard to himself alone and transforms everything into a question of his own utility; you must live for your neighbor, if you would live for yourself."
Seneca

"Two are better than one, because they have a good return for their labor: If either of them falls down, one can help the other up." (Ecclesiastes 4:9-12, NIV)

FINAL VOYAGE

MY OLDEST CHILD, Jacob, was born in Nebraska on June 26, 2003. He was long-awaited and celebrated like royalty by friends and family. We even got packages addressed to 'Master Jacob Vincent Metzner.' I shared a photo of newborn Baby Jacob with my medical school classmates. One observed, "It should be illegal to be that cute."

I happen to love the heat of the Omaha summer. Since Jacob was a summer baby, I frequently snuggled him into his stroller to go for a walk. On these walks, I had the luxury of staring into Jacob's eyes for as long as he could stay awake. I knew he was an absolute miracle, and I dreamed magnificent dreams for him. There was nowhere I would rather have been. This precious baby so completely enraptured me. I just wanted to be a stay-at-home mom. However, I did not dare to tell anyone how this baby had entirely changed my goals. Anyone could be his doctor. Only I could be his mom. I wanted to quit medical school, but I couldn't bring myself to do it. I decided to try to carry on. Many times, I have wished I did not. I could have been home with my precious baby. It's something I missed, something I cannot change. It's time I cannot get back.

At the time, I embarked on a frantic search for care for Jacob. In-home daycare? A traditional daycare setting? If so, which one is best? Close to our house? Close to the hospital? The myriad of decisions left me frazzled. As we looked for care, we visited a few homes. In one, there were two huge Dobermans. One of them was standing too close to Jacob in his baby carrier. I felt certain that a huge splotch of dog drool would splat down on his face at any moment. I was horrified. Of course, we would not be leaving our baby there! As we walked to the car, my husband Jeff said, "It didn't look too bad."

I now understand that women and men have very different kinds of instincts, especially when it comes to their children. After that debacle, we tried a more traditional daycare. I remember that as a room with infant beds, all lined up like in a hospital. Only this room was not bright and white like a hospital. It was in a dingy yellow basement. The rays of sunlight pouring in through the egress window only highlighted the dust and filth. I was crying as we left. There seemed to be no proper place for Baby Jacob.

I was getting desperate for someone to help with Jacob, as it was close to the onset of third-year rotations. I was now regularly asking every single person I met, "Who takes care of your kids when you are at work?" One day, I was taking Baby Jacob on his walk in the stroller. Just for variety, we turned to go left down the hill instead of straight to the corner. In one yard, there was a couple with a toddler.

After saying hello, I asked my now rote question, "Who takes care of your baby when you are at work?"

She answered, "A neighbor, her name is Chris. You may have seen her house, a couple of blocks up. It's the one with all the party signs in the windows and balloons."

No way! Turning into our neighborhood, we often saw this house on the left just down from the corner. Every so often, there was a huge party for kids. There were streamers and balloons and kids everywhere in the yard and on the playground across the street. I thought it looked like the most fun place on earth.

"Are you happy with your son being there?" I asked.

"Oh yes, Chris is the best, and her family is amazing. She has ten kids of her own."

My mind was like a slot machine going tilt, tilt, tilt. A huge family of kids suddenly became the answer I had been looking for. She told me, "I think Chris is full, but you can give her a call and ask, anyway."

I rushed home to call Chris. She said that she would like to meet with Jeff, Baby Jacob, and me that evening. When we went into her house, it seemed very calm and clean. I thought there must be some mistake about the ten kids. However, I did not yet know the power of Chris. Everything and everyone felt in order. Chris sat comfortably in her chair with her Bible close by. She looked like the picture of serenity. We sat across from her on the couch while she interviewed us. We had a pleasant conversation. Chris said she loved Jacob and could see he was such a good baby.

She told us, "I will need to talk to my husband, Mark, and get back to you."

Who was this superfamily-centric saint? Chris, one in a million. She was such a good wife and an outstanding mother. It felt like we won the lottery when she called back to say she would be able to care for Jacob. I was so delighted. I honestly don't know if I would have been able to finish medical school without her undying support and love. What a blessing it was for Jacob to be there.

Chris was equally a blessing for me, as I learned from her how to have a deeper and more consistent relationship with God. Chris taught me to take my troubles to God. She was compassionate toward people that others might judge. I remember one time she asked me if I would contribute to a fund for a mom friend. She proceeded to tell me how the mom was distraught. She had been sleeping with her baby and tragically rolled onto her during the night. Chris was constantly reaching out to hurting people like this. We immediately started a fund to help with the burial of the baby and other expenses.

I soon learned that the constant stream of 'parties' was of Bible classes in disguise. The Sjogren family would host these monthly 'Bible parties.' These gatherings were open to anyone who wanted to join. That was one of Chris's hallmark qualities; all were welcome and included. Her heart was open to everyone.

Chris especially loved to share the way God had transformed her life, which brought hope to others. Chris would tell me, "I was living a life full of sin. I was miserable. When I accepted Christ into my heart, everything changed." She would introduce her relationship with the Lord with so much joy and hope that it was infectious. She would ask the person checking out her groceries, "Do you know the Lord?" Soon, the conversation would involve tears, prayers, and hugs. The joyous exchange would conclude with Chris making sure they had a Bible and encouraging them to meet the Lord in daily prayer.

People from all walks of life were drawn to Chris and her well of joy. She would just say, "It's the Lord." The beautiful thing was that Chris did not walk on holy clouds. She was right here walking in the clay with the rest of us, and she was hilarious to boot. I have never seen anyone have more of a blast with kids. I learned to play by watching her example. Chris was free and silly with kids; she could also be stern if she felt they needed correction. But that was okay, because they knew she loved them. How did she prove this? Cookies, of course.

Chris was often found in her kitchen, baking her signature chocolate chip cookies. Vats of dough were stored in her basement freezer so that these cookies were readily available as needed. She started a little charity with her boys, Ben and Phil, called Two Boys and an Oven. They would bake a 'trillion' cookies and then sell them in various store parking lots. The money raised was for a cause the Lord placed on their hearts.

I remember one year they were selling cookies around Christmas time at a Lowe's parking lot. To warm up, the boys would occasionally go inside and play on an air hockey table that was for sale. Ben and Phil enjoyed it so much that they let Chris know that they wanted one, maybe for Christmas. So Chris looked at the cost and concluded that with all the folks they provided for during the holidays, they could not afford the extravagance of an air hockey table.

During this time, Chris was caring for Baby Jacob during the week. Chris knew that Jeff loved her chocolate chip cookies and generously bestowed them upon him. Clam shells of cookies were a common sight in our home, and they did not last long.

It was about five days after the Lowe's cookie sale concluded. Chris and I were chatting about the outcome. Single moms, underprivileged families, and children in need at the holidays benefited from their efforts. The 'icing on the cake' was that the manager at Lowes had noticed Ben and Phil enjoying the air hockey table. He was quite impressed with their character and efforts to serve. He told Chris that he had noticed the boys playing on the air hockey table and decided to give the display model to the boys for Christmas. So that is how it went. Another day, another miracle surrounding Chris. Her gratitude for the generosity bestowed on her was endless.

Near the end of medical school, Jeff and I decided to move with our two baby boys to Kansas City to be closer to family. Our last stop as we were leaving Omaha was, of course, Chris's house. There, we exchanged hugs with Chris and many of her kids. We cried buckets of tears as we left our Omaha family and headed to Leawood, Kansas, where my mom lived.

Chris and I stayed in frequent contact after our move. Some years more than others. On our birthdays and most of all when I needed her guidance with marriage, children, siblings, God, and anything else of importance. I liked to send Chris little gifts like dish towels. That was my 'jam.' I love to give gifts to people that are specific to their interests and their activities. I could make a career of this giving fest, and Chris was one of my favorite subjects. Knowing she was in that kitchen with her vats of cookie batter gave me a reason to send dish towels. She would thank me as if I had sent a new dishwasher or remodeled her first floor. Chris was grateful for the little things.

I had not sent Chris a little towel in a while, so when I came upon one that was good enough for her, I grabbed it. I stuck it in a brown paper envelope and mailed it to Omaha, knowing it would live the good life with Chris in her kitchen. Chris would undoubtedly call and say, "You are a stinker! How do you have time to go out and get a dish towel for me, get it packaged up, and in the mail? Girl, you are too much. What's going on with you? I miss you." Again, acting like I sent a Faberge egg or something.

Some weeks after I mailed her a gift, I received a card from Chris. This was in October of 2020. I immediately knew it was from her for several reasons. The card was adorned with several stickers of roses and other flowers. Then I saw her unmistakable handwriting that looked as though an angel had penned the words.

It was a sunny day as I walked back into the house from the mailbox, and I was in a particularly good mood. Additionally, I was delighted to hear from my dear friend Chris, so I ripped open the letter. Chris usually closed her writings with a Bible verse or two. This card was odd in that she penned four Bible verses right away at the beginning. The verses were about God never leaving our side. Then, because of her tremendous gratitude, she thanked me for the dish towel again and wished me well.

As I continued reading, my joy turned upside down.

Chris wrote, "I had not been able to get in to see my pulmonologist for a while. I called back in March, but he was so busy with COVID-19 patients that I could not get in. Then, in July, my breathing was still bothering me, so I called to try to get in again. This time, I scheduled an appointment and was seen. I was diagnosed with stage four lung cancer."

The letter fell from my hands. "No, No, No!" I shouted. My mind reeled; this cannot be true. No, Chris is so healthy, she eats healthy and exercises regularly. This did not make any sense at all. She has never smoked a cigarette ever. No, this could not be true. And why? Why would she tell me this in a letter? Why not call? This is some sick prank. But I know her writing. What is going on? Is this real?

I gathered myself and picked up the letter. I read from the beginning again, knowing now that the Bible verses were there to support me during the contents ahead. They were there to soften the blow of the punches I could not possibly tolerate. These were blows of hard truth. I read them slowly. Tears splashed onto the paper and blurred the words. I had to speak with Chris. I had to know how in the world this was true.

I plead with God.

"Why? Why someone who just lives to share Christ with His kids? Why someone who only has a kind word for every single person on the planet? Why a mom with ten kids and all these precious grandkids that adore her?"

The "whys" could go on forever. I needed to talk directly with Chris.

When I spoke with her, it was astonishing. She had accepted her diagnosis. She understood that missing out on her appointment back in March took her prognosis from bad to grim. Catching this kind of cancer at an earlier and treatable stage was essential for survival. In my mind, I knew that she was just as deserving of care as the COVID patients back in March of 2020. Chris's condition was no less important, not in any way. It was urgent. Caught at stage two or even three, this cancer could be treated. Now it was a death sentence. Chris held no bitterness about the months that passed without medical attention. She accepted how it was now.

She told me that she had decided not to have any treatment. "I want to live out my days with the health I have. I don't want to be some sick person, losing my hair, vomiting all the time, so weak I cannot even walk. I just won't do that. I won't do that to my family. I do not want to burden them like that."

"And how does your family feel about that?" I queried.

"They are supportive. You know, some more than others. But they understand. I want to enjoy the life I have. I want to spend real time with my kids, my family, my siblings, and make memories with them," she answered.

In typical Chris fashion, she did not disappoint. I remember that I could not see her until after Christmas. COVID was rampant, and she absolutely could not get exposed. She wanted to be sure she had time with every one of her ten children and grandchildren before seeing anyone else.

Then, in January of 2021, she made plans to go on a retreat with her siblings. No spouses and no kids. It was all of them and only them for the weekend. I honestly thought this was remarkable, something not even possible with my own siblings. Chris recounted to me how this was such a special and healing time for them to be together. She was still feeling good and fully took in the moments. She headed back to California to visit her sister's family. Chris traveled, enjoyed, and spent time with the people she loved most. She prioritized her time, as she knew these little blocks of feeling good were limited. Chris prioritized her time. It was her currency for life, and she spent it wisely.

In February, Chris was in the Kansas City Area to visit her son, meet his new baby, and attend a baby shower. She had promised to bring one hundred strawberry shortcakes for the event. She only had about an hour to visit with me, as her husband Mark would be back with the fresh strawberries very soon. She seemed like the same Chris I always knew, and she looked great. I wanted to do something special for her.

I told her, "I am going to miss you so much. I don't know what I am going to do."

There were no easy answers.

When she stood up to leave for strawberry duty, I noticed her purse was worn through in some places. Chris was never the type to splurge on herself. When we parted, I was determined to send her a new bag. She simply could not travel the world with that one. I walked into a store and immediately saw the right one. It would accompany her on this final leg of her journey on earth. I sent it as quickly as possible. Chris loved it and raved about how it was the perfect bag for her many travels.

I took every chance I could find to be with Chris. She lived in Omaha, about three hours from the Kansas City area. One of my visits after her diagnosis was in early May. As we chatted, I asked about our mutual friend, Sherri. Chris replied, "Oh, she is so great. I'm having lunch with her next week. It would be so fun if you could come. What are you doing on Thursday? This is ridiculous; I know you are so busy. I would love to be with you two. We will do it another time."

I know that putting things off for 'another time' is a fantasy, especially for someone with stage four cancer. When I got in the car to go home, I texted Sherri immediately. "Hi, Sherri. I know you are having lunch with Chris on Thursday. I wonder if you need alone time with her or if I could join? I understand either way. Love you!"

Sherri responded immediately, "Oh, I would love that. Of course, you can come. Let's talk soon." When we did talk, I told her, "I want it to be a surprise, so don't let Chris know I'm coming."

We planned it all out. We were meeting at Cozy Corners Restaurant for lunch. I asked my son, Nicholas, to join us. He said, "I don't know, Mom. I don't even really remember Chris. Now you want me to go to lunch with her, and she is dying? What will I even say?"

"You won't have to say anything. How about, 'Hi Chris, I'm Nick?' Chris is the most fun person. It's not like we will sit and cry for an hour. Please come."

With my plea granted, I had two partners for the journey: my son, Nicholas, who was in eighth grade, and Madison, who was in kindergarten. We arranged a perfect surprise plan with Sherri, making it happen on her end. We planned to arrive at Cozy Corners early to surprise them. Sherri called to tell us she was going to the best bakery in Omaha to get a cake for the occasion. When she arrived, she called us, "Okay, I am at *Deliciousness Now*. I told the woman working here about Chris. She is giving us the cake, the best in the place, but I don't know what to put on it."

"Oh, that is so sweet! Let me think about that and call you back."

I brainstormed with my kids, telling them, "It needs to say something about meeting Jesus because Chris is excited about this." Through our conversations, I pulled out the phrase, "Meeting Jesus is The Sweetest."

I called Sherri back with the idea, and she loved it. Sherri told us, "I will drop off the cake at Cozy Corners, so it's there when we arrive. Just ask the host to be seated at the table with the cake."

Our drive went swimmingly, and we proceeded to the restaurant to hide and surprise them. We needed to hide quickly, so I told the host, "We are here for the party, the surprise for Chris." She just looked at us like we were crazy people. So, I repeated, "You know the surprise party for Chris, where should we hide?" Still nothing. "The cake." I urged.

Again, the host returned a quizzical look. Suddenly, a light bulb in my brain turned on. "Wait, does Cozy Corners have another location?"

"Yes."

Nick, Madison, and I jumped back in the car and sped away. Now, we were not early by any stretch. We got there and ran in the door, ducking down to stay out of sight. Out of the corner of my eye, I saw Sherri and Chris getting out of a car parked in a handicapped spot right in front, so we dashed for our lives. I ran in and said, "The table, with the surprise? Cookie cake?"

They directed us just as Chris entered the restaurant, thinking this was simply lunch with Sherri. We all hid around the corner from the booth, and when Chris walked closer, we jumped up and yelled, "Surprise!" Chris almost fell over. She had a smile of amazement on her face and then tears. As we all hugged and sat down, Chris's gratitude was immense. She said, "I cannot believe you guys did this. This is the sweetest thing anyone has ever done for me." Then, looking at me, she said, "I can't believe you came." More tears. She was astounded that we landed back in Omaha only a few days after our visit. We laughed so hard we cried. Nick had a blast getting to know Chris. They are kindred spirits in their hilariousness. When the server came over, Chris said, "Oh, don't mind us; I just got out of prison, so this is a big day for me."

That tone continued during our time together. I sat across from Chris, wanting to soak in her beautiful spirit. My friend was glowing; she radiated love for us, God, and everything. I felt so blessed to be in the presence of these two amazing women and my two youngest kids. Lunch flew by too quickly. Then, we exchanged our lengthy goodbyes with hugs, smiles, and tears.

When we returned to our car to go home, Nick said, "That was not what I had expected. It was beautiful and uplifting."

"I know, isn't Chris amazing? She makes a terminal diagnosis look like nothing at all."

I was in contact with her daughters, who told me, "Mom has told everyone about your visit. That was the biggest deal in the world for her. She loved it!"

"I assure you, we loved it more!" I responded.

We had a couple more beautiful visits with Chris. She was the friend I could share anything with. She kept my confidence and directed my attention to what God would have me do in any situation. She would lovingly point out how I could respond when I presented my difficulties. I poured my heart out in a letter describing some problems I was having.

In the fall, Chris told me she wanted me to come and see her by myself. She wanted to talk with me alone. Chris's request for 'alone time' lingered in my spirit. I planned to see her in two weeks on a Wednesday. As our visit drew closer, I got a text from her daughter on the Tuesday before my Omaha trip. She said, "Mom wanted me to give you a call. She's not feeling great and wants to postpone your visit until Friday. She hopes to be feeling better by then." In my soul, I knew she would not be feeling better, so I responded, "I think I should come now, tonight, or in the morning."

"No, she says Friday is good. She's just in a rough patch."

Friday at 2:30 am, I received a text saying, "Mom peacefully went to the Lord this morning."

Through my tears, I told her daughter, Kate, "I guess she got a better offer for lunch." I felt so bad about this. I know she wanted to talk with me alone. I thought maybe she wanted to unburden something in the end. I'm sorry I didn't get to be there for her."

Kate responded, "Oh, no. That visit was for you. She read your letter, and it weighed on her heart. She wanted to talk with you for *you*, not for her."

"Of course, in her last days, she was thinking, 'Who needs my help?'" I was so relieved.

"Thank God. I'll be fine. I am so happy it wasn't something she needed."

"No, it was for you."

I could hear her smile as she continued, "And if it makes you feel any better, I was supposed to visit with her just before you, so she flaked on both of us."

As we hung up the phone, I thought, "Always the warrior for Christ. I should have known."

Chris's memorial service was beyond packed; people were spilling out the doors into the lobby. The eulogist began by saying, "Chris was diagnosed with stage 4 cancer about a year ago. Could I see, by show of hands, please raise your hand if, in the past year, you have had personal contact with Chris, either in a phone call or personal visit?"

At this point, almost every single person raised their hand.

"And in how many of these conversations did Chris have a goal of helping you?" Again, all the hands went up.

"So, in her final days on this planet, this extraordinary woman spent them helping you. If that isn't a tribute to the kind of Christly woman Chris was, I don't know what is."

The room was silent. Chris was better than all of us put together. She set the bar high and left it there. She placed it quietly and lovingly. Chris leaped over it first to give us courage and an example.

The roadmap was now ours to grab hold of.

"The comfort of having a friend may be taken away but not that of having had one." Seneca

"Life must be understood backwards; but...it must be lived forwards." Sören Kierkegaard

"When you go through a trial, the sovereignty of God is the pillow upon which you lay your head.". Charles Spurgeon

"A friend loves at all times..." (Proverbs 17:17).

UNDER HIS WING VI

How Many Solutions?

M Y DAD OWNED a successful construction company. As a teenager, this meant one thing to me and my siblings. Extravagant vacations? Nope, summer jobs for all the kids. My brothers worked in his equipment yard, and I worked in the office from 8 to 5 from the age of thirteen years old.

One day, Dad handed me a slip of paper with a name on it. He said, "I want you to find the contact information for this man. I need his phone number and address." At this time, there were no cell phones, iPads, Facebook, or Google searches. There were no YouTube videos to instruct me. Yes, these were the 'dark ages.' We had things called phone books that were about five inches thick. One was called 'the white pages,' and alas, it was made of white pages like tissue paper filled with personal information of people in your area. The other was called 'the Yellow Pages,' printed on yellow tissue paper, for looking up local businesses.

I marched out of Dad's office with that slip of paper to find the white pages and gain the information. This was going to be easier than I imagined. I went through the white pages with a fine-tooth comb. I scanned down alphabetically, and bingo! There was the last name: Paulson. This was easy-peasy. Now all I needed was the first name: Victor. I was going to have this back to the 'boss' in no time flat. I scanned again. Valentine, Valerie…Victoria. Wait, no Victor? I checked and double-checked, and no Victor was listed.

Well, this was an impossible task. I marched back to Dad's office to give him the bad news, dun-dun-duh! There was no Victor Paulson. I needed to break it to him easily, so I said, "I can't find Victor Paulson in the phone book." Case closed. I held my head high, awaiting my next directive. Instead of assigning me a new task, Dad grabbed this teachable moment.

"When you work for someone and they ask you to do something, like solve a problem, don't just hand the problem back to them. If you're going to present a problem, also suggest three ways to solve it. You can acknowledge the problem, as long as you bring your ideas for solving it. That will show you are really on your toes." Dad really wanted us 'on our toes,' using not only book smarts but street smarts. These were as essential as good character, and similarly, cannot be bought, only honed. Which, according to the *Oxford Dictionary,* is the process of "having been refined or perfected over a period of time."

In my personal thought bubble, fireworks were exploding.

In that moment, I realized that when a difficulty looked insurmountable, I was not going to just hand it back for someone else to figure out. *I* needed to find ways to solve it. This was the expectation of 'the Boss.' I took a very valuable piece of information from Dad's little lesson that morning. There are three solutions to every problem. Even when I cannot see them, they exist. Maybe there is a resource I have not considered. If I don't see the solution, I can ask other people for their ideas. God works through people. I can always say a prayer, "God help me." He never fails.

It turns out that Victor Paulson's information was available, even in those dark times with no internet and no apps to do the work for me. It was available in another kind of 'book' called a directory. Organizations would list members' names and contact information in hard-copy paper books and distribute them to their membership. Would Victor Paulson be in one of these? I failed to ask the questions that would lead me to solutions. These included, "How do you know Mr. Paulson? What line of work is he in? Where do you usually see Mr. Paulson? Is he a member of any professional organizations? Have you seen him at any community meetings lately?" These questions would have pointed me smack dab at Victor Paulson, a member of the Kansas City Builders Association.

There are generally three solutions to every problem, whether I see them or not. Three solutions became my foundation. I hope you will strive to find your own three solutions to every problem and never give up. I treasure my three-word prayers and solutions. I use them daily, and I love that they draw me toward the Trinity: God the Father, the Son, and the Holy Spirit. Three parts, one Being. This teaching can seem elusive and perplexing for even the most spiritual. I saw a children's book where they likened the Trinity to an apple. The Father was like the apple skin, covering and encompassing everything. The Son was the inside 'meat' or flesh of the apple. At one with the skin and at the same time different. The seeds were the Holy Spirit, remaining after the apple was gone. Small, yet powerful, and, if nurtured, had the potential to manifest The Father and The Son. So, the Trinity lives in me in this way.

Here are my favorite 'threes':

> *I give up.*
> *God, help me.*
> *Thank you, God*
> *Love you, God.*
> *Listen, Learn, Love.*

Take three breaths.
Pause three seconds.
I'm so sorry.
I forgive you.
Call a friend.
Be of service.
One more day.
Stick to facts
Feel your feelings.
You can cry.
Do three more.
Walk three steps.
Run three miles.
Swim, bike, run.
Never Give Up.
Ask three friends.
Say three prayers.
Dial three numbers
988
Ask for help.
Please help me.
Will you help?
Please join us.
May I help?
I give up.
I'm so sorry.
I forgive you.
I appreciate you.
I accept you.
I love you.

"I vow and consecrate to God all that is in me: My memory and my actions to God the Father; My understanding and my words to God the Son; My will and my thoughts to God the Holy Spirit." St. Francis de Sales (from a consecration prayer to the Trinity)

"Until now you have not asked for anything in my name. Ask and you will receive, and your joy will be complete." (John 16:2, NIV)

"And when you pray, do not keep on babbling like pagans, for they think they will be heard because of their many words. Do not be like them, for your Father knows what you need before you ask him." (Matthew 6:7-8, NIV)

Number One

HERE WAS a narrow hallway that led to Dad's office. During the summers I worked in his office, I often found myself waiting just outside that hallway for a chance to talk with him. There was really nothing to do but stand there with the documents I held, awaiting his signature. Before cell phones, people like me just stood and waited patiently. If a co-worker walked by, we had a real face-to-face conversation.

Many times, I was alone, waiting in the hallway. I believe that my time in the hall had a purpose. Dad was not about wasting time, opportunities for growth, or the dissemination of information. His way was always teaching, never preaching. He taught us the lessons that were important to him.

The indirect method is often the most ingenious way for a parent to instill information. I apply this with my kids. Since the knee-jerk reaction from a child to a parent may be one of negativity, judgment, or rebellion, plant the answers so your kids think they have discovered them on their own. There are skads of ways to get the messages delivered covertly to your kids. I have used, "Let's watch this video together" method or "Let's read this together." One of my favorites is to pre-call the coach or instructor so they know what's going on. Then I ask my child, "Why don't you go talk to your coach?" I set up the conversation and let the proverbial magic happen.

My parents were big on leaving things around for us to read. Books were strategically placed, so I thought I had found them. One was a book about the birds and the bees. I thought I had unearthed a secret cache of information. I would read it and hide it right back where I found it, sure it belonged to one of my siblings. I didn't want to get in trouble for looking at such obscene complexities. In actuality, it was a textbook intended for me, quite brilliant, really.

Waiting in the hallway to see Dad provided a similar type of classroom. To pass the time, I would read what he placed on the wall. There was a piece of writing framed in a nondescript wood frame. It read:

Vince Lombardi: What It Takes to be Number One

"Winning is not a sometime thing; it's an all the time thing. You don't win once in a while; you don't do things right once in a while; you do them right all the time. Winning is a habit. Unfortunately, so is losing. There is no room for second place. There is only one place in my game, and that's first place. I have finished second twice in my time at Green Bay, and I don't ever want to finish second again. There is a second-place bowl game, but it is a game for losers played by losers.

"It is and always has been an American zeal to be first in anything we do, and to win, and to win, and to win. Every time a football player goes to ply his trade, he's got to play from the ground up-from the soles of his feet right up to his head. Every inch of him has to play. Some guys play with their heads. That's O.K. You've got to be smart to be number one in any business. But more importantly, you've got to play with your heart, with every fiber of your body. If you're lucky enough to find a guy with a lot of head and a lot of heart, he's never going to come off the field second.

"Running a football team is no different than running any other kind of organization - an army, a political party, or a business. The principles are the same. The object is to win - to beat the other guy. Maybe that sounds hard or cruel. I don't think it is. It is a reality of life that men are competitive, and the most competitive games draw the most competitive men. That's why they are there - to compete.

"The object is to win fairly, squarely, by the rules - but to win. And in truth, I've never known a man worth his salt who, in the long run, deep down in his heart, didn't appreciate the grind, the discipline. There is something in good men that really yearns for discipline and the harsh reality of head-to-head combat. I don't say these things because I believe in the 'brute' nature of men or that men must be brutalized to be combative. I believe in God, and I believe in human decency. But I firmly believe that any man's finest hour -- his greatest fulfillment to all he holds dear -- is that moment when he has worked his heart out in a good cause and lies exhausted on the field of battle-victorious." - Coach Vincent T. Lombardi

I must have read this hundreds of times while working for Dad. He meant it for me, and I appreciate its deliberate placement.

May I never come second off the field.

"Some people say I have attitude – maybe I do… but I think you have to. You have to believe in yourself when no one else does – that makes you a winner right there." Venus Williams

'There are always new, grander challenges to confront, and a true winner will embrace each one." Mia Hamm

"Start children off on the way they should go, and even when they are old, they will not turn from it" Proverbs 22:6 (NIV)

THE BUCK STOPS HERE

I OWE MY DAD, Vincent, a huge debt of gratitude for leading by example. He was a Depression-era World War II veteran. In the War, he led a group called 'the go-ahead men.' Dad drove a tank out ahead into enemy territory to locate enemy nests before his platoon advanced. Later, he told me that he feared for his life every single day in this high-danger position. Dad rarely said two words about the War, but the memories of it ran deep within him. Once he survived that, the rest of his life must have felt like child's play. Vincent was a fearless entrepreneur and would start a business and make it fly. He had the work ethic of a stallion, and the word quit was not in his vocabulary. I cannot remember when I questioned or talked back to my dad. He demanded respect. He gave discipline and love.

When it was snowing, Dad would wake me early to shovel the driveway before school, but not some little driveway. No, this was a circle driveway up a massive hill to our house. I wish I could tell him how much I appreciated my training. I am thankful he made me go out with the boys to accomplish this arctic chore. As far as he was concerned, if the boys were up shoveling, so was I. I would bundle up and grab my personal snowplow. These were not just any shovels. They were Vincent S.D. specials. He invented these tools in his personal machinery shop in our basement. They had wooden handles and giant green blades. He added a stopper on one side of the blade so the snow would stay contained and not trail out the other end when the scoop was full. This scoop allowed us to lift and dump the heavy, wet snow. We cleared the snow from the driveway, shoveled the sidewalk, and put down salt. Only then could we grab breakfast and get ready for the day.

Our chores continued year-round. Each week, crabgrass had to be painstakingly removed from our yard. Apples had to be picked or picked up off the ground. The rose garden needed watering and plant food. Cherries needed to be harvested, cleaned, pitted, and made into pies. Work was in style, and laziness was passé.

On Sundays, we attended church and often made meatballs, sauce, and pasta. Then we visited Dad's parents whether we wanted to or not. When we got home, we did homework and got to bed early, as the morning would come fast. We needed to be up in plenty of time to make our beds, clean our rooms, have breakfast, and walk to school. It was about 1.5 miles each way, and our feet were our 'cars.' Could Mom or Dad take us to school? Sometimes, if Dad took us, we had to be ready to start the day by attending mass before school.

As I crept into my teen years, summer jobs were mandatory. At age eleven, I was babysitting during the day. At age twelve, I cared for a family of six children. By fifteen, summer was a time to make money and save it. I worked forty-plus hours a week at Dad's construction company. There was no opting out of this work ethic training ground. It was not punishment but Life Lesson 101. Vince Lombardi's words were in full effect: "The only place success comes before work is in the dictionary." Honestly, I appreciated the structure. It kept me from indulging my vices.

I set my alarm for early morning to be ready to leave with Dad by 7:30 am. We journeyed to the east side of town, where the construction company had its home. This part of town looked different. The houses were small and shabby. There was trash and rubbish on the streets and in the yards. There were hungry people outside. My heart would go out to the many children we saw outdoors as we drove home in the evenings. Some of them looked sad, tired, shoeless, and dirty. Their eyes looked vacant, and their expressions were downhearted. It wasn't always gloom and doom as some played joyfully with siblings. Other kids traveled the sidewalks with bright cherry popsicles, splashing drops of red as the hot summer sun beat down. My parents did not shelter us from the harsh realities of the world. I knew that other kids had it rough. My life seemed privileged and carefree in comparison. I did not take that for granted.

Under Vince's rules, food was used wisely and kept if it was edible. One of the best reminders of this was the 'Crisper.' If chips went stale, as they often did, you put them in the 'Crisper.' This must have predated the invention of the chip clip. Carless teens and kids routinely placed half-eaten, open bags of chips and crackers in the cabinet. The bags were left gaping open to welcome the snacker. Less popular chips would sit unfastened for days or weeks before rediscovery occurred. When this happened to a pitiful bag of potato chips, the 'crisper' came to the rescue. Whatever claims the 'crisper' promised did not come to fruition. The whole 'like new' tagline was simply false. The point was, 'Don't throw good food away.' It's still delicious food. 'Waste not want not' was possibly invented by my Depression Era Dad. He piped, "One man's trash is another man's treasure." Dad also taught, "A penny saved is a penny earned." When he observed extravagant expenses like a diamond belt buckle, Dad would say, "Some people have more money than sense."

There were more enforced activities. None of us can forget getting a call to come downstairs, kneel on the floor, and say the rosary. These urgent prayer sessions were mainly in the evening and in the middle of more exciting endeavors. Again, this was not an optional family fun time. I hear Dad saying, "The family that prays together stays together." We were securing immediate help for a suffering person. Prayer became a refuge and safe depository for our concerns. And 'only if you want to' was not a parenting style in our house. Fortunately, Mom and Dad taught us to do the right thing, not the convenient thing. Today there is so much discussion about what the child wants to do. What child will feel compelled to choose the hard work necessary to become a productive member of society unless it's required?

I coach swimming, and I know it's an activity that my parents respected. Unlike soccer or tennis, swimming is a safety issue. There is no threat to your life if you suddenly find yourself in the middle of a tennis court. However, falling into a pool is a different story altogether. Swimming is challenging and requires skill and discipline to learn. Our children must swim from age one, and our youngest from six months. The swim team starts at age five and continues until they are eighteen. At age six, Madison complained about going to swim team practice. Our oldest, Jacob, said, "You might as well get used to it. You only have twelve more years to go." I smiled, but Madison was not laughing. If I am honest about it, I cannot even do the swim practices that she is now doing at age nine. It's an entirely challenging sport.

I was intrigued when a fellow swim coach asked me to join a pilot program to teach swimming in the inner city. I gave the condition that I would do it only if my son, Nicholas, who was sixteen that summer, could coach alongside me. We were a package deal, so all or nothing. The program director wanted both of us. We found out that these were kids with little to no swimming experience. In fact, there was a culture of fear of water that they would be working against. We would have to travel at least 30 minutes each way and get paid next to nothing. But Lee Lee's biblical training echoed in my ears, "To whom much is given, much will be required" (**Luke 12:48**). We traded in a summer at the country club for a summer at the Boys and Girls Club of Kansas City on 43rd and Cleveland in Kansas City. These kids are my heroes. They bravely faced their fears each time they stepped into the pool.

I asked one swimmer how she came to be in our group.

She said, "My mom just signed me up. She didn't ask me or anything."

"That's a good mom who just signs you up to do hard things," I said, beaming.

Some people might disagree with this idea. They claim we must only have our kids do things with their 'buy-in.' But what part of weed picking would I have 'bought into' at age eight? I had a brown bag from the grocery store and was instructed to fill that sucker with crabgrass, period. I am so thankful for every shovel of snow and blade of crabgrass. It gave me time to consider the suck of it. It let me know that I wanted a much more significant role than picking weeds. I still shovel snow and enjoy sweating on a cold, snowy day. I would also give anything to be that little girl with my mom picking cherries on a warm summer day. I took great pride in the cherries I pitted and the resulting delicious pie. As important as finding things you love includes the process of ruling some things out. I thank my parents for this lesson.

The rosaries and visits to the grandparents help me now. There are times my kids don't want to visit LeeLee in her nursing home. Not because they don't love her. It's quite the contrary. They adore her, but the place smells 'funny', and it can be depressing to be there. I tell them, "That's okay. You don't have to want to do something to do it. We need to think about LeeLee, who has none of the freedoms we have now. She can't go anywhere and relies on visitors. Can we not sacrifice thirty or sixty minutes of our day to bring her some good cheer?" We don't go because we 'feel like it.' We go because it's the right thing to do. Dad taught me how to treat people who might feel alone and forgotten. He respected them and assisted them in any way he could. We were constantly stopping by nursing homes after work. We would pop in to see a priest that was no longer able to say mass. We would check on his brother, Buddy. He fought in the Korean War and never recovered from the trauma. He returned to the United States as a broken and mentally disabled man. We frequently brought Buddy a carton of cigarettes.

I asked, "Why do we bring Buddy cigarettes? Aren't they bad for him?"

"We bring them because that is what he asks for. He has so few pleasures. This is what he asks me for, so I get them for him."

It was that simple. I can still see Buddy's yellowed fingernails and stained teeth. He enjoyed cigarettes, and my dad, his legal guardian, would ensure he got them.

It wasn't all work and no play. There was seemingly endless fun available after work and chores. We belonged to a beautiful country club where I swam and played tennis in the summer, and ice skated in the winter. We traveled extensively to New York, Niagara Falls, Canada, San Francisco, Oklahoma, Dallas, and our lake house. We enjoyed our lives. The vacations were fun and a nice contrast to doing the things we didn't feel like doing. I learned that we sacrifice our time for those we love. We go out of our way for the marginalized and forgotten, even within our family. Dad taught us to do our job and do it right. He loved to say, "Let's get er' done." If we had a project to accomplish, we started early and stayed late to clean up.

Christmas was a time of radical giving. Everyone deserves love and kindness. Dad hosted a massive Christmas Party for all his employees and their families. Not just the office staff, but all the guys who worked out in the field on construction sites. At the end of the night, each family got to select a huge frozen turkey to take home for their Christmas Dinner. It was like *A Christmas Carol* on steroids. My parents didn't have to tell us that they were students of Saint Francis, who said, "Preach the gospel at all times, and when necessary, use words".

They took 'faith without works is dead' to an entirely new level. The list of kids they sent to Catholic high school and college seemed endless. Family members and friends would call my parents for everything from vacation houses to burial plots. They would fill the needs quietly and without fanfare. I recall Mom getting off the phone with one of our relatives.

I asked, "What was that about?"

"It was Donnie asking if we had a spare burial plot for his mom"

"What did you say?"

"I told him yes, we'd give him one, but don't these people think ahead about anything?"

I laughed thinking, I guess it's not really on the to do list: apples, milk, burial plot.

As a child, I would go to Dad's office with him on the weekends. I loved to explore. He had a sign on his desk that read, "The Buck Stops Here." I was about seven years old and asked him,

"What does that mean?"

"It means that when there are problems, they may travel through the whole office. But I am responsible for the final say once they hit my desk. I've got to make decisions and solve problems."

Right there, Dad earned a new nickname: Bucky, as he exemplified the place the Buck stopped. The name stuck with him for many years. Bucky became a term of endearment used only by me and Mom.

One summer, I worked at our family-owned construction company. My job was to follow the stocks Dad owned and graph their progress. This information is now instantly available on multiple websites. What was available to me? A newspaper, *The New York Times*. I learned the ticker symbols and reported weekly back to Dad. I was about fifteen. I was also assigned to find obscure facts, names, addresses and phone numbers. Remember there was no internet, so I relied on paper sources. There were no computers for this, and apps and cell phones were far in the future.

Sometimes after five or ten minutes I gave up and brought dad my, "I can't find it" expecting to be moved on to a more doable task like counting paperclips.

He drove home the lesson again, "When you work for someone, don't just bring them the problem. No one wants to hear about more problems. So, if you bring one, bring three ideas of how you can solve it. Then, you can present the problems and your solutions, making you indispensable."

Yesterday, my daughter, Madison, pointed to a place in our car and said, "Someone needs to clean that out." Instantly I thought of Dad and, "When you think someone should take care of that, the someone is you."

I responded, "If you are going to show me the problem of the crumbs in your seat in the car, then you had better be ready to solve it. If something is dirty and you say it needs cleaning, it's your job to take care of it. Don't just bring me problems; find solutions. You can go ahead and clean those crumbs."

The complaints about the dirt in the car quickly ceased.

Now the buck stops here. Thank you, Dad. I love you.

"Few things can help an individual more than to place responsibility on him, and to let him know that you trust him." Booker T. Washington

"Whatever you do, work at it with all your heart, as working for the Lord, not for human masters." (Colossians 3:23)

"Each one should test their own actions. Then they can take pride in themselves alone, without comparing themselves to someone else." (Galatians 6:4)

PROMISES KEPT

YESTERDAY I WEPT BRUTAL TEARS. Not the tears of physical pain, hurt feelings, or the sadness of bad news. No, these tears refused to dam. I tried to rein them in with logical arguments to no avail. These were tears beyond the comfort of, "It will get better soon." They were the tears of, "You missed your chance." They were the tears of *regret*. There, I have said it, the R word. Let's get it out on the table: regret, regret, regret. People say they have no regrets. They say the very Zen thing that I also like to say, "Everything needed to happen exactly as it happened for me to be right here right now." While that is true, I still wish I had made better choices at various points in my life.

Babies are one of the few human conditions with the luxury of living regret-free. They beautifully exist in a state of perfection from our Father. They are living without sin. They are neither selfish, nor rude, nor proud. Babies exist in and for delight. But for the rest of us, there is regret. What's my proof? Look no further than confessions poured out in a Catholic church on a Saturday afternoon worldwide or those sweetly disguised as fifth steps in recovery programs. There, you will find expressions of unbridled remorse.

In both cases, you will find regret and the souls that carry it. Growing and improving necessitates the admission that what I did was not for the best and highest good for all. I can call it by other names: remorse, compunction, or guilt. However, the thesaurus blurts out that these are a few of the "Eighty-four ways to say REGRET."

Sometimes, lack of sleep or an effort to control life rears its head, and regret immediately slaps me in the face. Other times, it sneaks up like a tiger stalking until allowed to pounce, and when it does, it rips me to shreds like a slab of raw meat. Yesterday was that kind of regret. It showed up while I was simply going about the business of my Sunday.

I recently read an author describing her writing process. She wrote one chapter while sitting in a lounge chair in Bali. Another was written from her hotel room in New York City while eating her room service meal in bed. In contrast, I write standing at my kitchen island, where I serve grit and hard work. My Determination Café is open 24/7. I'm especially busy from 6:30 – 9:00 am and again from 3:00-11:00 pm. On weekends, my little café is slammed from morning to midnight, often feeling like Grand Central Station. A constant parade passes through my catch-all cafeteria: kids with backpacks, shoes, wet towels, water bottles, clean clothes, dirty socks, goldfish, homework, permission slips, scraped knees, injured egos, stories to share, and hunger to address. There are also adults with bags of trouble to unpack, in desperate need of solutions. Since this was a bustling weekend day, I was nomadically searching for a quiet place to find respite and to write.

My body does not agree with sitting to do my work; I need a desk to set my computer on and stand to type. I wish I had one. Then, like noticing an old photo hanging on the wall for eternity, I saw the desired furnishing. It was in my bedroom, standing quietly in its place like a soldier outside the British Parliament. I had not thought of it before because it was a desk all dressed up in a beautiful costume of inlaid swirls of wood in the shapes of flowers and cherubs. No, this was not a utilitarian desk, but a work of art better placed in a gallery. My parents purchased it on their dream vacation to Europe. The only person I saw who used this intricate escritoire was Mom. I can still see her sitting there in an elegant Chanel suit, with thick ivory embossed stationery, holding her fountain pen, and writing a letter to a friend. She looked perfect. Sitting down in that ornate chair covered in damask blue fabric in my sweats seemed inappropriate.

I opened the pull-down part of this elegant treasure to place my computer on the surface. The desk itself rejected the idea as the imperfection of the handmade surface refused to let the computer sit flush. So, instead of writing, I was now down a rabbit hole, looking through the photos and papers neatly placed in the demure drawers of the desk. A few essential treasures were stacked neatly in the two larger drawers on each side. There were leaves I gathered while walking the beach in Florida, and a few other papers neatly tucked into a Ziplock bag. I told myself *I don't have time to look through everything I found right now. I will need to come back to this treasure cache later*. But before I surfaced again to the tasks of my day, I noticed a few white sheets of paper neatly folded together and quartered.

I unfolded the contents to find a copy of Dad's journal. It read: Vincent S. D. The first thing that struck me was the handwriting. His penmanship was perfectly executed in all caps, and it reeked of authority and confidence. Each location was documented with precision, giving me a step-by-step guided tour of Dad's service in World War II.

The dossier took me step-by-step from Fort Leavenworth to Fort Bragg to crossing the ocean on the USS Pasteur. Then, there was the tour of duty in Europe. I don't know why I previously thought of soldiers in war going to a single location and setting up shop to defend the Allies. This reminded me of the show *M*A*S*H*, where the enlisted did stay in one place because it was a military hospital. Now, it dawned on me that the hellish reality of war included the constant uncertainty of the unfamiliar and unfriendly.

The journal outlined the seemingly endless array of locations methodically scribed. The words marched down the pages: June 13, June 14, June 17, June 18, each with its separate location, providing a predictable cadence amidst unpredictability. The one constant was the absence of stability, familiarity, and routine. There was the rare event of a skip in the chronology of the dates, cuing me to an extended stay in one place.

Several things jumped out at me:

- BATTLE OF THE BULGE, WE RETREATED
- APRIL 13, 1945, HEARD OF PRESIDENT ROOSEVELT'S DEATH (HELPED CAPTURE 6 JERRIES).

There was one whimsical entry. This entry was after September 2, 1945, when Japan formally surrendered, marking the end of World War II, also known as VJ Day. It read:

SEPTEMBER 26, 1945. RECEIVED A PASS TO PARIS (A NICE PLACE THAT PARIS). OCTOBER 5, 1945. RETURNED FROM PARIS.

I smiled. Calling Paris "a nice place" was like calling the ocean 'wet.' The journal then returned to moving to a tent city outside

Frankfurt, Germany. There was no other lighthearted entry. Pages fifteen and sixteen of the journal conclude:

> December 26, 1945, LEFT FOR LE HAVRE AND BOARDED SS MT. VERNON AND SAILED AT 16:00 HOURS ON THE 27TH. ARRIVED IN NEW YORK AT PIER 51 ON JANUARY 3, '46, at 16:30 HOURS...LEFT ON THE 6TH FOR JEFFERSON BRKS. ARRIVED ON THE SEVENTH AND DISCHARGED ON 9TH DAY OF JANUARY 1946.

Starting May 11, 1945, I saw this list of names: RICHENBACH, GREIRWEIDA, RAVENSORGA, STREGGA, EISENACH, STOCKHAUSEN, EISENACH, MARKOUL, HAUSEN, NUR-NURG, TAUS, LANOTA (PIZEN), HAVOLICE. I selected a name that sounded familiar to me, and I chose Stockhausen. Dad was there from May 13, 1945, until June 7, 1945. I landed on the starting point for my research, and here is what I learned.

Sachsenhausen- For these purposes, it is believed that Sachsenhausen is the full name for the Hausen Concentration Camp mentioned in my dad's journal. Within each camp, there were often forty sub-camps. This camp was " in operation between 1933 and 1945, Nazi Germany and its allies established more than 44,000 camps and other incarceration sites (including ghettos). The perpetrators used these locations for a range of purposes, including forced labor, detention of people deemed to be "enemies of the state," and mass murder. Millions of people suffered and died or were killed. Among these sites was the Sachsenhausen camp and its subcamps.

The SS established the Sachsenhausen concentration camp as the principal concentration camp for the Berlin area. Located near Oranienburg, north of Berlin, the Sachsenhausen camp opened on

July 12, 1936, when the SS transferred 50 prisoners from the Ester-wegen concentration camp to begin construction of the camp. [1]

In the spring of 1944, SS authorities began to bring thousands of Hungarian and Polish Jews from ghettos and other concentration camps to Sachsenhausen as the need for forced laborers in Sachsenhausen and its subcamps increased. Many of these new Jewish prisoners were women. By the beginning of 1945, the number of Jewish prisoners had risen to 11,100."

Of course, I knew Dad was a WWII Veteran. I knew he drove a tank and was involved in go-ahead operations scouring for Nazi presence. He told me, "I feared for my life every single day." I knew Dad's duties included releasing people from concentration camps. I knew he was a highly decorated war veteran. I knew he served this country without faltering courage and that he was rewarded for his service. But seeing this hit me differently. Now, there were names and lists of places and, more importantly, people. Human lives that he was willing to die for. People he had never met and never would meet. His actions were worth everything. He freed real people, innocent men, women, and children, from a literal hell.

Dad rarely spoke of the war. He mentioned it to me a grand total of two times in my life.

I remember, in my childlike innocence, that I asked him, "Was it so great letting those people out of those horrible concentration camps?"

"It's not like they came running out. They walked out slowly and just stood there. They didn't have anywhere to go, no families, no homes. They lost everything," he gravely explained.

After reading this journal, I felt like such a fool. I lived with this amazing man, a hero of war. What did I do about it? Nothing. I just acted like he was a regular dad. Maybe I was a wonderful child, but

---

1   (https://encyclopedia.ushmm.org/content/en/article/sachsenhausen)

now that felt like not enough. I felt he deserved more. Why didn't I ask him more about all this? Why didn't I honor him for it? No, I just trotted off to school, tennis team practice, friends' houses, or whatever activity my teenage brain told me was extremely important. I regretted the time I lost and could not get back.

I was curled up by my bed, crying, when Nick came in from Mass. He tenderly asked what was wrong, and I told him what I had learned about my incredible dad.

"He was amazing. I could have honored him for this, but I was just some jerk kid."

"No, Mom, you were a great kid. You did honor him. Besides, all kids are jerks. No, you were good."

"But he was right there every day, and I missed this."

"Mom, you were good."

The tears would not stop. "How did I miss this? Why is it so easy to overlook what is right under my own roof?"

I prayed: *God, what do you want me to learn? What do you want me to do with all of this?*

I turned to Nick, "I may have missed it then, but not now. We need to share this and help other people. I can still honor my dad. I missed this opportunity when he was alive, but not again. I can do better right now, and I will. Will you help me?"

At that moment, Nick gave me an "I love you, Mom." Nick uses this phrase like the word *chaio*. For him, "I love you, Mom," can mean yes, no, goodnight, good morning, and several more. This time Nick meant, "I've got your back."

I was grateful and thought of the time Nick came home from school and asked, "Do you think you can love someone you have never met?"

"Sure," I affirmed.

"Because I love Papa D even though I never met him."

It's been several years since I last visited Dad's grave. Two weeks ago, we were in a part of town near the cemetery.

"Nick, would it be okay with you if we stop by Papa D's grave?" I queried.

"Sure," Nick responded.

While at the grave, I looked around and noticed many of my dad's good friends were buried nearby. I remembered the hilarious Bob Alyward and his wife, Wanda, now buried feet away. I thought, *Dad's in good company. Those two were a blast.* I thanked God for my dad's life and all the lives he saved. A promise of AA recovery came to mind: "you will no longer regret the past nor wish to shut the door on it." The peace I felt let me know that this promise came true for me.

There was a small voice in my head that left me with a shred of curiosity. I thought *it would be nice to visit my sister Maggie's grave, too. I thought they were buried together, but I don't see her headstone. Maybe I was mistaken.* T

The next day, I met up with one of my brothers. I asked him, "What about Maggie? Where is she buried? Is she there?"

"She's right there. She's with Dad. When Dad died, they exhumed her little coffin and put it in with his. She's right there."

I thought *that was so fitting. Even in death, Dad keeps his baby under close watch, always looking out for others.*

"Life's most persistent and urgent question is: What are you doing for others?" Dr. Martin Luther King, Jr.

"The best way to find yourself is to lose yourself in the service of others." Mahatma Gandhi

"For even the Son of Man did not come to be served, but to serve, and to give his life as a ransom for many." *(Mark 10:45, NIV)*

LeeLee VII

Epic Mom

I HAVE NOT SAID VERY MUCH about my mom so far in this book. I asked myself why, and the answer was easy. I consider her life to be an epic tale. I would need to sit down and prepare to write *The Iliad* or *The Odyssey*. It would be a Herculean task to choose the outstanding moments of her ninety-eight years of living. Mom's life is so compelling and unbelievable that I would like to try to tell at least some of her story as she shared it with me.

Marilee DiCarlo Mitchell was born February 18, 1927, on a farm in Axtell, Kansas. At that time, they lived with her grandparents, Joe and Maggie Mitchell. She was the oldest child of Frances and Leo Mitchell, who would have ten more children. When Mom was a girl, her papa rented farms to work. They moved around Kansas, from Summerfield to Corning to Centralia. Mom said, "During this time in my life, things were really touch and go."

My mom is not the type to tell stories of weird or scary things that happened, so maybe that is why this story stands out. She told me, "We rented one farm and a farmhouse. We brought all our things into the house. At one point, we were standing in the dining room, and this huge, wooden dish cabinet lifted right off the ground."

"What do you mean, off the ground? How far?" I asked her.

"Well, not that far, probably about five or six inches. But it was far enough for us to know we were going to get out of there. We turned around and never went back."

When Marilee was 12, her father purchased a farm for $35,000, which translates into approximately $794,837.41 today. Leo thought it would never be paid off, but it sold in 2015 for 1.5 million dollars.

As a child, Marilee would come home from school, bring vegetables from the garden, start dinner, and go to the basement to begin laundry, which would be done by hand and put through a wringer. The wringer was a contraption with two rollers to squeeze out water. When the wringer was on, the machine made such a loud noise that it filled the entire cellar. Once flipped on, clothes needed to be fed into the thin space between the two spinning rollers. Mom explained, "I went down to do the day's laundry. I got the washing tubs going. Next, I turned the wringer on to get the water out of the clothes before hanging them on the line to dry. My tiny fingers squeezed through with a shirt as I fed the clothes into the wringer. My arm was trapped up to my elbow. I was young, so I could not reach over to turn the wringer off. I stood there helpless as the wringer continued to squeeze down relentlessly. I yelled and screamed for help; all the while, the wringer was burning the skin off my arm. Finally, my mama came down to help me, but it had been a while. I was badly hurt."

Anyone who knew Mom back when she wore short sleeves would know about the fierce scar on the inside of her right elbow. As a little girl, I liked to feel the glassy smooth area and then the surrounding circle of dark pink tissue with many small lines. It looked like a fossil from a sea creature, maybe the underside of a starfish arm. The scar was always there as a physical reminder of how hard those times were. It would fade in color but never resolve, just like the other traumas she endured.

She once asked me, "Is there anything I did to hurt you or anything I need to apologize to you for?"

"No, Mom, no," I warmly replied.

"When I was young, I was always really scared. My mom would beat me every day," Mom elaborated

"For what?" I asked, shocked.

"For anything. I never knew what for. Just something would set her off, and she would start hitting."

"Where? What do you mean?"

"She would slap my face from when I was very young."

"How often did that happen?"

"Nearly every day, so I never felt safe."

"Do you feel safe now?"

"Yes, I am safe now, and not scared."

"Good, because you deserve to be safe. I'm so sorry that happened."

"Oh, it's okay. My dad was always really sweet to me, and my mom felt bad about it later."

Mom's chores were never done, even once the laundry was hung on the line. Next, she had to complete and serve dinner, wash the dishes, and begin baths for her siblings. Once they were all settled in for the night, complete with clothes ironed and ready for school, Marilee was done.

She told me, "One time, I took a test in school, and the headmaster came to talk with me. He said, 'Marilee, we can tell from your test scores that you are highly intelligent. Why don't your grades reflect this?' I told him that I wanted to study, but by eleven at night, when I was done with all my chores, I would just fall into bed, exhausted. I could not even hold my eyes open to study, but I sure wanted to."

Marilee and her family lived in a house that was no mansion. There were three bedrooms: one for her parents, one for the five boys, and one for the six girls. There were no screens, not even television. For entertainment, they sometimes gathered around the radio, but mostly, they went outside to play. Marilee rarely had time to play. Her favorite outing was to the Axtell County Fair, where she enjoyed riding the carousel horses. One year, the whole family piled in the car to go.

But her mom announced to Marilee, "You won't be going."

"Why didn't they take you?" I inquired.

"Oh, I don't know. I did something, and that was my punishment. My dad was saying, 'Let's just take her.' But Mom was firm. I watched, crying, as they drove away.

"It was the Depression then, but we never went hungry because we had cattle and grew most of our food. We had plenty of meat and milk. We canned vegetables and fruits in the summer, so we had some for the winter. One year at Christmastime, I saw a Shirley Temple doll in a store window. It was so cute, with the curls and the sweet, pink dress. I wanted that doll so badly. It cost three dollars. I decided to be the best little girl I could be, hoping Santa would bring me that doll. I was so good. I mean, I really watched it. Christmas came, and no doll was under the tree. I was crestfallen. When I returned to school in January, I discovered another girl got that doll for Christmas. She was a mean girl, unkind. I could not understand that. Those were some hard times."

Her papa would always tell Marilee, "Don't worry, things are going to get better."

She would ask him, "How do you know that?"

He replied with a smile, "I just know; they can't get any worse."

"Times were more civilized then," Mom said, "My dad went to the store. It was the Depression, and we did not have any money. He asked the grocer if he could take some things, just to get our family through. Papa told him, 'I'll write everything down. You can be sure I will pay you back every penny.' The grocer replied, 'Leo, you do not need to write anything down. I know you are good for it. Take whatever you need.'

"Since it was close to Christmas, the grocer gave us a small bag of gumdrops, and we each got one drop. Another time, when one of the girls was born, the grocer sent a bag of jellybeans, and we each got one. We had not had candy for a couple of years, and he gave us two bags of candy. To this day, jellybeans are my favorite."

The farm was not an easy place for Marilee. She was a beautiful girl, which did not go unnoticed. She had a long walk to and from school every day. One time, she got caught in a barbed wire fence. There was no one to help her, so she freed herself after some time. She was hot, exhausted, and injured as she continued to walk the dirt roads. A man slowed down and offered her a ride. Marilee was hesitant.

"You are that Mitchell girl, aren't you?"

"Um-hum," Mom answered.

"Well, looks like you are bad off. I know your dad, Leo. Hop in, and I'll give you a ride."

Trusting that this man knew her papa, Marilee got into the car. It soon became evident this was not a good Samaritan but a man with horrible intentions. He abused Mom. She had no one to tell, but this haunted her for many years as more trauma piled on.

She would also tell me about her dad's dog, Spike. They loved Spike, especially her papa. "That dog was always right there at my dad's side. He was his constant companion in the fields, and they worked the farm together. Dad loved him. Spike got sick and needed a vet. My mom told him that there was no way we were taking that dog to a vet. She said, 'We do not have money to spend on a dog. Take him out in the field and shoot him.' Of course, my dad resisted wholeheartedly, and Spike got weaker and sicker. Dad grew hopeless. He pleaded to take that dog in. Mama was firm, and finally, he relented to her orders. He took Spike out back and did as he was told. That changed Papa; he was never the same."

Maybe Mom was not, either.

When people asked my own dad, Vince, why we didn't have a dog, he would reply, "We raise people, not dogs." Mom never argued with this.

Marilee has always been very forward-thinking. As a young woman, she had many goals and desires. She loved education; for her, it was the way off the farm. She wanted to be a nurse, but explained, "At that time, you could not be a nurse and have a family. I knew I wanted a family, so that was not in the cards for me. I moved to Kansas City and went to business school." Marilee attended the Sarah Shawn Business School in Kansas City in 1944. She began working at Patti Construction Company in 1945.

One fateful day, Vince DiCarlo walked into Patti Construction. She reminisced, "I was at the front office. Vince came in, and another good-looking guy named Jim was already waiting in the front. I asked Vince, 'Who do you wish to see?' and your dad said, 'I wish to see you.'" A beautiful smile lit up Mom's face when she recalled this.

The next thing she knew, the two men were arguing. "Vince said, 'I'm taking her out Saturday night.' Then Jim said, 'No, you're not. I'm taking her out.' To which Vince said, 'I am.' They were fussing about this in another room, and I could hear them. Well, neither of them had asked me out yet. Don't you think I could decide who I was going out with on Saturday night?"

After securing the two offers, Mom politely declined Jim's offer, saying, "Thank you, but I have plans. Maybe another time."

Mom continued, "Vince took me to the Continental Hotel for dinner that Saturday night, and I thought that it was pretty good. I never did go out with anyone else after that."

"When it came time to get engaged, I wanted an emerald-cut diamond. It was $2000 in 1947." $2,000 in 1947 = $28,534.51 in 2024.

Dad said, "Hang around a while, and I will get it for you."

Some years later, he delivered on that promise with a flawless six-carat, emerald-cut diamond. Marilee also told Vince, "I want to live in a big colonial brick house with pillars in front." He said that would happen, too, and it did. He told me he wanted me to have everything I wanted in that house. It's still a great home. I wish I could be there."

My mom took very good care of herself and was still a stunning woman in her sixties when my dad died. Several eligible men asked her to go out.

"Why didn't you go?" I asked.

"Oh, I guess I really didn't want to. No one could live up to Vince. Plus, I don't want to train another man. It took so long the first time," she laughed.

Dad would tell her, "I love you more than yesterday and less than tomorrow." This was even engraved in her wedding ring. 'More than yesterday, less than tomorrow' was all that fit, but she got the idea.

"The flower that blooms in adversity is the most rare and beautiful of all." Robert D. San Souci

"Without the fire, the phoenix never rises from the ashes." Forrest Curran

"I know what it is to be in need, and I know what it is to have plenty. I have learned the secret of being content in any and every situation, whether well fed or hungry, whether living in plenty or in want. I can do all this through him who gives me strength." (Philippians 4:12-13)

IRISH BLESSINGS

T HIRTY YEARS HAVE PASSED since Dad died. In those years, my mom has been the matriarch of six children and seventeen grandchildren. The words 'superhero' and 'trooper' drastically understate her strength. She envisioned and built two custom homes. She traveled to Asia, Ireland, and Paris. She has lost her hearing, most of her sight, and her ability to walk. She lost her homes, all of them. She has sacrificed happiness and endured suffering for those she loves. Yet, she still has a ready laugh and graceful smile to share.

When Mom first became a grandparent, it was clear that she was far too young and beautiful to be called 'grandma.' We all agreed to call her Mama Lee, from her name Marilee, and my dad would be Papa D. Twenty years ago, with my son, Jacob, we began calling her LeeLee, which has stuck ever since.

Everyone who works with LeeLee loves her because she is kind, grateful, and cheerful. Never in her life has she looked at some- one as less than her. The people who helped in our home were her equals. One woman worked as a housekeeper for us for seventy years. Day in and day out, Mom would prepare or buy her lunch. LeeLee had some very wealthy friends. She once said, "Bessie does not allow her 'help' to eat in the kitchen. She will tell her, 'You can take your things and eat in the ironing closet.'" I was aghast. These people had huge, gorgeous houses, and the 'help' could not be at the kitchen table? This behavior would never occur to LeeLee as appropriate. She had a gift for making everyone feel right at home. In fact, one of her favorite sayings was, "Mi casa es su casa," and she meant it.

When I tell people at her senior living community, «Marilee DiCarlo is my mom," their countenance changes: they soften, smile warmly, and say, "Oh, I know your mom." I will tell my friends, "I don't know how she does it. She does not complain and says she is feeling pretty good." She has a sound mind at age ninety-eight, which is no small feat.

Of all the losses of independence I have witnessed Mom tolerate, one of the worst has been her loss of hearing. Talk about feeling alone; you have no clue what others are saying. That has got to be so disturbingly isolating. It's horrible to feel you are missing out; now try missing out on every word all the time. She's a heroine for how long she has held it together. For decades, she's been letting go of things without a gripe and always with a tenacity to overcome all obstacles. There has been a level of acceptance, never resignation. Mom would consistently reinvent, improve, and pursue what she could do next until now.

Mom has been on a decline for the last few weeks. She refuses to get up and even attempt walking. The occupational therapist stops in, but Marilee insists she cannot leave her chair. She tells them, "Not today, I am really tired." When I arrived to visit her, I found her asleep in her chair with the television on. I am upset that they have given up on her walking. She fell a couple of times, and they just confined her to a wheelchair. It's less risky for them. Instead of working to help her get stronger, they let her muscles atrophy to the point where she could not walk even if she wanted to. When this began, I asked her why she was no longer walking with her walker. "Oh, I would like to, but they won't let me. They say I must be in the chair," she would reply.

Even a saint would be worn down by what Mom has gone through. She has been an absolute trooper while being moved from independent living to skilled rehab, to skilled nursing, to assisted living, and now back to skilled nursing. They didn't have a better room ready for her, so they moved her to a temporary room for six weeks while they were waiting for someone to die. That is seven moves in one year. Then, Mom will get her room in long-term care. When she was temporarily placed in that wing of the building, Mom said, "I don't like it over here. All these people are dying." I know what she means. These folks are predominantly in wheelchairs. They wheel them out for meals, and many cannot feed themselves. The aids feed them. Then they wheel them across the hall to the television room for the next hour, where most are fast asleep. It smells funny. I can't say it feels like an upbeat place.

The last time I visited Marilee, she said she was feeling down. Who can blame her? She is just sitting there alone all day. She is one of three people who keep their door wide open. It's like the space is beckoning, "Come on in." Mostly, the call is unheard, and LeeLee remains in her solitary space.

On Tuesday, we had a care meeting with my mom's nursing home team. I was not able to attend in person but called in to participate. They told us that they were struggling to move her around. Essentially, they said, "Marilee needs to go to long-term care because we don't work that hard on the assisted living side." Further, they do not expect her to ever return to assisted living. This means, "We are sending her over to the other side, permanently, to die."

I hated this. My mom has always had such an exuberant will to live. She has kept her goals and dreams alive and consistently looks to the horizon for what is next. The team also told us they would need a 'sling' to move her, something that only the long-term care section uses.

I brought up that Mom has been feeling down. She mentioned this twice to me in the last three weeks. In the care plan meeting, I requested a doctor's order to increase her antidepressant dose. The whole discussion was deflating. I lost my unfailing optimism that Mom would regain her strength to the point of walking and not need the help offered in long-term care. I felt like they were saying, "She really is dying now." I went to bed, just sad about this, and woke up in a funk, not rested from my few hours of sleep. I knew I had been feeling down for a while now, and I was starting to get concerned about my mental state. Too many consecutive days of feeling blue weighed heavily on me. The icing on the cake was this dreadful news about my mom. That morning, I had to rush to my yearly physical. I filled out a mental health assessment. and wondered if I should say how bad it really was. I didn't want to because it would then be too real. I don't want to be hospitalized by an overreaction. I did indicate I was struggling, but not to the extent I felt.

My doctor is an absolute jewel, a woman about my age. I never feel that she is rushing to check off boxes with me. She has all the time in the world to discuss my concerns. For my visit, I am usually there for an hour. She asked me how I felt, and I told her I was not great but in no immediate danger. I wanted to feel better, but felt forced to drag my suitcase of sadness everywhere.

I got into my car and called my brother, John, to discuss Mom's situation. He said, "We have seen her accept changes, but this time, it's more of a resignation."

"It does not sound like they expect her to improve over there."

He threw me a necessary bone by reminding me, "She has consistently done better with that level of care. Many more people are coming to her room, and the attention seems to help her. But she seems resigned, so we will see what happens."

John's assessment gave me a tiny glimmer of hope that she might improve. Then John generously added, "Your idea of increasing her medication was smart. She needs that. She talked to me for a while about how bad she felt. That was a good idea."

"Thanks. I am concerned about Mom. She has been a champion, going through all this with minimal complaint. I would have been complaining much more, and about twenty years earlier."

John added, "There is no doubt she has been a trooper. I would also have been complaining way before now."

"Can we ask her to stay alive for us? Hasn't she paid her dues?"

"No doubt she's plowed through so much adversity. But I think she may do better with this move," he added.

"I feel like we are moving her around like she is an eighteen-year-old college student. We are just moving her from one place to another. I know it's hard for her."

John agreed. It was good to talk with him. I said, "I love you," as we hung up. I love John, no matter what happens. There have been some significant misunderstandings in the last thirty years since Dad's death. He's made some horrendous errors in judgment, and no doubt he believes I have, too. Some of them are so severe that people have asked me, "Why do you even talk to him?" That is one choice, but at the end of the day, we are family. We need each other. We need each other as we navigate this time with Mom. For me, it would be ten times harder without John's support.

I realized in this moment that I love John unconditionally. I see his positive qualities and his downfalls, and I love him. Why?

Because I remember when I was a lonely kid. I was the seventh child by a mile, and my parents were tired and done in many ways. John and his lovely fiancée came to my rescue. If I had school projects, they helped. If I needed new clothes, they took me shopping. I would spend the night at their house on some weekends. His wife was very kind to me, and I adored her. She was an art teacher in the urban core, and her talent was only matched by her compassion. They were my second parents.

When they married and had babies, I still spent the night babysitting those little cuties. I loved every minute of it. This was how it was for years. I even took care of their kids when they went out of town. I would prepare the kids and bring them to camp or whatever activities they had. I made all their meals, packed their lunches, and ran their baths. I tucked them in at night. I love those two kids.

Things changed; I got older and left for college. There was a lot of water under the bridge. Despite all the changes, I always knew I could count on John, and we all did. When it came time for me to walk down the aisle at my wedding, I asked John to give me away. He made the kindest toast, saying to everyone, "Elise is the best of us." I also talked about family and Dad. I could see the tears well up in John's eyes. We were united in our tragedy and suffering. These are just some of the reasons I love John. He has been there for our mom and for all of us. He's a good man. I am grateful he is my brother. Life is too precious to carry anger around. I wanted him to know I love him.

When I hung up the phone, nothing had changed in the physical realm. However, I started to feel better. I still had my sad suitcase; it was just a little lighter. Later that day, I took my son, Will, and daughter, Madison, to the Royals game. We had seats in the Diamond Club, which, as the name suggests, are extraordinary. We had four seats behind home plate. But when Jeff asked, "Are you excited about the game?" I responded, "No, I am going for the kids. I am doing this to be a good mom."

I was thinking about the piles of work I had to do and how I could not touch them for at least four and a half hours. My next thought was, I am not rich if I cannot take time to go to a Royals game with my kids. I have decided to say, "I am rich," because I found out what being rich means to me; it is that I have time for the people I love. So, I will say, "I am not rich if I cannot do crosswords with Jacob. I would not be rich if I could not work on a puzzle with Nick. I am not rich if I cannot take my daughter to cheer. I am not rich if I can't go to lunch with Will." Then, because I do these things, the opposite must be true. I am wealthy and grateful for the freedom that prosperity brings me. I have worked hard for it. I need to share great experiences with the people I love. It's a good thing.

On this day, however, I found my lack of enthusiasm for the baseball game concerning. I love my kids and the Kansas City Royals. I was going through the motions, getting ready, and driving to the ballpark. Surprisingly, I felt both better and worse when we got there. Memories of being with my dad in this section behind home plate flooded in. I even got a little teary as I looked around at all the changes that have taken place with the club over the years.

Mostly, children get to innocently enjoy life. They don't have to look back with nostalgia at every change. They enjoyed last year and this year. As adults, we see the changes and must make peace with them. This is required to enjoy the present without constantly pining for the past.

I was horrified when I realized my daughter had not been to enough games to understand baseball. No child of mine will be without knowledge and love of the game of baseball. With enthusiasm, I began tutoring her on all the rules and nuances of the game. It was nearing the end of the game, and Bobby Whitt Jr. was up. I told Madison, "Whitt is a solid player and will do something special." Will said, "I would love to see him jack this." No sooner had he finished than we heard the crack of the bat. It had that perfect sound of a well-hit baseball. We watched it sail over center field, beyond the outfield wall, and over it for a home run.

Everyone jumped to their feet to cheer. Will's expression of joy was utterly priceless. The game was great fun. I felt sunnier. I remembered how important it is for mental health to go outside, be with people, do something you enjoy, and take a break from routine.

This brought me some joy. When we arrived home, I still did not feel my baseline level of happiness. The more I chased it, the farther away it was. Then I felt my inner voice saying, "It's God. There's still no other solution than God. Good try with all the other stuff. You need to go to God." I can't say I had a profound moment of closeness with God right then. It was as if I just needed to acknowledge that God was my source. When I did that, I felt the fear dissolve. I set down my sad 'suitcase.' God doesn't want me carrying that around, just like I wouldn't want one of my kids carrying that thing. Finally, I realized that everything was worse because I had gotten so little rest. That can make everything feel bleak. Once I realized that, the best option was to go to bed. So that is what I did. I read to my daughter until I could not hold my eyes open another minute. We both fell asleep in a blink.

The next thing I knew, I was awakened around eleven pm by a phone call from my son, Jacob. We were having a great conversation. We bantered back and forth about our conversation, then I realized, wait, I feel good. Like normal me, yay! This is what I had been longing for. Nothing was happening that was earth-shattering; it was just a lively scientific dialogue with my son. It didn't cost a bunch of money. I did not need to go anywhere or get dressed up. I was in my pajamas and in bed. I smiled. It made sense. God would not make it so I could only feel better at the Diamond Club. The

Diamond Club is a luxury that not everyone can afford. I can't get there anytime I want. No, He would make our happiness entirely more accessible. I could not feel suddenly made whole by the game. The game did not suddenly make me feel whole. I would have gotten the false impression that the answers were outside myself. Then, I would always be chasing. Instead, I was able to stop and rest and let the answers come to me. I just needed to receive God in my heart again.

Today was good. There were some highs and lows. As my friend Mike says, there are still situations that "I did not ask for, I do not like, and I cannot change." I am constantly aware of the waning days of my precious mother, LeeLee. Yet, I do not despair. I have God, and I love Him entirely. He has given me the absolute best parents. How blessed I am to have my mom all these years.

We have a routine when we part:

Me: "I love you."

Mom: "I love you."

Me: "You are the best thing that ever happened to me."

Mom: "You are the best thing that ever happened to me."

This time, I added, "You are a national treasure."

She laughed and received the compliment without brushing the content aside.

"Let us not say goodbye but farewell until we meet again." And "May the road rise up to meet you, may the wind be ever at your back. May the sun shine warm upon your face and the rain fall softly on your fields. And until we meet again, may God hold you in the hollow of his hand." Irish Blessing

"As the Irish say, 'May your glass be ever full. May the roof over your head be always strong. And may you be in heaven half an hour before the devil l knows you're dead.'" Irish Proverb

"The LORD is my shepherd; there is nothing I lack. Even though I walk through the valley of the shadow of death, I will fear no evil, for you are with me; your rod and your staff comfort me. Indeed, goodness and mercy will pursue me all the days of my life; I will dwell in the house of the LORD forever." (Psalm 23: 1,4,6, NIV)

SIDELINED?

"IN THE NAME of the Father, the Son, and the Holy Spirit," began my daily rosary meditation. The leader discussed the very human fear of being 'sidelined' because of ailing health or failing mind. He said, "No one wants to be sidelined, just watching everyone else still in the game, knowing they are not getting back in." He went on to discuss the suffering of losing control of our minds and bodies. This was a downer topic I had not expected.

I knew that I needed to go see my mom and had been thinking about it for several days. On this day, I had a packed schedule. However, I had a cancellation, which left my afternoon open. I knew that this would be a perfect time to go to the nursing home where Mom lives, but I just really did not want to go.

I do not like nursing homes.

There, I have said it. The smell is indescribable. As I entered the hallway with the locked door, I felt instantly trapped inside. I took the long walk on the brown sea of carpet to Mom's room, 1913. Today when we entered, she was asleep. I brought my daughter,

Madison, who, at 9 years old, brings lovely levity to the situation. We awakened Marilee and she said that she was feeling, "pretty good," which must mean something totally different at age 97. This did not look like 'pretty good' to me.

We were there for about ten minutes when the aide came in to take Mom to dinner. She was there to get Marilee situated in her wheelchair for the journey to the dining room. As the aide wheeled her chair over, I saw a clump of something stuck to the chair. It was food from God knows when. This only reinforced my disgust with this place and the fact that no one is watching or caring about the details for LeeLee. With the clump cleared, we tried three times to get Mom into her wheelchair. She couldn't make it, and she shook with weakness as she tried to stand. Each time she flopped back down into her chair, exhausted from the process. I told Madison, "I need to get outside for some air." Thank God for the beautiful sunshine that greeted us just outside the doors. I felt like a fish just freed from a hook and thrown back into the safety of the water where I could breathe again.

When we reentered the building, Mom was at her place at the dinner table, a place where elderly people stick to their routine. They sit in the same place at the long table each night. They eat in silence, no longer trying to fill the quiet space, but resigned to its presence. I was now perfectly uncomfortable as Madison, and I grabbed a couple of extra stools to join the group. No sooner had we sat down than the man across from us pointed out our violation of the unsaid rules. He told us, "There is another lady who sits there."

I brushed him off, saying, "Okay, thanks." When we did not move, he was perturbed and repeated, "There is another lady who sits there. You are in her place."

I responded, "Okay, when she gets here, we will move."

"Why don't you just move now?" he insisted.

"I promise we will move when she arrives," I assured him.

Time was passing by, and the mystery woman did not appear. The table was filling up and finally I was informed that the woman had arrived and was sitting at the other end of the table. She was an adorable elderly woman and seemed perfectly content with her radically changed location at the dinner table. However, we had promised we would move, so that is exactly what we did. Now all was well, and the man at the table seemed much more at ease. In fact, everyone was, except me.

I asked, "Mom, can we move to the end of the table, where there is space for all three of us?"

"No, we can't move once they have set us up at the table. It's just part of their rules."

I wanted to scream, "Oh my goodness, whose rules? You are paying an exorbitant amount a month, and you can't move to another seat at dinner?" Absurd. But I was feeling defeated by this point and just continued to stand. Madison was spinning on her little stool and happily awaiting her grilled cheese sandwich. She was enjoying the gift of youth with the innate ability to make everything fun. She finds the fun. She was spinning away and enjoying life. I was not. I was so uncomfortable. I came to visit with my mom, and all I have done is stand outside while she was getting cleaned and stand behind her at dinner. I just wanted to go home, but for me, leaving my mother there at the table was not an option.

I tell my kids, "She has no one. She cannot go anywhere. She is completely bound to that place. She is under their rules and their schedule. So, it's not an option for me to just say, 'I feel like leaving now.' That would be entirely selfish.

We had planned on staying twenty minutes. We were now into our second hour. I had not been able to visit with Mom. At dinner, since there were no available seats, we were not able to chat or converse. I stood; she ate. This felt like a lame waste of time. My thoughts were engulfed with negativity. I said to myself, 'Please pull yourself together. What can you bring to the situation? Where is your gratitude and your joy? How can you be part of the solution?"

I was just stuck in pathetic thoughts about how these people were sidelined, permanently. They were not waiting to get back into life. This was their life. I watched as their hands shook while they tried to eat a hamburger or pick up a cup of coffee. My mom was now holding her fork and eating with her left hand. I needed to extricate myself from my thoughts. Say something! I tried to start conversations and use humor. One woman, Nadine, had been waiting for her hamburger the entire time I was standing there.

I said, "Maybe they had to go out and get another cow." She smiled.

Then to Mom, "I like how you are left-handed now, when did that happen?"

"When I had to, probably a couple of years ago."

"You just switched from right to left?" I added, amazed.

"Yes, I'm used to it now," she explained.

This idle chit-chat was not comforting. I was focused on the mustard getting all over Mom's fingers as she ate her burger. I handed her a napkin, and still the mustard was stuck under her fingernails. She ate the next half without mustard. I needed to get out of there. What is wrong with me, I questioned? Why am I so ill at ease? I realized that I had come here hungry, tired, and needing a shower. I needed to take care of myself, but too bad I was already here. I came expecting personal time with Mom. That is not what happened.

After Mom got her lemonade, I asked her if it would be okay to take her key lime pie to her room. She agreed, and I unlocked the wheels so her chair could move. Madison cheerfully asked, "May I push her?" I knew Madison was in a completely different world in her headspace. She just ate a small salad and a grilled cheese sandwich while sitting on a spinning chair. All was well in her world.

I prayed, "Why is it so difficult for me? Lord, I'm sorry." I knew I was just absorbed in the impending sideline for all of us. It was in my head, and here I was seeing it firsthand. It did not look fun. When I am uncomfortable, I need to ask, "What is this bringing up in me? Why am I so disturbed by this situation?"

As much as I projected out into the future, LeeLee is living this now. She's not able to do any of the things she loved. I remember when she was young, active, energetic, strong, and current on everything. I imagined her dressed in her beautiful clothes and regularly attending social events. I recalled her traveling and adventuring. That is the woman I know is still living inside her, and it broke my heart to think of her sitting here alone most of every day. I was considering my visit today a wash.

Maybe I needed to visit when I was not exhausted, hungry, and tired. I needed to avoid the dinner hour with its set-in-stone routines. Most importantly, I needed to pull it together and continue to act much better than I felt for now.

As Madison was pushing the wheelchair back to Mom's room, part of me urgently wanted to leave. Yet, I knew I could not. I kept thinking of the mustard stuck under her fingernails from picking up her hamburger. I also knew she could not clean herself. I was consumed with the urgency of finding a wet wipe. We also needed to find someone to help Mom get back out of her wheelchair, as they use a sling for this. In my bleary-eyed exhaustion, I turned to my capable nine-year-old and said, "We need someone to help us with the chair and her hands. Can you find someone?"

I need to hand it to my girl. When she needs help, she goes right to the top. She found the highest-ranking employee in this place, not an aide in scrubs who would usually perform this task. Instead, an angelic woman dressed in professional clothing appeared as if an apparition from heaven.

When I saw the woman's name was Amanda, I introduced myself, "Hi Amanda, I am Marilee's daughter. I met you on a conference call before."

We exchanged pleasantries, and I said, "I don't know who to ask, but my mom needs a wipe for her hands, and she needs help getting back in her chair. I know this is really below your pay grade."

"Oh, one hundred percent I can do that, and get someone to help me. As she walked away, I told Mom my goodbyes, "Mom, we need to go home. I love you."

As I leaned down to kiss her, she said, "I love you so much."

I cannot remember a time when Mom said *I love you 'so much'* like that.

I was as if she said, "You have no idea how much I love you. You have no idea how much it means that you come at dinnertime and just stand there. You have no idea how much it means to me that you bring your daughter, whose brightness of heart lights up everybody's face."

God, I got it. I see it, she's not on the sidelines, not at all. Mom still has an incredible well of love that lives inside of her. She gives what she has and shares it freely. I was standing there, stunned by her generous outpouring of love and kindness. She's like the widow in the Bible who appears to be stripped of everything. However, she puts that one tiny coin into the collection.

In that time, people gave their money to the temple for show. They dropped the coins into buckets, and as the money was placed in them, it clanked and clattered. The more coins, the louder the cacophony of sound, the bigger the bigshot. It was for show. But a tiny mite? A mite hardly makes a twinkle as it lands. I have one and it's light, like a tiny dot of bread that could be fed to a small bird. Yet Jesus said that her gift was worth more than all the others. They gave from their surplus, the interest, what they had left over. She gave all that she owned, and this sacrifice was precious to the Lord.

This sentiment of love from Mom was everything. It was so honest and straightforward. It made me feel deeply loved and appreciated. It filled my bucket. The whole place, the smell, the stains, the mustard, the grouchiness, faded away. My life lens went from telephoto to zoomed in on Mom. In the end, it is everything to feel that someone loves you completely and appreciates you entirely. It's my dream to make people feel like that, and Mom's example in that moment taught me well. We can love people so deeply, sincerely, and sweetly that they will be forever changed. It's the highest calling. Mom's love changed me in that moment, as in my entire life. I owe her a debt of gratitude, and I feel blessed to call her Mom. For those who love, far from being sidelined, are most certainly in the game.

"To live in the hearts we leave behind is to live forever." Carl Sagan.

"Love is a fruit in season at all times and within reach of every hand." Saint Mother Teresa.

"And now these three remain: faith, hope, and love. But the greatest of these is love." (1 Corinthians 13:13, NIV)

LOBSTER TALE

LET ME give you a snapshot of the last 25 hours. Right now, it's 8:14 pm on Christmas Eve. The whole holiday season has changed so much for us through the years. Before bed last night, December 23rd, I felt very run down, as I often do at this time of year. As a mom, wife, daughter, friend, author, counselor, business owner, and more, I want to get everyone I care about the perfect gift. For my daughter, it is the ideal pair of roller skates. For my mom LeeLee, it's the gift of time and Kentucky Fried Chicken. For my college kids, cash is king. I know I am aiming for an ideal, a fantasy, but that will not keep me from trying.

I knew I needed to attempt to get to bed before midnight. I offered to do bath and stories with Madison. In theory, this was a solid plan. However, it slipped my mind that kids cannot usually get to sleep without tranquilizers, the couple of nights before Christmas. There were no big yawns, quiet stories, eyelids closing, and gently drifting off to night-night land.

This December 23rd was also fraught with anxiety because Bunny was lost. This kind of crisis ramped up our holiday bedtime routine to a new level of frenzy. The ever-spinning merry-go-round of most important stuffies complicated the scenario. One night Bunny is essential, and then, without warning, boom, it's a Puppy night. When the coast seems clear, it's suddenly Giraffe and Duckie night. You get the idea, and last night was Bunny night. But not just any bunny; it was *Teal* Bunny. In Madison's mind, the color teal was loosely held. *Teal* was in the color range from mint green to turquoise, and one needed to intuit what color teal represented that night.

The search continued as I was wearily lying in bed, offering my prayers for a safe recovery of Teal Bunny. Finally, Teal Bunny was recovered in the nick of time. I began to breathe easily. Then Madison told me, "I'm hungry. I want corn." It was after 9:00 pm, still December 23rd. I was fighting a cold and fierce exhaustion from too many nights of scant sleep. I had stayed up addressing Christmas cards, wrapping and hiding presents, helping Will move, making extra trips to visit Mom in her senior living facility, and delivering gifts to school, sick friends, and loved ones. These are just some highlights. So, getting up to make *corn* was not on my radar. But if you know Madison, once she decides something, it's happening. Late-night corn was going to be a thing, no question. I just wasn't willing to be a part of it. Also drifting through my consciousness was that our eldest, Jacob, was not feeling well. He thought he felt feverish, but it was not confirmed because none of our seven thermometers had working batteries. We were left to rely on the untechnical, hands-on-the-forehead method for gathering data. And in my most doctorly voice, I concluded that he was febrile. Did I pout and think, *Wait a second, it's Christmas, and my kid is sick, and my other kid wants Teal Bunny and corn? Woe is me.* Of course not. I know that Christmas is not exempt from snags. On the contrary, it magnifies them.

I know that illness, tears, stress, exhaustion, and missteps are a part of the holiday terrain. It's not that I am a Grinch; far from that,

I LOVE CHRISTMAS. I just dial down my expectations to stay sane. I got up this morning, Christmas Eve, in *go* mode. I needed to make homemade mashed potatoes, a crust, and cheesecake. I got down to brass tacks immediately and began at 8:30 am. I will spare you the details and let you know I cooked non-stop, in my pajamas, until 1:30 pm, and still had to clean up.

All the while, I was checking on Jacob, who was now confined to his room and needed a constant flow of Gatorade, Emergen-C, Goldfish crackers, and the like. I also sprinkled in making meals, discussing "life, liberty, and the pursuit of happiness" with my brilliant son Nick, answering emails, and finding Shrinky-dinks, markers, thread, tape, and other essentials.

Next, it was off to meet LeeLee at 4:00 pm mass at her senior living facility. Nick was kind enough to stop at KFC to pick up dinner for her. She wanted her usual: chicken, mashed potatoes, gravy, and lemonade. I didn't want LeeLee to eat institutional food on Christmas Eve, not on my watch. After convincing Madison that pajamas were not acceptable for Christmas Eve mass and packing a few snacks, we left to meet LeeLee at church.

When I got in the car, Nick called, "Hey, is LeeLee supposed to be at church?"

"Yes, why?"

"Well, she is not here."

"What do you mean, she is not there?"

"I'm looking around, and I don't see her."

"Oh great, did they forget to bring her to mass? I'll call over there."

After several calls to various aides, it was clear that LeeLee had been taken to church. That is all we knew. You can imagine the added stress this caused. I called Nick and said, "Maybe they forgot to bring her. Maybe they took her to another chapel. Either way, I am sure she is safe, so we need to go to Mass. We will figure it out afterward."

Wow, who was this chill woman? I'm just taking this in stride. I remembered Christmas masses from a few years ago. I was upset if we were not all together and in the main church. But I now accept that I don't get to control the actors and the play, not on Christmas or any other day. Instead, I get to show up for reality, whatever form that takes. If LeeLee was not at Mass, meeting up with her afterwards was okay.

We did find LeeLee in the front of the chapel. Nicholas was kind enough to wheel her back to her room. As Madison and I reached her room, Nick was already settled in, chatting away with her. Soon, the KFC was all set up. I needed to go to the dining room for more napkins and forks. That was when I saw a plate of food in front of a resident. It stopped me in my tracks, and I spun around to look at the stack of menus with "Christmas Eve Dinner" printed at the top. Each night, residents are given a sheet of paper at mealtime. They write their name at the top and circle their food selections.

The menu for tonight was unlike any of the hundreds I have seen before. It was on thick white cardstock printed in red and black in a formal font. It confirmed what I thought was plated for several residents. Right there it was: Prime Rib with Lobster Tail. Since my meals were all protein shakes and apples that day, the Lobster Tail jumped out at me immediately. *When was the last time I even tasted a lobster tail?* It must have been when I lived at home with my parents as a teenager. I promptly picked up a menu and began circling items.

The teenager working in the dining room instructed me to return in fifteen minutes for my food. As promised, it was there, all boxed and bagged for me. Mom taught me to take all of it, as the

KFC hit the spot for her. It was getting late, so Madison and I proceeded home. All the while, I was immensely excited to get inside and savor my Christmas Eve lobster meal. I didn't even rush into the house. I wanted to savor each moment as I looked forward to my lovely meal. I don't eat meat, so the Prime Rib was for Jeff, and the lobster tail was for sharing. I was thrilled.

I opened the bag and pulled out the white Styrofoam container.

I popped it open, ready to eat. There was NO lobster tail, just a slab of meat and a roll. My disappointment was palpable. *Excuse me, God, didn't I just cook and care for everyone all day? Where is my lobster tail?* Immediately, I felt how ridiculous I was acting. I'm not supposed to get a prize for doing the right thing. No, doing the right thing is its own reward. Why don't I *look forward to my time with God like that? I looked forward to that lobster tail as the decade's most extraordinary treat. I was looking forward to it more than God.* Food can become an idol, which I did with this meal. That is why it was not mine. Still, I was having a mini tantrum about another protein shake dinner on the way to check on Jacob.

As my sanity returned, I thought about God's sovereignty. He never wants to take something good from us. He leads us only to better and better. I was grateful for my kids. I checked on the ailing Jacob and brought him more Gatorade.

"I'm sort of mad, so I'm going to exercise."

"What are you mad about?" he sweetly inquired.

"Nothing. It's not anything. I just need to sweat it out."

It was now dark and cold outside, so I went to the indoor workout room. I flipped on the TV to finish a movie I was watching while I biked. However, a Nate Bargatze show appeared on my Netflix choices. I really appreciate this comedian and his use of clean humor. Jeff, Nick, and I are consumers of comedy. I told Nick, "Crass humor is for a true novice. Anybody can string together some profanities and get an awkward laugh, but clean humor? That is very funny, that takes genius." Enter Nate Bargatze, funny man, no cussing, real-life humor. So, I decided to see how his material would affect my crabby little mood.

As I watched, I laughed so hard that it hurt. I identified with his frugal wife and could not stop laughing at his hilarious retelling of anecdotes. I biked, sweated, and laughed out loud for forty minutes. The whole experience was so much more enjoyable than a lobster tail. I thought," *Okay, God, I get it.* I needed to miss out on the dinner that I felt I earned, go on a self-pity jag, get angry about those feelings, decide to work out, turn on the TV, see that Bargatze had a new show out, and have the best laugh I've had in years. I would not trade that for even the best lobster tail."

I completed my biking and went upstairs. Then I gratefully grabbed a protein shake and sat down to write, knowing that I need to continue to distinguish between my wants that are never met and my needs that always are.

"You can't always get what you want, but if you try sometimes, you might find, you get what you need." Mick Jagger

"And do not be conformed to this ¹world, but be transformed by the renewing of your mind, so that you may prove what the will of God is, that which is good and acceptable and perfect."(Romans 12: 1-2, NASB)

"And we know that in all things God works for the good of those who love him, who have been called according to his purpose." (Romans 8:28, NIV)

Lessons From The Course VIII

EXIT THE WATER

SPORTS SERVE me as a microcosm of life. Things do not always go as planned. You can prepare and prepare, but God owns the day and the weather too. I read that Bob Bowman, the renowned swim coach of Michael Phelps, would hide Phelps' goggles or crush them before important meets. Champions in sports and life are made in adversity. Everyone can smile when things go as planned. I find out who I am when the plan gets scratched. It can be a good habit to manufacture challenges. A long hike that requires stamina and strength can be an instructor. Unfamiliar waters on a triathlon can serve as a teacher. When equipment breaks, tires leak, or a thunderstorm begins, a graduate level lesson begins. I give my dear friend adversity a hug. I know she has not arrived to defeat me, but to insure my strength in all things.

I was recently in a triathlon, and I psyched myself up for the swim. Of the three disciplines of triathlon -- swimming, biking, and running-- for me, swimming is the most demanding and nerve-wracking. I told myself all the right things, "I can do this.

Swimming is so fun. I am strong in the water. I have a strategy. I will not leave the water last."

Now that final statement is tricky because to be one of the first to exit the water, it follows that you need to be one of the first *in* the water, too. That's intimidating because all the downright super-human athletes are stacked up at the start just chomping at the bit to conquer the swim. There is no way I am placing myself in that pack to be swum over and submerged, potentially swallowing water instead of air. The extremes of the front or back of the pack are quickly eliminated. I need to get in the middle and stay in the middle. I need to shove that bully fear aside and take hold of my swim. It does not belong to anyone else.

Recently, I asked a friend who trains triathletes for a living, "How can I approach the swim? Do you have any suggestions?"

"First of all, go out easy. Don't go charging out there at a pace you can't hold. You can get out of breath that way. You just need to be consistent and do what you do. Also, sighting is essential. About every eight strokes, you need to look up to make sure you are on course."

When you run or bike, there are these sweet little arrows on the ground that guide you. Also, volunteers are charged with keeping you perfectly on course. The open water is different. If you swim 50 yards in the wrong direction and double that to 100 yards to get back on course, now you have an 850-yard swim instead of 750 yards. You can imagine how much time and dis-tance this adds to a swim. This goes against the commandment to get in and out of the water as quickly as possible. No one wants to commit such a 'sin.' This is where sighting becomes all-im-portant. Sighting the buoy out in front of me is like following the essential path of the North Star. In theory, this sounds all fine and good.

However, at the Kill Creek triathlon, another plan was brewing. It was a cold morning, and the water temperature was warmer than the air. I looked up to sight and had a rude awakening. My goggles were completely fogged, and I could barely see a foot in front of me. My 'North Star' was veiled behind a cloud of fog. It was still there; I just couldn't see it.

Could I stop to clean my goggles? And stand on what? Water? I'm not Jesus. I gave myself a firm talking to: "Suck it up, Elisemarie, this happens. It's an unwelcome obstacle you did not see coming." This is one of those times I can't afford to ask 'why?' Instead, I ask, "What now?" What are my options? Keep swimming or raise my hand to be pulled into a boat. I refused to quit. I began to count, one, two, three. I methodically pulled water with my arms while my eyes lived behind my opaque goggles. This was a challenge I had not expected, and I did not want it to throw me off course. I was able to exit the water with my head held high.

"Obstacles don't have to stop you. If you run into a wall, don't turn around and give up. Figure out how to climb it, go through it, or work around it." Michael Jordan

"Being challenged in life is inevitable, being defeated is optional." Roger Crawford

"Therefore keep watch, because you do not know on what day your Lord will come But understand this: If the owner of the house had known at what time of night the thief was coming, he would have kept watch and would not have let his house be broken into. So you also must be ready, because the Son of Man will come at an hour when you do not expect him." (Matthew 24:42-44, NIV)

BE LIKE METZNER

WHEN MY KIDS were only four and five, playing soccer, I heard kids complaining, "That's too far to run. I don't feel good. I need to rest. I'll sub out now. I'm too tired to play anymore." When the coach called these same kids to get in the game, they would charge onto the field with the enthusiasm of petrified wood. I knew that this was not a recipe for success. I have a plaque in my kitchen engraved in marble with the words, "Never, never, never quit." The letters are painted in gold. I think it's no coincidence that we always hear people say, "Go for the gold." More than bronze or silver medals, gold medals are exponentially coveted. Why is this? Maybe it's because the first place is associated with winning. The saying is, "It's not winning or losing that matters; it's how you play the game." Try saying that to five-year-old boys after a soccer game. You will receive a sea of eye rolls and smirks. Winning feels amazing, and that is why we are willing to put in the pain to accomplish it. There is also the apparent value of gold. If I offered you an ounce of gold or silver, I'm confident the gold would win every time.

The mentality I saw in those five-year-olds gave me a teaching moment for my children. I said, "When a coach tells you to do something, just do it. It may feel like it's too much or too demanding. But I was hoping you could listen and do what the coach asks. If you want to complain, do it only inside your head."

My boys adopted this doctrine for sports. It's one of the reasons Jacob got "Hardest Worker" on the Blazers Swim Team. The coach said, "That was unanimous; I mean, not even a question." Jacob went on to be a team captain of his high school swim team. For Will, this meant receiving the "High Point Swimmer Award" year after year. No one was going to outlast or out speed Will in the pool. He thrived on first place and nothing less. He calculated the points available for winning each of his swims and methodically conquered those races individually.

Now, my son, Nicholas, is a Junior on the swim team at Rockbridge High School in Kansas City. He gets up at 4:30 am to arrive at practice by 5:30 am. Then has a full school day, only to return to practice from 3:30 pm-6:30 pm. I make a point of asking him every day about each practice. They are grueling, and I want him to know I care. I rise early for those morning practices, too. You will find me shouting, "I'm so proud of you!" as Nick cuts through the grass to his car carrying two huge backpacks, one for swim and the other for school. Yes, this fantastic kid also carries actual schoolbooks back and forth every day.

Last week, I did not hear much about practice. I do hear about the fabulous breakfasts that the moms supply. I may not know the main swim set, but when warm monkey bread is served, I hear about it. Their coach us Mr. Fisby, some say he demands too much of the boys and is too hard on them. What I can tell you is that he 100% has a plan. He knows how to motivate these boys and does it passionately. Sometimes, that's a hug, and sometimes, it's a kick in the boot. Either way, they have thirteen state championship titles and are consistently on their way to the next.

On Friday, Nick came in the door from practice, and I asked my routine question, "How was practice today?" Instead of "brutal" or "killer," I received real-life sentences. I prize this from my boys.

Nick went on, "Fisby talked to the group after practice today. He said, "More people need to be like Metzner. Do you know why? He NEVER complains. All I hear from the rest of you is moaning and complaining. Well, take a note from Metzner!"

"Really? People complain to Fisby?" I said in amazement.

"Oh yeah, all the time," Nick responded.

"I would think they would be too afraid to do that."

"No, there is tons of complaining," Nick confirmed. "Yeah, so it was really cool when he used me as an example of not doing that. He pointed it out to the entire team. I was not expecting that, and I sort of felt like I could almost cry."

"Wow, that is amazing! I am so proud of you; great work!" I exclaimed.

Nick may not be the fastest swimmer on the team because he is mortal, unlike some of the genetically fast, sheerly gifted 'fish'. I thought I would rather have the most determined, hardest-working swimmer with the best attitude than a fast and haughty swimmer any day. Speed can be bought and trained, but character cannot. I am so proud of my kids for taking a 'get it done right with a good attitude' work ethic into the world. I adopted that from my dad. I hope that on my best days, they have seen it in me.

Not to mention the incredible Coach Fisby. He sees everyone and has the unique ability to extract their best qualities for the team. It's like making metal, Fisby burns away the imperfections until he forges pure compounds. Only the best remains to create unbreakable bonds. A State Championship organically emerges from the process. Fisby's swimmers, divers, managers, and families are the better for it. Thank you, Fisby. Thank you for seeing my son and saying something about it so generously. Your attributes make you a great coach, leader, and man. Thank you for your able example.

Nicholas, thank you for making my life fulfilling and rewarding every day. I follow and cheer gratefully as you lay the steppingstones in your path to success.

I love you, Mom.

"I do not know anyone who has got to the top without hard work. That is the recipe. It will not always get you to the top but should get you pretty near." Margaret Thatcher

"Opportunities are usually disguised as hard work, so most people don't recognize them." Ann Landers

"All Scripture is God-breathed and is useful for teaching, rebuking, correcting and training in righteousness, so that the servant of God may be thoroughly equipped for every good work." (2 Timothy 3:16, NIV)

NEVER, NEVER DO THIS

HE SHAWNEE MISSION Park in Kansas hosts a large national qualifying triathlon. I did this triathlon as a team with my son, Nicholas, last year. I knew doing the entire race myself was still out there for me. Swimming in the open water made me nervous. We had a lake house where I swam in open water all the time, but this was different and without a life jacket.

There was another triathlon last August, appropriately named Kill Creek. I practiced the open water swim in another lake. I felt great. My son, Nicky, was near me in a kayak. I felt good going into the race. However, it was a small race. Not many swimmers entered the water, and we went in one at a time. I became anxious during the swim. I needed to breathe, so I turned over to backstroke. This was perfect, but without lane lines, I was veering right and left. This made my swim extra-long. At one point in my panic, I thought, What am I doing out here? I have a family. I have kids. I cannot die like this. I just kept on swimming and being hard on myself. My self-talk was full of fear, and I got the results of all my stinking thinking.

I exited the water, thank God. All I cared about was that it was done. I mounted my bike and took off. What a relief to be on a bike! I could breathe whenever I wanted, and all was well. The bike ride was beautiful. Sometimes, multiple riders, going both directions, packed the lane. Other times, it was a solitary ride, and I embraced the serenity. Then my bike betrayed me. With miles left to go, the tires seemed flat, and the gears clunked as I shifted. None of the volunteers had an air pump. After a wrong turn that lengthened my already miserable time with this bike, I finally made it to the transition area.

I was so happy to rack that piece of junk bike, grab some water, and run freely. Once on the run, I was at my best, no black lake water, no bike to nurse along the way. I was keeping track as I knew I needed to go two laps on the run course. As I was running out on the course, I told the person at the turn, "Remember me when I come back by for my second loop." As I approached that point for the second time, the volunteer was gone.

The new volunteers told me, "You need to go another lap."

"No, this is my second time at this station."

"We haven't seen you. We think you need to go one more lap."

Upset that they did not believe me, I came to a complete stop, something that is against my personal code of 'always keep moving.' As I was standing there perplexed, the woman I had seen before reappeared like the apparition of an angel.

I was elated and shouted, "There she is! Remember me?"

She turned toward me and the other volunteers and said, "Oh yeah, you go on, honey. It's her second time through."

Thank you, Jesus. I was ready to get to the finish line.

My kids were waiting there to greet me. That was one happy moment, and I felt so blessed with my fantastic crew. It was all high fives and hugs. Of course, I needed photos to record this historic moment. My teenage boys were ready to leave. "Great job, Mom. See you at home." I was grateful they drove all that distance in the early morning to be there for me. I am a blessed mom.

I thrive on continuous progress mentally, physically, and spiritually. The following summer, I knew that Shawnee Mission was still out there for me as a solo competitor, and I was intimidated. This event is really for the big boys and girls in the multisport world. I had only four weeks to train instead of the 'required' 12 weeks. Still, I wanted to do the Shawnee Mission Triathlon with the big kids.

It's a race of me versus me. If I want to conquer this thing, then it's on me to do it. I know that if you want to do something then do the damn thing. Don't think about it. Thinking and researching are the two most significant ways I know to stay stalled out of achieving goals. How many people do you know who say, "I'll think about it," and rarely end up at the top of the mountain? I love how Vince Lombardi puts it: "The man on top of the mountain didn't fall there." They work like no other.

I worked at boiling my fear out and solidifying confidence within. As the race approached, my daughter asked, "If you are afraid, why are you doing it?"

I told her, "Because I don't want to let fear define me. I want to conquer my fears."

I'm doing this for me. I know that when I challenge myself physically, the mental and spiritual growth will follow. I gain confidence I cannot get from anything else. I feel the satisfaction in doing hard things. This is just how I am wired. I also learned that spiritual growth is difficult to see in the immediate. It takes time and effort. It takes work, prayer, and surrender. Growth in the spiritual is not linear and obeys its own trajectory.

Early In recovery, I was reading about spiritual growth. The book suggested attempting physical goals first, as spiritual growth can feel painstakingly slow. Physical improvement is an easy place to see results. Going to the gym, pounds fall off, muscles become defined, and mood elevates. I also developed perseverance, which helps in the spiritual gym as well.

In the spiritual, I know God protects me and loves me. He would never let anything terrible befall me. I am the apple of his eye, and so are you. However, I knew I needed a plan to handle panic, should it arise. I wanted my kids to know they can not only face their fears but conquer them.

I felt ridiculously nervous the morning of the race. Mine had been moved to 30 minutes earlier because of the impending heat. However, lightning flashed outside my window, and I was not sure what the race directors would do with the weather. As the storm continued, Nick helped me load my bike onto my car rack. We set out toward the park while it was still raining. When we arrived, we learned that the race had been postponed 30 minutes due to the thunderstorm. This gave me all kinds of extra time to get into my head. Soon we saw lightning in the distance and the race was postponed for another 30 minutes. All this standing around left me totally stuck in 'hamster wheel' brain mode.

I spotted Samantha, a friend I had not seen in a while, as she had moved to another state. We greeted each other with hugs. Then what did I do? I started to vomit out all my negative self-talk. This is something I warn my kids about: "You can *think* negative things if you need to. You can even share those with someone to try to get them out of your head. But you can *never let them out of your mouth* in a serious way. Never. Never."

Here I was putting myself down right and left. For those who don't believe in manifesting your life, take a guess at what happened for me on the swim. There was good news and bad news. The good news: I did not panic. The bad news: I couldn't get in a groove with my swimming. Just think of all the negativity that I was carrying for those 500 meters!

This course is a long swim out and then a short swim back to the transition area. Once I turned that corner, I was sick of myself. A switch flipped in my brain. I was suddenly relentless. I was a *competitor*.

For God's sake, what was I doing? This was not some Sunday walk in the park. I was in a triathlon, for the love of God. I was back. I started swimming a fast freestyle. I wanted to beat the woman in front of me out of the water. I did not want to be last out of the water. As much as I don't want to admit I care, my pride was now at stake. She was far ahead, and I began to catch her, but my late effort cost me. I was the last swimmer out of the water. I received the dreaded sympathy claps from the onlookers.

The biking leg of the race was uneventful. I ran toward the transition area, grabbed some water, and got onto the run course. Now my self-talk was totally different. In sharp contrast to my earlier rant about swimming, I was saying, "I love the run. Running is so easy. I can breathe whenever I want, and I feel totally free." This created a wonderful start on the run course. Soon, I had conquered the 'dam hill.' As many runners stopped and walked, I was able to run up that beast. After my humiliation during the swim, I was thankful that I could maintain some dignity on the run.

Then a kid, maybe 10 years old, blew by me. This kid was absolutely booking it. I thought the kid was awesome!

The next thing I knew, I was yelling, "You look amazing! Tell me how to be fast like you."

As he blew by me, he called out, "Just pick up your feet and let the run…"

My mind was thirsty for those last two words. I thought hard. What did I hear? I finally settled on "and let the run take you." I liked that ending to his words of wisdom, so I made them mine. I kept repeating in my mind, "Pick your feet up and let the run take you." I started to pick my feet up higher and faster. I realized I was holding myself back. I was running cautiously and gingerly, careful not to trip on a branch or crack in the blacktop. Was this the best I could do? Was this what that boy was thinking? Was he telling himself, "Better hold back and stay under control. You don't want to fall."

I seriously doubt it. I imagined he was saying, "I am a cheetah. I run faster and faster. I destroyed this course. It's no match for me." Could I let loose like that? Could I just have fun and see how fast I could go? I wasn't sure, but this was as good a time as any to try. I gave myself permission to speed. It felt exhilarating. I looked at my watch, and I was on pace for a 7:45 mile. This was much faster than my average pace. I was pleasantly surprised.

The hardest part of the run was ahead. It's all uphill to reach the finish, and the course is rude that way. I saw many people walking again and encouraged each one. I saw one man who was walking and looked spent.

I said, "Keep going. You are only one mile from the finish."

"Really? I needed to hear that," he cheerfully replied.

With that, he took off jogging again. We were on the difficult last portion of the run with a steep incline. I had slowed down from my top pace, but I would not stop and walk. A woman, about 19, ran by me and said, "Keep going, you're doing great."

Goodness gracious, that was like wind beneath my wings! I surged forward. Her words made me feel seen and noticed. Some runners were saving their legs for that final stretch to the finish line. Everyone wanted to look their best when family and friends were

NEVER, NEVER DO THIS

watching. However, I had been climbing and climbing this uphill battle. The nearing finish line wore me out. I could hear my kids, "Go Mom! Go Mom!" I crossed the line. Mission accomplished!

As I approached the tents filled with sports merchandise, I saw the awards tent. About fifty people were in the line to see how well they did. The top three in each age group would get an award. I said to myself, absolutely no need to get in that line. There is no way I got any award. Don't even think about it. I hugged Samantha, who had finished before me, and said goodbye to my family as they walked to their car. I spoke with some friends and fellow competitors and exited the park.

The next day, I told my husband, "I was the last person out of the water."

Knowing that it had been a staggered start, he said, "Well, were you the last person in the water?"

I suddenly realized that during my swim, I had only been passed by one swimmer, as I was the second to last to enter the water. I hesitantly looked up my overall results. I was pleasantly surprised. I did better than I thought. A couple of days later, a friend asked me how I placed. I didn't know because I didn't think that was worth looking up. Then, I received an email from the race director that results had been posted with a link showing the winners in each age group. Curious, I pressed the link. There was my name: Elisemarie, Age Group Place: Second. I had a trophy to pick up. I also qualified for the National Triathlon Championship in Atlantic City.

Next, Kill Creek was approaching, and I felt compelled to do it. Why? Because of the absolute trash I was thinking and saying in this triathlon. I was telling my friend, Samantha, last night, "My goal, and it will be a win for me, is if I can go to this race and not say a single negative thing about myself. In fact, I want to say some positive things about swimming and how much I love it before

I get in the water. I want to see what happens. I am running an experiment."

I am continuously running this type of experiment to gather data on myself. I need to see where I am when pushed far beyond my comfort zone. I can talk a challenging my mental game when I'm lying in bed. But what can I do when I'm in freezing, dark waters by myself? This is where I want to maintain peace. But I still had not registered for the race. A few nights before the race, my dear friend, Samantha, whom I had seen at Shawnee Mission, texted me. She said, "Are you planning on doing Kill Creek?"

"I am thinking about it but not really sure."

"Same here. I registered, but now work has started, so I don't really know if I can do it. Would you want my registration? I called the race director, and she said it could be transferred to you."

"May I let you know tomorrow?"

The next day, I told her I would assume her registration. She needed to call the race director to make it happen. I asked Samantha, "I will need your Venmo so I can pay you."

Samantha replied, "Oh no, you don't have to do that. I can just give it to you."

"Really, are you sure? "

"Yes, it will just be my gift to you as a thank you."

A while later, I received a text from Samantha that read, "Thank you!! Consider it a thank-you gift for getting me into running."

Well, this felt like one of the sweetest things anyone had ever done for me. It was so full of thought, consideration, and generosity. I loved the gift, and I loved what it means to me.

My hope is to go and have my experience without judgment. I want to simply notice my thoughts and actions and process the data afterwards. I consider much of my time running, swimming, and biking to be meditation. This is where I hear most clearly from God. I want to be able to hear the still, small voice under great physical, mental, and spiritual duress. It's my training, not for some race, but for the race of life itself. Things get difficult, and many voices compete for my attention. I am learning to keep my attention on God's voice as the only voice of true consequence. When I do this, I have clarity under pressure. For me, the teacher is the triathlon. The tuition is high but worth its cost.

> "that you may love the Lord your God, listen to his voice, and hold fast to him. For the Lord is your life, and he will give you many years." (Deuteronomy 30:20 NIV)

> *"The true test of a man's character is what he does when no one is watching." John Wooden*

> *"Far away there in the sunshine are my highest aspirations. I may not reach them, but I can look up and see their beauty, believe in them, and try to follow where they lead." Louisa May Alcott.*

> *"Indeed, the very hairs of your head are all numbered. Don't be afraid; you are worth more than many sparrows." (Luke 12:7)*

Talk Back To Your Brain

I URGE YOU to take command of your mind. Choose your thoughts and talk right back to those negative voices. Why? Aren't they trash-talking to you all the time? Are you going to let that bully taunt you forever? Maybe it's time to say, "Back off and cut it out. I'm in charge now, and you have overstayed your welcome for the last time. Don't let the door hit you on the way out." It's about time you stood up for yourself and said it aloud whenever possible. Your mind is your thought neighborhood, so pull the weeds and plant beauty. Get the trash-talkers and hooligans out once and for all. Make your mind a beautiful garden with a locked gate around it.

This saved my life, and it can save yours too. I had to realize that all sorts of thoughts were living in my brain, rent-free. They needed to be evicted and excised from my awareness. The work was painstaking and so worth it. I sorted through the messages in my brain one by one. My goal was to become the most optimistic and positive version of myself. If they no longer served me, I told them,

I am not thinking like that anymore. I said this by faith until it was true. I befriended positivity and took it with me everywhere.

Last night at dinner, my daughter wanted everyone to open a fortune cookie and read their fortune. I was the only one who played along. She opened her fortune, which read, "Your optimism brings you great fortune."

Then she said, "Mom, can I trade with you? You are always being positive."

I happily accepted the swap. I thought, "Thank you, God. My daughter knows me as this person. Madison recognizes my optimistic mindset." Victoriously, I washed the dishes as I let this wave of gratitude splash over me.

"When there is no way, find a way." Coach Tony Severino

"Watch your thoughts, they become your beliefs. Watch your beliefs, they become your words. Watch your words, they become your actions. Watch your actions they become your habits. Watch your habits, they become your character." Vince Lombardi

"For we live by faith, not by sight" (2 Corinthians 5:7)

NEVER GIVE UP

SEARED IN my mind is the day from grade school when I struggled to run around one city block. I was humiliated. I did not see myself as athletic or talented in any way that involved physical strength. I once read, «It is your responsibility to ensure that your child is excellent at a minimum of one sport by middle school." In other words, find their strength. This did not happen for me, so I wrote myself off as 'unathletic.' I felt less than my peers. Debbie was amazing at volleyball. Amy was an incredible soccer player, Rachel was a tennis player, and Kathy was a runner. You get the idea.

By fourth grade, I was overweight, and I had to wear glasses. To top that off, braces, pimples, and underarm hair were next. It wasn't easy to feel good about myself. Additionally, I became physically ill with an incurable disease that gave me extreme pain. Then there was the humiliation of a wheelchair in the Dallas airport.

I did not want to use the chair. I knew I could manage the airport just fine on crutches. However, a gentleman greeted our plane upon arrival with a wheelchair. I said, "Oh, I don't need that. I have crutches, and I will be fine."

My parents insisted, "This is the Dallas airport, and it's huge. You will be happy you have this."

My spirit was crushed by my thirty minutes in that chair. Gobs of people stared at me with pity. I felt useless and defeated. I thought, I am in a wheelchair, and I'm 14; I can't walk. My life will never be good again.

I did not recall the carefree days of being healthy to run, skate, and play as I wanted. I stared down that metaphoric black hole but didn't dare talk about it with anyone. I felt hopeless, trying to scrape my way out, my nails encrusted with filth as I clawed my way up the sides, only to slide down into a cesspool, time and again.

When I run, it's with the privilege of being alive and able to move freely. According to medical science, this should not be possible. I am so grateful for my healthy body and mind. I become euphoric at the mere fact that I am indeed running. To top it all off, I am pain-free. It's hard for me to relate when my children do not want to run or exercise.

Running changed my life and kept me alive through many trials.

Now, I have qualified for the National Triathlon Championships -- swimming, biking, running. For me, it's the most demanding sports competition in existence. It pushes me mentally, physically, and spiritually every time I compete. The training requires a degree of self-discipline and grit that is beyond normal. When I found out I qualified, I was over the moon. Yet two close friends gave me expressions of complete disbelief. The way they made eye contact told me they thought I was a scam. Slowly, the air trickled out of my shiny balloon that said, "I DID IT!" As it fell to the ground, I crossed out the joyful words and mentally wrote, "I can't do it." This did not sit well with my belief system about myself. My skin crawls when I believe the lie that I am not good enough.

Later, I questioned my two deflators separately. The first man said, "Yes, I was thinking that if you qualified, I mean, who didn't qualify?" The other man said, "No, I think it's really cool." I knew this was not true. His look of disbelief and scorn could not be explained away that easily. The first guy at least had the guts to tell me what he was really thinking. I wrote off the Championships as impossible for me. I convinced myself that there had been an error, and my invitation was a mistake.

A couple of days later, I received a text from my friend Mary, stating that one of the swimmers on our team had qualified for nationals. This was fantastic—what an accomplishment for this young woman. I stood in awe; she worked her tail off and deserved to go. I responded to the text, "That's amazing. I did, too, but I'm not going."

Mary replied, "It's an accomplishment. You are always doing for others. You need to do this for yourself. You should go, do this for you."

Her words echoed in my mind. I had written off the idea, but which part of the data I received was true? The reactions of the two men, or Mary? I often ask my patients to return to facts, not feelings. I revisited my invitation to Nationals. To be included, I needed to place first or second in my age group in a national championship qualifier. I did that. I had as much right to be there as anyone else.

I could get in my head and debate my attendance way past the date of the actual event. From the comfort of my bed, I did it and did not do it five times. How did I get out of that spinning wheel? I purchased a plane ticket. Still, I felt my qualification was undoubtedly an error. I increased my swimming distance and speed. Now, I was only partially an imposter. My running took on another level of endurance as I increased my pace. I booked a hotel room. Still, I was uncertain. I asked someone very close to me what he thought. He said, "If you want to go, I support you, but I'm not going myself." I did not want to go alone, but I knew I was equipped. I've done plenty of things in my life solo. I was not going to balk now.

All the while, I continued to run harder, swim faster, and bike longer distances. I took my eyes from the floor to the optimistic horizon. I shut out the negative voices, both internal and external. I fought them with my actions. To further prepare myself, I added the element of adversity by creating 'rails' to jump over. When I did not want to swim, I swam in frigid waters. Before submerging myself, I would say, «Embrace the suck!» I made 750 meters my new home distance in the water. I needed it to feel easy and simple, and it was. When I was exhausted from the five hundred things I do every day, I willed myself to run at least 3.15 miles when I just wanted to stop.

At my last triathlon, a woman in her twenties set up her bike in the transition area next to me. There was a man with her; I assumed he was her husband. He wore a thick gold band. The woman was cold, so he took off his fuzzy pullover and gave it to her. He was giving her last-minute tips and reminding her to stay hydrated. They made plans to go out to breakfast with friends afterward. I conversed with them and found out that they were brother and sister. I instantly longed for such a person. I scrolled through the list of my brothers and knew this was impossible for me. Although saddened, I knew I had to accept my despair quickly and move on, like swallowing a slimy oyster.

I pulled gratitude out of my toolbox and began thanking God for the wonderful people in my life. I told myself, "My son, who loves sleep like no other, assured me he will be here by the event's start at 8:00 am on a Saturday." As a complete surprise, there was a mom friend of mine there to cheer on her son. She is kind and intuitive and waited at the finish line after her son finished to cheer me on. The Lord always supports me and provides for my every need.

I longed to have someone with me at Nationals who would be supportive and excited to take part in my experience. This helped me gently dip my toe in the waters of sharing my plans to attend this event. First, I did this by texting my business mentor, John. He texted his congratulations, and when he saw me, he made a point to reiterate, "Nationals, that is just so cool." I knew I could finish this monster task with no one at the finish line. I also knew it would be so much more rewarding to share this accomplishment with those I love.

I recalled the words of my sweet niece, Alaina, who often tells me, "You've got all the athletic genes in the family. I so admire how athletic you are; you inspire me." Then she will text me, "I just ran two miles, feel great!" or "I just ran three miles before work—game changer!"

It dawned on me why I was in this game in the first place. It's not about me. It's about paying it forward. There have been countless people who offered me inspiration purely by example. David Goggins, Eddie Penero, Dr. Robert Schloegel, Cecile Schloegel, and many others I don't know by name. Fifteen years ago, I saw a woman training in the pool where I also trained. I still think of her determination to slay her triathlon race. When I asked her how it went, she said, "It was awful. I didn't hydrate properly. I had dry heaves for the last nine miles. I would go to the side, heave, and then run as far as I could. It was miserable, but I finished." Her only goal was completion. Sweet Alaina said, "You are going to win!" I responded, "Finishing is winning."

That is why I wanted my daughter, Madison, and Alaina at the finish line. If I could give some part of myself to each of them, a part that says, "Just keep going; you are stronger than you believe; you can do this!" Then, my journey would be a success. I gently dipped my toe into the ocean of vulnerability and asked Alaina if she would like to come with me. "Yes!" she replied without a moment's hesitation. Now it's all locked in. I go for myself, for them, and ultimately, for God, whom I love above all else. I know God will have 'appointments' already lined up for me on the journey. There will be someone who needs my encouragement, my smile, and my simple prayers. I will give this willingly and gratefully. God has a reason for my accomplishments and always points to His greater glory. If I, a crippled, insecure kid, can compete on the national level in my fifties, anything is possible.

Not only for me but for you.

"Everyone has the will to win but very few have the will to prepare to win." Vince Lombardi

"Believe you can and you're halfway there." Theodore Roosevelt

"With God all things are possible." (Matthew 19:26).

WHAT ABOUT THOSE
ALL-IMPORTANT FEELINGS?

I SHARE MY journey with you so will not be a slave to your limiting beliefs about yourself. If you are healthy, you have the privilege of being in control of your emotions, thoughts, and actions. Of course, your first feeling or thought may not be true. It pops up without your permission. That thought gets a pass, but only that first one. The rest of the thoughts and actions are yours for the choosing. These you can control. You cannot sit around and wait to feel better, as I did. I wanted to sit on my couch and wait until I felt better to act. One of my sponsors used to urge me to get a job. It sounded good in theory, but I didn't want to work. My feelings won out, and I was basically broke. I had a grand total of two dollars allocated for lunch and ten dollars for my weekly trip to a small hole-in-the-wall market in Brooklyn, New York.

The key I missed was that I needed to act, and my feelings would follow not vice versa. In my defense, before I got sober, I was constantly working full time and going to school. Then I would add another job when I could. I really needed to stop just desperately taking all the work that fell in front of me and figure out what I wanted. But that was not going to happen by analysis and paralysis. I needed to get moving into the world to meet with my destiny. It was not going to come knocking on my door. I have started four businesses. They are all successful. I needed to try things I felt drawn to. I learned it's not important where it goes, it's more important *that* it goes. All learning is forward motion. I am either learning what works for me or what does not. Both pieces of information are equally relevant to progress. Sometimes I hit a wall in the process. That's okay, as I learned from it. When I was willing to ignore my discomfort and my fear-bound perspectives, prosperity followed.

Now I think of my feelings as Information that just comes spilling out like a continuous printout of my mind. It gives me a record of my feeling at that moment. I need to take a glance at the paper and acknowledge the feelings. They are neither good nor bad in and of themselves. I cannot control those first impulses. I can control what I will do with information. I can give it power or throw it in the trash. The choice is mine.

I told my first sponsor in AA, "I don't really like that meeting. I don't think I will go anymore." To my horror, she responded, "The thing is, we don't really care how you feel. We care that you stay sober. You can quit that meeting only after staying there for an additional month while adding another meeting to see if you like it."

I thought, "But what about my precious and all-important feelings?" Recovery and life are about growing up. Growing up into the person God wants me to be, not a person living out my character defects. To accomplish this growth, my feelings about doing the right thing are completely irrelevant. I think the right thoughts, and take the right actions, PERIOD. If this makes me feel sad, misunderstood, or humbled, well, too bad. I spent too long pretending I was above you as I stared up at you from the sewer. It was time to put down the bottle and live here and now. And what if the here and now sucked? Well, too bad. It was up to me to do something about it and stop feeling sorry for myself.

Sometimes I ask Mom, "What did you do yesterday?"

"I didn't have any visitors, so I had a pity party, but no one came," she tells me with a smile.

Humor is considered a mature coping skill and it's one that LeeLee has down to a science. I follow in her footsteps whenever possible. Another way out of the bad neighborhoods in my head is to act. I talk back to my negative thoughts. As a teen, I used the idea of ending my life as an escape to get through my pain. As an adult, that option lived in my neural pathways. It was there, loudly saying, "Today is the day you do it. You end it. You will hurt yourself." Those ego-dystonic thoughts are very painful to endure. I needed to shut that path down by saying aloud, "I am not thinking like that anymore. I am an adult with tools. I can handle having problems. I can tolerate discomfort and pain." It was a revelation to me that I can be simultaneously uncomfortable and comfortable. When I feel discomfort, I tell myself, "I can handle this feeling, maybe only a day, an hour, or a minute at a time. The difficulty will pass. I have no idea when, but it will pass.

Sometimes our brains get very black and white. It's either wonderful or terrible. These extremes are distortions. It's also a distortion of thinking when our brains tell us, "It will always be this way. It will never get better." 'Always' and 'never' are practically guaranteed to be illusions. Instead, I can tell my brain, "This is how it is right now. It could change at any time."

I will feel that I cannot wait another day for the outcome I want. Again, here is a lie. My first sponsor taught me, "Feelings are not facts, but it's a fact that you have feelings." I truly disdain waiting; that is a feeling. How about living? That's what I love, so I *live* until the event occurs. As an example, I can use my current desire. I am drawn to a farm with a barn, horses, green space, a garden, and beauty all around. I feel like I need it immediately. That's false, I have everything I need. If I believe I need those things now, I ask myself, "Where can I go and experience some of what I am looking for? Can that bring me some joy as I continue to search for my farm?" Of course it can.

There can be many feelings conflicting within me simultaneously. For example, sadness and happiness. Life is like a big soupy mix of feelings. Sometimes I get an unexpected hot pepper or a slimy snail. When I get lucky enough to have a purely delicious bowl of all wonderful ingredients, I stop right there and thank God. I did this at dinner last night with my family. It was the conclusion of a particularly busy day. I made time to see Mom in her care facility. This consistently brings me right back to gratitude.

In the middle of dinner, I said, "I am so happy right now."

My husband said, "Why? Do you love your food?"

"Not just that. The food is great, and the people are amazing. I'm just so lucky."

I ate the food I chose, went to the bathroom unassisted, and heard and saw well. None of this is available to LeeLee at this time in her life. My house is free from unescapable stench. I have a roof over my head, clothes, and running water. I have hardwood floors and soft carpets. My neighborhood is safe and quiet. There is a grocery store two blocks away where I can get anything. I have people who love me, and I love them. I do sacred work in my counseling and writing that I love. My children are an endless supply of joy, pride, and learning. I am humbled to have these four divine assignments from God. I am free from illness.

I am beyond grateful for what I have right here, right now.

"Acknowledging the good that you already have in your life is the foundation for all abundance." Eckhart Tolle

"Gratitude is not only the greatest of virtues but the parent of all others." Cicero

"Rejoice always, pray without ceasing, give thanks in all circumstances; for this is God's will for you in Christ Jesus." (1 Thessalonians 5:16-18 NIV)

First Mile, Worst Mile

YESTERDAY I SWAM, so today was a running day. I did not particularly feel like running, expending high energy for an extended period of time. I knew I could not finish unless I started, so I began on the bike. I warmed up for two miles. Then I remembered that in triathlon training, there are literally no free rides. There are no easy activities within the three choices of swim, bike, run. Biking is the impostor of the friendly guy in the group. Don't be deceived. By the time you add resistance, incline, wind, and fatigue, he's more of a hoodlum than a friendly chap.

Now I feel like a jerk for even writing this, because of what I just witnessed. I was in my car in a parking lot with the door open to stay cool. I repeatedly heard a loud sound that resembled the honk of a goose. Only this sound was more sustained and guttural. The sound grew louder and louder, repeating at set intervals. Finally, the source of the sound was right in front of my car. It was a severely disabled boy. He was ambulating with the assistance of three adults and braces on his wrists, where he leaned on them for support. This made me want to cry. What must he and his parents go through daily? Hardship, struggle, frustration, sadness, and agony came to mind.

The boy was participating in physical therapy. The three women who assisted him communicated with him by holding a paper in front of him. I had no idea whether it contained words or pictures. I only gathered that he did not like what it said, as he made more noises in protest and would occasionally collapse to the ground and hold his head as if blunt force trauma was occurring. The entire group stopped in front of my car a couple of times. Soon, I realized that one of the women working with him held a sign that said, "SAFE BODY." Each time he protested and fell on his knees to the sidewalk, she would calmly say, "Safe Body," and help him to his feet again. Another woman supported him on his left side. She rubbed his shoulder as if comforting him. The third woman followed closely behind for support. Clearly, this saintly trio works with severely disabled kids. I could see the signs of exhaustion in the expressions on their faces. The woman on the right, with the paper, had sweat rolling down her forehead. Her lovely strawberry blonde hair was thrown into a disheveled ponytail, and strands were falling out. Their work must require excruciating patience, perseverance, and determination.

It made me feel stupid and small for complaining about the miniscule issues I have with my amazing kids who are all healthy and well. I sometimes overlook my countless gifts and forget how incredibly blessed I am. In the reading today at church, the Israelites were disgusted with the manna God gave them to survive. The priest asked, "Don't we often do the same when we do not prepare ourselves to meet Christ? We come into Mass and just experience it by rote. We don't really ensure we are in a state of grace to meet the Lord."

I felt a little prideful that I had been to confession within the last seven days. I was congratulating myself for all the 'extra' Masses

I had attended during Lent. But these are not things worth trophies. These are the things I *get to do* for my soul, just as I *get to run* for my health.

Today, when I didn't feel like running, I told myself to go half a mile. I went .52 miles and abandoned the treadmill for the bike. I was disgusted with myself. How was I going to run a half marathon in three weeks if .52 miles seemed a challenge? I got back on the treadmill. For the next mile, I was convinced that I needed to quit. My brain totally chimed in with 'stinking thinking.'

My calves hurt. My shoes are too worn out. That pain in my glutes seems worse. I am not even sure this is good for my joints. My toes are jammed at the end of my shoes. I need new shoes. Maybe it's the insoles? I need new insoles. I can't do a good long run anyway right now, so what is the point? On and on my head protested while my feet kept moving. First to two, three, four, and then I needed to stop at five miles to go pick up Madison from school.

At that point, I realized I had forgotten a crucial fact of most exercise: Starting is the hardest part. For me, getting in the pool and enduring those first few lengths of freezing water is miserable. When I run, it takes at least a mile to sweep out all the negativity and get into a pace with my body and mind. Biking is not hard. It only *feels* challenging at times, and I can't let that record play too long, either.

I get to do all these things because I am healthy and well. I know what it's like to be seriously ill and to lose the freedom of health for an undetermined amount of time. Now I relish the fact that I run freely. I can use my voice to express myself and to help others. That boy is deprived of the luxuries I can entirely take for granted. Many days I am identical to the ungrateful Israelites. I am ashamed to say it's so, and when I see this boy his 'cross' looks massive.

I told Madison about the boy and the utter sadness I felt in witnessing his struggle. Later, we were on our way to track practice. I announced, "Let's pray three Hail Marys."

"Who are they for?"

"One for you, one for me, and one for LeeLee."

"What about that boy you saw?" she asked.

"Yes, let's pray one for him, for his parents, and for the people who work with him," I affirmed. There was no reason to stop praying, and I began a second Hail Mary for the boy.

"We already prayed for him," Madison pointed out.

"Well, let's pray another. It's not like you can pray too much. You can't over-pray."

"Yes, you can," she argued. "What if you spent all your time going to Mass and praying and never saw your family? You would need to skip Mass one day and see your family. Family comes first."

Not wanting to start a debate, I just said, "Hail Mary full of grace..."

I quietly prayed.

God, I am sorry for my childlike tantrums when I whine and complain like a spoiled child. Please forgive my ungrateful heart. Please take me back into Your arms of forgiveness and grant me another chance to make my heart unto Thine. That first mile is a gift.

"Our greatest glory is not in never falling, but in rising every time we fall." Oliver Goldsmith

"I am not afraid of storms, for I am learning how to sail my ship." Louisa May Alcott

"Thanks be to God for his indescribable gift." (2 Corinthians 9:15, NIV)

Abandoned

Y ESTERDAY WAS SUNDAY, September 15, 2024, but unlike any other Sunday, I competed in the National Championship Triathlon, sprint distance, in Atlantic City, New Jersey. I was there to push myself and do something that was a million miles from my comfort zone. Why do this? I am seeking to better myself.

My triathlon began Saturday morning, September 14th, as I arose at 3:58 am to catch the plane to Philly. I quickly packed my last toiletries and made sure my 'team' was ready to go. Jeff was taking us to the airport, about an hour away. Will, my 19-year-old son, was joining me, as was my 9-year-old daughter, Madison. The icing on the cake was that my 25-year-old niece, Alaina, was also going with us.

I said goodbye to my son, Jacob, who would typically be at the University of Alabama. However, he was tucked in his bed, sleeping before a national exam that he needed to take in Missouri on this exact morning. I was sad to miss the time with him, but these two events coincided, and they were not in the same part of the country. I gave him a couple of extra hair scruffs and told him, "You are the best. I love you." We took a quick selfie as I documented my day. Later in the car, I looked at it. Jacob's eyes were closed, not to blink but closed as his eyelids rebelled at being awake at that ungodly hour. It was perfect, and I smiled.

We arrived at the airport without a hitch. However, my daughter's ticket listed her as an unaccompanied minor, so we needed to check her in at the ticket counter.

When I told Jamie at the American Airlines desk about the flight we needed to board, he said, "No, you cannot get on this flight. Let's see if we can find you another."

Knowing the day was timed down to the second made me object.

"We need to get on *this* flight," I firmly stated.

"Well, you have to be checked in forty-five minutes before take-off or we can't put you on the plane."

I thought, where exactly was that information in the email I received? It simply said, "It's time to check in." It in no way states, "Now or never, suckers!"

I told him, "I did not know that. We need to be on this flight."

A sudden flurry of dramatic sighs and communications took place.

"I'll see what I can do," he added with dramatic flair.

He alerted the staff at the gate to our presence. He furiously punched the keys on the computer, releasing them with firm clicks. Another call to the gate, more numbers, and Morse code exchanges took place. After a series of dots, dashes, and a 'singing telegrams,' he was able to secure our seats on the plane. Satisfied with the opening act of today's play, Jamie's activity ceased. He handed us four freshly printed boarding passes, and I gleefully called out, "Thanks, Jamie!" as we began our sprint.

The next stop was TSA. We quickly placed shoes, computers, cell phones, keys, and other personal items in the bins to go through the x-ray machine. Then we put our bags flat on the belt. We started to walk away to go through the metal detectors when the man working the conveyor belt operation called us back.

He said, "You have to put your own stuff through."

My mind whirled. Okay, this guy's job is to push these plastic bins onto the conveyor belt. Now he's telling us we need to put our own bins through the machine. So, his job is actually to tell *us* to do his job. This place is nuts. All the while, the clock is ticking. Will gets stopped for a pat-down. I think they must have decided he looked way too chiseled to be innocent. We laughed at the fact that Will, a person who works for a security company, was selected for a pat-down.

Once he was cleared, we took off running. When we got to our gate, the woman was on her little radio saying, "Final boarding call for flight 2464 for Philadelphia. All passengers must be boarded at this time. We are closing the doors in 1 minute."

We ran up to her and I fanned out the boarding passes. She gave me an uppity look that said, "You are late, Mama." There was no time to try to earn her approval, we needed to get on this plane. I was fine with being judged, I just needed on that bird. She reluctantly accepted our boarding passes as if we had personally inconvenienced her with caring for a hundred-pound grizzly bear.

Finally, we were in our seats, and all was well. We landed in Philly without a single bump along the way. It felt like we were on glass the entire flight.

Madison said, "I loved that plane ride. Can we take the same one back?" I loved the simplicity of her thoughts. "If it's good, let's get the same one," makes perfect sense.

As we were leaving the plane, I saw the cockpit was wide open. First, I thanked the pilots for a flight that I could fall in love with. Then I asked if Madison could go in. The pilots were all about being friendly. They let her come on up and sit in the pilot's seat.

One pilot with white hair said, "All the buttons are just for show. It's really not that complicated. Besides that, it was my first flight."

I smiled in reply, "That was great for a first flight. I think you have a future in this."

Madison was enamored by the plush seat covers in the cockpit and thoroughly enjoyed her time in the driver's seat, where she likes to spend most of her time anyway. Then it was off to the rental car. Most of the rental car companies had their own brightly identifiable buses: Avis, Hertz, and Enterprise. We stood looking for the Budget shuttle, only to realize that there was a half-scratched-off Budget sticker on the Avis bus. When we inquired, the driver told us, "I'll take you. Budget is just across the street from Avis." While this presentation was not seething with professionalism, it would do for now. I got a little wink from God as I looked up at the television monitor in the Budget office. It was the Alabama football game. I smiled as I thought of my Jacob. Roll Tide!

We got in our rental car and headed for the shore – Atlantic City. When we arrived at our hotel, we were pleasantly surprised to find out that two of our three rooms were ready for early check-in. We went up to our rooms on the eleventh floor. My peeps were in front of me, so I was riding the elevator up and down by myself. My kids know that I consistently walk up in hotels, etc. I get uncomfortable in small spaces. But here I just said to myself, "Get on this sucker like you're totally okay with it." The cool thing was, I felt fine and not the least bit anxious.

When we were leaving the hotel, Madison said, "Mom, you would not have liked those elevators. They zoomed so fast."

"What do you mean? I rode those elevators constantly." This was shocking to my crew and to me.

Where was my definite fear of elevators? Not to mention, where was my fear of flying? I was feeling awesome about my newfound fearlessness. But there was no time to pat myself on the back. I needed to get to the bike shop to pick up my wheels for the race and get my bike into transition by 2:45 pm. The person at the front desk suggested I use an app for my rides. Did you ever notice that when people say, "It's so easy, it will take about 2 minutes to install," it actually requires seventeen passwords, two photo identifications, a birth certificate, and a recent photo of fifteen of your nearest relatives. While I am struggling to install this "simple" app, sand is slipping through the hourglass, and I have no bike to show for my efforts.

I was wishing I just had a car to go pick up my bike at random location A and drop it off at completely unknown location B. Suddenly, my brain, going on three and a half hours of sleep, kicked in. I do have a car, a rental car, that we upgraded to an SUV at the last second. I did this on a whim and realized later that it would be perfect for hauling my rented bike around town.

With this information, I jumped up, got to my car, and headed to the bike shop. I passed Baltic Avenue and Atlantic Avenue on the way to Ventnor Street. Convinced I was in a real-life Monopoly Game, I hoped I would not land on 'Go to Jail'. I took a right on Ventnor as I passed Park Place and Treasure Chest. Seriously, my faith in this bike shop hit an all-time low. There was a door, and it said the name of the shop above it. I was expecting a Target size store. This mom-and-pop bike shop had about five bikes sitting outside. They were all beach cruising bikes with big baskets up front. I thought, great, I will be the laughingstock when I cruise up to transition on this contraption next to all the twelve-thousand-dollar carbon bikes.

When I walked inside, I told them my name and that I was there for my bike for the triathlon, hoping against hope that my bike would weigh less than two hundred and fifty pounds. To my surprise, Jordan, a lovely woman working there, marched directly to a great bike. She tore the paper with my name on it from the cross bar and said, "Go for a ride and see what you think. We can make any adjustments you like."

I was stunned; this bike was better than any bike I had ever thought of owning. It looked beautiful and was spotless. The gears shifted like butter; there was no clanging or chains falling off in the middle of my ride. I rode around the block back into the bike shop's workroom. I saw a man with hands covered in black grease working on a bike. He asked me, "How did you like the bike?"

"It's amazing. I love it! Best bike I have ever ridden," I gushed.

"I completely took it apart and rebuilt it. It's like a brand-new bike."

I thanked him profusely for his great work and loaded the beauty into the car to head to Bader Field. I stopped in at WAWA just across the street to grab a Gatorade for race day. I had learned about WAWA hours earlier; it is the QuikTrip of New Jersey. With my liquid fuel in hand, I ran back to the car. On the way back, the guys from the bike store saw me and said, "You don't have to run."

But in my mind, I was minutes away from the transition area closing behind a huge iron gate with my bike just outside, too late, and no race for me. I could not let that happen. Time was of the essence. I set my GPS for Bader Field and found it quickly, only running one red light on the way. Before you judge, in Monopoly land, there is a light at every corner, and if you hit one red, you will be on the timer to hit all of them. I could not afford to be a completely law-abiding citizen, but I did look both ways. I parked and jumped out of my car with my bike and wetsuit because after packet pickup and bike check-in, there was an inviting 'swim familiarization' in the frigid waters off the Atlantic.

At this point, I was lost. There was a sea of athletes, bikes, vendors, arrows, lines, stickers, and wrist bands to navigate. Once in the transition area the rows were designated by gender and age group. I have never seen so many bikes in one place in my life. I likened it to a baseball field covered in bikes. I finally found the spot to rack my forty-dollar-a-day 'rebuilt' rental bike, and I was right next to a woman with a twelve-thousand-dollar rolling machine. I had to remind myself that I am here to have *my* best race. Not to impress or dominate externally, but to conquer the parts of myself that stand in my way.

Next, it was time to head over to the dreaded murky water. I pulled on my wetsuit with the ease of patting down a cactus. It's supposed to fit tight, but at this point, I was not sure I could breathe, and it was extremely snug around the neck. This only caused me anxiety about not being able to breathe before getting in the water. For this practice swim, athletes entered the water at any time between three and four pm I prepared for the shockingly cold temperatures and found that it was not extreme. There was a 350-meter loop set up for us to follow. I noticed a man next to me treading water. Was he nervous like I was?

I put my face in the cold water and started swimming. I could not get into a groove and was berating myself for it the entire way. At the 'swim out' ramp I saw that man I had seen in the beginning of my swim. To get a feel for my own time, I asked him, "What was your time?" He responded, "I don't know but I have been around twice." With his response, he singlehandedly extracted my confidence.

Great. In the time it took me to go around once, he'd done two laps. I kept walking up the ramp out of the water and noticed a man next to me. He had only one arm and instantly gained my respect.

My perspective shifted. I was grateful to be there. I was unhappy with my swim, so I decided to do something about it and get back into the water. I turned to go back down into the churning waters.

I swam in a calm and assured way. Where was that stroke five minutes ago? Where was this totally chill human? Here, with the pressure off, I was swimming as I always do. Then I saw many swimmers without wetsuits, so I tried that and again swam normally. Why couldn't I swim like that in a race? I left with mixed feelings. I was reassured that I knew how I wanted to swim and that I had succeeded in it for a few minutes. Then the thought dogged me that I wouldn't be able to do that race morning. This annoyed me.

I called my sponsor, Diane, and told her my dilemma. She said, "What about God? You need to talk to God. You are there for a reason. Just say, 'God, you have brought me here with the ability to do this, so please help me do it.' It's incredible you are there. You are making memories with your kids that will last forever; it's special. I know you want to be perfect because that's the way we want to be. But it just doesn't go that way all the time. I ask God to help me use my abilities, and then it goes as it goes. Okay, honey?"

This helped me tremendously. I still felt frustrated and insecure. I was upset with myself; I get paid to help people through these sorts of feelings. I help them to stay calm and perform their best under pressure, but I could not do it for myself. I was humbled as I realized I am asking my patients to do hard things. I'm so proud of them for their courage. I called my husband, Jeff. Maybe he would see the solution I was missing. He told me, "You got all the kinks out today. You will swim well tomorrow."

"That won't work for me. Whenever I get into the open water races, my swim falls apart. So my brain is telling me that is the way it's going to be."

"Just because it did today, does not mean it will tomorrow. Just go in with confidence that you will do it better tomorrow. Where is your confidence? You can do this," he encouraged.

Suddenly, I saw the error in my thinking. I started to believe that because it had always been a certain way, it would always be that way. That is all or nothing thinking. It's black and white, always or never. These distortions are rarely true. I started thinking that tomorrow could be totally different. I envisioned what I wanted for the swim. Most importantly, I prayed a rosary as a meditation to slow down my mind. It worked so well I decided to pray another one and fell asleep after two Hail Marys.

I awoke at 5:00 am to head over to the race. As I drove into the parking area of Bader Field, I was struck by all the little things that needed to come into place along the way for me to be where I was. Each step led me here. I took in the clear, crisp morning air. The sky was particularly beautiful with the sun shining and a few perfectly drawn clouds. I made it through all the plane tickets, boarding passes, hotel reservations, rental cars, bike rentals, wet suit squeeze-ins, elevators, planes, fears, doubts, and uncertainties. I stood in awe, thinking of each person and their amazing stories that brought us all together today for one amazing event.

Thank you God. I love you.

There was a short time for me to get everything situated by my bike, so I hustled over to the transition area. Athletes were placing their towels, folded small to fit tightly into the space, and setting out race equipment. I placed my towel down and added my helmet for the bike, shoes for running and biking, race belt with number, sunglasses, hat, and water bottle. After checking and double-checking, I walked away from the area to slide into my wetsuit and surrender my belongings to the baggage area. It didn't exactly feel like I would ever see my personal belongings again, as my bag was placed in a huge garbage bag and loaded into an unmarked truck. I needed to let that go. I slathered Vaseline on my feet and ankles for maximum slipperiness and carefully pulled my wetsuit on inch by inch. Next, I headed over to the staging area for the swim. Every swimmer I watched enter the water looked fantastic and fearless. But when I spoke to those who were waiting to get into the water, it was another story.

Many talked about their fears, their panic attacks, and their feelings of breathlessness. I related to all of them, and here we stood about to get into the very waters that plagued us before. I had not seen my family yet. Maybe there was some sort of hitch in transportation? There were hundreds of people there, maybe they just could not find me. I told myself, "It's okay if they don't make it to the start." Pulling me out of my head was a voice calling, "Mom, Mom!"

It was Will, and next to him were Alaina and Madison. My heart leapt with joy upon seeing their faces. I got to hug them tight and said, "I love you," to each of them. Will, often quiet, was outspoken and supportive. "You got this, Mom. You are going to do great!" Our fun reunion came to a halt as the 'lilac swim caps' were called to prepare to enter the water.

The announcer stated the distances of all the legs of the race and said, "Twelve miles on the bike." I thought it was ten, so my mind went into a mini frenzy to adjust my race plan. Again, there was nothing I could do about that now. As my age group bunched close, most were high-fiving and cheering. I was quiet. Did they not know what they were about to do? I knew the mountain ahead, and my face was serious. I would smile at the end.

The woman next to me said, "I love this age group."

"Why?" I asked.

"Because it's not competitive like I hear in other groups. We are all just confident," she explained.

I was feeling far from confident and blurted out, "Confident? I don't know that I feel confident now."

"Well, we are all nervous. That's not what I mean; we are confident in who we are as women, so we can be supportive of each other. I love that," she expounded.

This was true. Every other woman in this group that I spoke with gave me a "you got this" or "good luck out there." One friend of mine, Sarah, said, "Listen, we are just going to get through this any way we can. This is such a small percentage of the population. No one even does this, so do it anyway; you can get it done. We are blessed to be here." Sarah is so uplifting. She brought me the truth that I could stand upon. As we moved down to the edge of the water, I watched everyone dive in confidently. I prayed.

God, you have brought me here with my abilities. Thank you. Please help me be an example for someone or inspire someone. Thank you for being with me.

I felt a voice directing me, "Do what they do."

With that, I followed them to swim to the start. We were to swim out to the middle of the water, about 100 meters to some orange buoys, and tread water until we heard the horn to start. I thought this was incredibly ungracious; it turned our 750 meters into 850 meters and treading. Can't we just call it the start when we start swimming? I conceded to my perceived punishment and swam out. I was feeling good and didn't even mind the treading. The current was pushing us forward, so the announcer asked us to swim back to the line. The motivation to swim in any other direction than the swim exit was tough to muster. We all backed up a couple of strokes to appease him. Then the horn sounded, and we were off.

I was swimming well. In fact, I started to have fun, and when I looked up, I was close to the first of the six buoys we needed to pass. I looked at my watch and realized I was going fast. I swam on.

Then I lost it. After a few women swam over me and I swallowed mouthfuls of salt water I was less optimistic. The waves were bigger today, and the buoys seemed far apart. When I swam, I kept hitting a swimmer near me. I decided to swim breaststroke and realized that would take me forever. If I wanted to get out of this swirling sea, I needed to go fast, and that meant freestyle. I stopped a couple of times to ask the lifeguards on their paddle boards the way to go. I was past the halfway mark and pushed myself to get to the 'swim out' arch as quickly as possible. I was so relieved to touch my feet down on the ramp. I ran to the transition.

I peeled off my soaking wetsuit, strapped on my helmet, tied my shoes, and headed out on the bike course. I expected the bike segment to be easy-peasy. I was surprised by the effort I needed to exert as my bike was buffeted by strong winds coming off the Atlantic. Keeping steady was a job. The course took us to an on-ramp to one lane of the Atlantic City freeway. We biked a few exits down, then biked around and turned back on the corresponding on-ramp to return to Bader.

On a twelve-mile bike ride, there was plenty of time to think, reflect, and pray. The course mapped a gorgeous ride beside the ocean, with lush areas of untouched waters and foliage.

Thank you, God, for all this beauty. Thank you that I am here. Thank you for the incredible gift of my health that has brought me here. I can still hear the voice of authority, my physician telling my mom, 'She may never walk again, and definitely not run.' Yet here I am, a miracle of the healing power of the Great Physician. I want people to know that they are stronger than their diagnosis. They can blast through a bad prognosis. They can refuse to accept the voice of an authority figure telling them it's over. As a fifteen-year-old in a wheelchair, being in any race, much less a triathlon, was way beyond my dreams. I was reminded of the verse that says, "God can do exceedingly beyond all that we think, hope, or imagine."

Just after I passed the police cars at the turnaround, I heard a siren blaring that almost startled me off my bike. As the sounds grew closer, I thought, What did I do? I soon realized that it was an ambulance. Was I in the way? I was unsure of what to do, so I followed the bike in front of me off the highway and onto the shoulder. The ambulance sped by, followed by another, and more emergency personnel continued. I realized that someone must have passed out or something. I started praying Hail Marys for the person's safety.

Please, God, make them okay.

Thoughts rolled through my mind of all the dangers of the sport: dehydration, heat exhaustion, panic, mechanical malfunction, distraction, high speed, low blood sugar, equipment failure, the list could go on. I kept pedaling and saw the destination of the multiple emergency vehicles. I saw a young man sitting on a protrusion near the highway. I was relieved, he looked shocked but was upright. The man in front of me put on his brakes, looked over, and kept biking. Then he turned back to go to the scene. I thought that guy was awesome. He's giving up his ride, his precious personal best time to turn around and check on this guy. He's my hero. I debated with myself about what to do. I knew, at that point, that there was an army of trained EMTs at the scene. Although I am a doctor, they really don't need my two cents, and the guy may have just needed some IV fluids.

Knowing that I was not essential personnel on this one, I thought of my family waiting at the finish line and our impending date with a plane home, so I biked on. I returned to Bader and racked my bike. Then it was off to the 5K run. I had not anticipated making it this far. I had not even looked at the race map of the course and had no idea where I was going. Luckily, I saw some runners headed back, and I asked if it was an out-and-back course. "No, just straight out all the way to the finish!" one man yelled.

This kept it simple, and I was running at a good pace. Soon, I arrived at the boardwalk in Atlantic City. I love running alongside the ocean; few things are as breathtaking and exhilarating. It's my happy place, and it's the part of the race where I excel. Thank God I have one. Now it was my turn to encourage all those who had succumbed to walking the rest of the way. I started yelling out, "You are doing great! Push through this! You can do this. Let's go!" Soon, I was exiting the boardwalk onto an incredible blue surface that was attached securely to the sand. It made the run easier than just running on the soft sand. The beauty was heightened. The run was more challenging than anticipated, but I could taste that the end was near, so I kept forging forward. The course ran along the ocean and out and around the pier, and then looped back. I saw women in their seventies walking. I was amazed that they were on the course at all and looking fantastic.

One man had a black compression sock on his left calf. I ran beside him for a while as he told me, "My calf just froze up. It's killing me and did you see the ambulances on the bike course? I was right behind the guy."

"Really, what happened?"

"He shouted, 'On your left' to pass someone, but he was looking down at his GPS and not ahead. He crashed right into an orange pole and flew out onto the highway traffic."

"No way, that is awful!"

"Yep, his face hit the pavement, and it was gone. He immediately went into a coma. For me, I was so shaken up. My race was over."

"That is just terrible. I am so sorry to hear that."

Our conversation closed as I surged ahead, leaving him with a word of encouragement.

I'm so blessed and lucky to have made it this far. There are pitfalls all along the way. That is why they call it 'the agony of defeat.' I am here knowing that it is a gift from God to even be running at all. I biked safely, not on my own strength but by God's grace.

I made the turn around and knew every step was taking me closer to the finish line. I was in the lane to the finish. Beside me was the lane with runners still heading out to the turn. I encouraged them, which only pushed me to go faster. I was excited to see my family at the finish and imagined our victorious embrace. I ran faster and faster, yet I did not see them at the finish line. Again, I pushed back disappointment and told myself anything could have happened. I will find them soon, and with that, I sprinted over the line. Relieved, I kept moving, and a woman from the Air Force, Special Warfare Division, pulled a cold towel out of a huge bath of frigid water and placed it around my neck. Our eyes locked with mutual respect and admiration. I wanted to let her know that she was a fantastic woman who, being in the military, had to overcome some serious obstacles. I wanted to thank her for her service, but in the flood of emotions, no words came out. The look we exchanged would have to suffice.

Next, a heavy medal on a thick ribbon was placed around my neck. Someone handed me a bottle of cold water, and another took my timing chip from my ankle. I went to the nutrition tent and wondered why I had not seen my crew. As I exited the tent, I realized that, obviously, it was blocked off for athletes only. As I continued following the path away from the finish line frenzy, I was greeted by my family with cheers and hugs. My son Will said, "I am so proud of you." Alaina echoed the chorus. I am not sure what Madison said, but she was buzzing around happily. We took loads of photos and parted ways again as I went back to retrieve my bike and possibly my belongings as well.

The people who attend these events with loved ones are called sherpas. Sherpas are Tibetan people living in Nepal, and they are known for the crucial role they play in supporting those attempting particularly difficult treks. Will, Madison, and Alaina were my sherpas, providing their support and asking nothing in return. They came all this way to see me for five minutes at the start and for me not to even spot them as I finished. They are precious, and I am forever grateful.

As I spoke with other athletes on the buses back to Bader Field, they consistently talked about the high winds on the bike course. It was a fight to stay on, pedal fast, and stay locked in mentally. This type of race is a physical challenge on the surface, but the mental stress cannot be underestimated.

Reflecting, I realized that I did not believe I would be able to complete this race. That Unbelief snapped at my ankles and tried to pull me under the waters several times. Each time I attempted to pull away from his razor-sharp teeth they dug in further. Finally, I successfully pried his jaws back and extracted myself from his bone-crushing grip. Still, he followed closely, nipping, so I tucked him into an urn and carefully carried him on my ride and into the run. Every person I talked to believed in me; it was I who lacked belief. Although my 'sponge' was filled with the waters of faith, I could not squeeze out the drops of belief that would quench my thirst. As I crossed that finish line the urn of Unbelief toppled from my grip. It seemed to spin as it landed on its side, smashing into tiny shards. It stopped me in my tracks, and I stood silent and stared. What to do? Unbelief was gone, destroyed beyond repair. I refused to carry him any further and abandoned him there, dying on the pavement. I now welcomed my new ally, Belief. We victoriously walked away arm in arm into the bright sunshine of the boardwalk.

"There is only one corner of the universe you can be certain of improving, and that's your own self." Aldous Huxley

"The greatest explorer on this earth never takes voyages as long as those of the man who descends to the depth of his heart." Julien Green

"'If you can'?" said Jesus. 'Everything is possible for one who believes.' Immediately, the boy's father exclaimed, 'I do believe; help me overcome my unbelief!'"(Mark 9: 23-24 NIV)

CHEERS

RAINING FOR A TRIATHLON involves discipline in physical training, strict nutrition, and mental visualization. Between training sessions, muscles must be rolled, iced, stretched, and compressed. Treats are a distant memory. An easy two-mile run seems like a fantasy.

Knowing it was all behind me was part of the joy of crossing the finish line. After completing the National Triathlon Championships in Atlantic City, I walked along the boardwalk in amazement. I was still determining where I might pick up my belongings or get a bus back to pick up my bike. I floated along into another athlete as I asked, "Are you walking back or taking the shuttle?"

In a lovely South African accent, she answered, "Well, the walk is twenty minutes. Are you up for that?"

"I'm not exactly looking for a twenty-minute walk at this point," I replied.

We both smiled, and Stasia introduced herself, saying, "The shuttle appears to be right over there. Brilliant, I'm going to hop on."

I needed to pick up my belongings from the baggage tent. After I grabbed them, I decided to run for that shuttle. Walking back was looking less and less appealing. I was just in time to grab a seat, conveniently right across from Stasia. We started chatting again about many things. She was quite fascinating and had lived in South Africa, then Russia, and now in Chicago. When we got off the bus, she said "Cheers" to the driver.

"That's so great, I love cheers."

"Yes, in South Africa, we say, 'cheers' instead of 'thank you'. Then, instead of you're welcome, we say, 'pleasure,' she explained.

"Oh, I love that, pleasure! I am going to start using that."

We walked back to the transition area to get our bikes with this monster accomplishment behind us. We happened to be in the same age group, so our bikes were parked close together. The once bustling area filled with bikes, helmets, wetsuits, running shoes, and hopeful athletes was now a ghost town of abandoned visors, t-shirts, and water bottles. We shared a little celebration of "We just finished the National Triathlon!" with a few whoops and woo-hoos. Then we went to grab our bikes off the racks.

Stasia commented, "Now we can do whatever we want! We did it! A big bag of peanut M&Ms has my name on it."

"I was thinking more like a bag of diamonds," I smiled.

We laughed. Then I thought, I don't need any reward. The experience was its own reward. Meeting so many great female athletes from South Africa, Florida, Colorado, and more was a blast. Swimming with that positive group was priceless. The freedom and space of the bike trail provided miles of time to spend with God. The glorious run along the ocean was breathtaking. All the athletes were pure inspiration. I honestly did not need a bag of M&Ms or diamonds. I packed my bag with memories, accomplishments, growth, belief, and an abiding love for my crew.

Peace and a deep sense of gratitude washed over me. I returned home feeling everything was different, but I was changed. Everything seemed so easy, which was a welcome shift in my perspective. My life was not an intercostal waterway; it was the same block I had lived on for nineteen years. It's my comfort zone, and I'm happy I stepped out of it.

"It's good to go, and it's good to come home." Dad

"We cannot become what we want to be by remaining what we are." Max DePree

"Let us with confidence draw near to the throne of grace." (Hebrews 4:16, NIV)

OLYMPIC-SIZED LUCK

HAVE YOU ever seen the stories they show during the Olympics that feature an athlete as a child looking up to a certain sports giant? Then, as in a fairy tale, they are taking the podium in that very same event. In the 2024 Paris Olympics, Michael Phelps placed a gold medal around Léon Marchand's neck. Marchand just broke Phelps› world record in the 400-meter individual medley. How amazing would that be, to have the most decorated Olympian of all time crown you with your gold? Not to mention that each medal contained a piece of the original Eiffel Tower in it.

The most surreal person for me to meet would be David Goggins. He reigns in the world of ultra-athletes as Michael Phelps does in swimming. Goggins has taken his unrelenting strength and turned it into millions for himself and his philanthropic causes. The big publishing houses said they did not want his book and questioned him, "Who wants to read a book about a fat black man becoming a Navy SEAL?" Goggins proceeded to self-publish his book, *You Can't Hurt Me*, to the tune of seven million copies sold worldwide. It's his second book, *Never Finished*, that has left an indelible mark on me. I understand his feeling of not fitting in and finally being okay with that. His message of "I just needed to be me. This is what God planned for me" resonates wholeheartedly in my soul.

Last summer, I relied on Goggins' book. David's peals of inspiration rang in my ears as I trained for my triathlons. I would listen over and over to the chapters that filled me with courage. I related to David in many ways: how family members can divergently view the same exact situation. I never quit. The bar is ever rising for me and those I love. I am grateful, while I look ahead to the next rung on the ladder.

I always felt different, and, as a teen, that meant being alone. It was too difficult for me to bear, so I watched the popular kids and followed suit. I needed them to validate me. I was a chameleon, turning into whatever I thought they wanted. That left me exactly zero minutes to be me. Now, I am secure alone or with people. I don't drink and have not had a drink in twenty-nine years. My scene and my posse are God, family, and myself. A massive chunk of being me includes caring for others and serving them.

In medical school, there was an excellent doctor and teacher. He was in the field of psychiatry and took athletes and students under his wing. He died tragically, and at his funeral, the priest said, "Who would do this? Who would go into the depths of people's problems? Who would journey beside them in the darkness of their minds? Who cares to do this work?" I thought to myself, I do.

For many years, I prayed, "God, help me be your servant today. When I want my way, remind me to serve. Help me be a servant like you."

I wanted to be like David in the Bible. He is referred to as "A man after God's own heart." I thought that was the highest compliment a person could hope to receive. I wanted to be a person after God's own heart as well. Goggins appears to be on this path as well; he takes five months out of the year to parachute out of planes, rescuing people. He could easily sit back on his yacht, sip cool drinks, and enjoy his wealth. Alternatively, he could go on a speaking tour and make millions. However, he takes these five months every year to continue to give back and provide on-the-job mentoring to his rescue team. He studies to become the best Emergency Medical Services-trained rescuer ever.

The key to his passion? He wants to be the best at whatever he does. I want that too, but it's a big ask. If you want to be the best, you have got to be willing to do the things that other people might not do. You must sleep less, go out to dinner less, visit friends and family less, and buckle down. For me, I cannot be my best if I am overly concerned about what you think. I also need to be vulnerable and transparent if I am to help others. When you see how flawed I have been, and I openly share it, I hope it frees you.

I share my alcoholism so that you might look your addiction in the eye and smash it. I desired that drink, but I thank God I needed to stay alive more. I wanted your love and approval, but I needed God's and my own more. I wanted to listen to all your views and agree. I needed to learn my views and stand firm. I wanted to look like you and act like you. I needed to look like me and take the actions God has for me. I wanted to be everything for you, but this left nothing for me. I wanted to take care of you, but I needed to take care of myself. More times than I can count, I wanted to quit, but I needed to carry on. I dove back into the dark waters that daunted me. I stayed in them until I could move as freely in that water as on solid ground. I have discarded the world of secure paychecks and positive quarterly reviews for God's review.

I follow the path where it leads me. Just before Dad died, he shared with me a cassette tape. It contained a study on Psalm 91, beginning, "The Lord is my Shepherd, I shall not want." Later it says, "Yea, though I walk through the shadow of the valley of death I will fear no evil." The instructor pointed out, "It does not say, 'You can just relax, I'll be there to take you around all the hard stuff.'" However, the Psalmist continues, *when*, not *if*, we go through the 'valley of death,' we don't need to be afraid because God is with us.

First, doesn't the 'valley of the shadow of death' sound inviting? Then it tells us we are going there, for sure, on our little tour of life. The fact is that God will be with us to guide us.

Why do we need to go through suffering? Suffering has given my life meaning and purpose. It has forced me to grow spiritually, mentally, and physically in ways I would never have approached from the comfort of a soft fluffy pillow. From it I have learned and grown. According to Soren Kierkegaard, we need suffering for our spiritual and mental growth. These experiences can give our lives more profound meaning. He indicates that in the wake of our angst and despair, we develop meaningful relationships. We strive for "achievements in a well-lived life."

If you could get a doctorate in suffering, David Goggins would have a PhD. This is a massive part of why I have chosen to be a student of his life. With all the physical abuse with a belt buckle that he suffered as a kid, he does not have a victim bone in his body. He doesn't feel sorry for himself or anyone else. He uses all the horrible parts of his past as fuel for good. This is precisely what I am doing with my writing. I want to take all the dark moments of my life and demonstrate how I used them for good. I faced my trauma and its collateral damage. As I grew spiritually, I traded my defects for assets. I hope this frees you to take a fearless look at yourself and become who God created you to be.

You truly can change, but not while carrying a hefty load of self-pity, self-doubt, negativity, addictions, people- pleasing, mean, angry, king- baby attitudes. I want you to let all that go and soar. Trust me when I say that from where I came from, I am the least likely person to get sober, grow strong, be positive, live a healthy lifestyle, be responsible, serve others, and strive to better myself daily.

However, here I am doing it. Today, I was the kid with the Olympic dream meeting my inspiration, David Goggins. I could not believe he was greeted with a smattering of polite claps. It was an honor to be in the room and hear his story in person. As the interview was completed, I immediately jumped out of my chair to give him an ovation. I did not shyly look around the room to see what everyone else would do. David looked over and said, "Thank you," and waved. Although he was walking away, I saw a few kids run up to him. He signed an autograph, grabbed a photo with the kids, and said, "I am sorry, I can't" to everyone else.

Goggins' last act of generosity before walking away was to take a photo with me. I was overjoyed because I wanted to have a record of meeting this physical, mental, and spiritual giant who has taught me valuable lessons. It felt surreal to shake hands with the actual, in-the-flesh David Goggins. I thanked Goggins for inspiring me on my journey. I thanked God for my day. I thanked Him for the insane luck and perfect timing that made all of this happen. Am I blessed? For sure. It is with my whole heart that I say, "Goodnight, world, sleep tight. Dream great dreams and make them come true."

"Even the struggling, suffering religious believer is on the right path; his or her sufferings in fact indicates that he or she is on the right path." J. Watkin

"The struggle you're in today is developing the strength you need for tomorrow." Robert Tew

"Cast all your anxiety on him because he cares for you." (1 Peter 5:7 NIV)

Cows

5:42 AM ON A SATURDAY, that's what time my alarm roused me from my slumber. *Why is this beeping so early?* I was running a half marathon with my son, Nicholas, and we needed to travel to the race location. As I forced myself out of bed and dressed, I noticed my hands were shaking.

Gosh dang it! Why am I nervous? This is so ridiculous! I admonished myself. I've run half marathons before. I've done triathlons in the churning waters of the Atlantic. What was I afraid of? I was going to be on *land* the entire time. But fear is not rational, and it was having its way with me. I was scared and nervous. When I feel this way, I must admit it to myself first. The more I push it away, the stronger it holds on, so I needed to calmly acknowledge what was happening in my body. Then I needed to tell on myself. I told Nick, "I'm all nervous for this run."

Instead of telling me, "Don't be nervous," which is sure to make me feel shame about being nervous, and then I have another layer to work through, Nick did the best thing: he made me laugh. I felt lighter as we journeyed out to the race location. However, as

I approached the start, I determined I was an absolute impostor. I had no right to be there. Everyone else *looked* like a runner. The women wore tiny running shorts and tank tops. One woman had on a tank top that said, "BEEF." Her calf muscles bulged, and her skin was golden tan. Her EarPods were in place. Now, she was a 'real' runner ready to go.

I felt like the Velveteen Rabbit when he meets the 'real' rabbits in the briar. They have hind legs and ears that twitch. The Velveteen knows right there he's only a fraction of a living, breathing rabbit. It was the same for me. These were living, breathing, tough runners who took on the fifty-degree weather with bold shorts while I donned a long-sleeved shirt and a sweatshirt. I also wore my compression running leggings and track pants layered over the top. I didn't look like these scantily dressed Greek goddesses. I was an overdressed pseudo-runner. I didn't even have the right earbuds for my music.

"Mom!"

Nick's voice called me out of my insecurity rant and back to reality. "Mom, come on up here."

Nicholas lined up with a pacer. Pacers carry signs saying how long it will take them to complete the entire 13.1 miles. Then runners can stay with that person to run consistently to finish in that total amount of time.

Nicholas was with the 2:10 pacer. "Mom, you can do this. You're good," he encouraged as he put his arm around me and pulled me in close for a squeeze of support. I talked to myself, *Quit playing small. You have been running for forty years and have every right to be up here.* "And we will start in ten, nine.." The announcer's words boomed through the crowd.

The next thing I knew, the countdown was complete, and we ran. Nick further cheered me on, "Remember, Mom, the first mile is the worst."

This is a little something I taught *him* about seven years ago. We were running our first longer race together—a 10K race in downtown Kansas City, Missouri. As we approached the start, Nick had a panic attack. He said, "Mom, forget it. I am not doing this. I will see you at the finish."

I responded with all my coaching tricks. I told him, "I can't do that. I won't be able to do it without you. I need you to run with me." I thought maybe the old "I need you" would speak to his servant heart.

"No, Mom, you don't, you can run this without me, no problem."

Then I tried to get him out of his head by talking to other runners. I started introducing him to some younger runners near us. I found a puppy for him to pet. I was desperate to help him get out of his head and into his feet. As the race started, he stood beside me, and we began jogging. Nick worked out all the kinks in the first mile and raced well. He finished before me. Nick also had a similar experience the last time we ran this half marathon.

But not this time. This time, he was more than prepared mentally and physically. He was no longer a scared ten-year-old. He was a confident, strong, physically fit athlete of seventeen. Nick knew his mind and body were ready for the task, and it showed.

Nick quickly pulled ahead of me, and gradually his turquoise t-shirt became a small dot that disappeared over the horizon. Now I was on my own. I'm no stranger to running races alone. I comforted myself, *I'm good, I'm okay.* Nick has been running ten to fourteen miles regularly. I was sick this past week, and I spent three days in the hospital with my son and missed my final week of training. But no excuses. I planned to show up and do my best because I committed Nick to do this.

I love this particular race, called Running With The Cows. It's in a beautiful small town of green fields and farms. Everyone who lives there also volunteers, and they are so welcoming. There are signs every mile, and enough water stations to hydrate a small nation. These people are not going to let you hurt. They stand out there holding cups of Gatorade and water. Sometimes they also offer fruit snacks and energy goo. They bring their cattle to the edges of the fields so everyone can enjoy seeing them. There is constant cheering and the ringing of cowbells along the course. Not to mention the best home-cooked buffet immediately following the race, complete with tables full of homemade desserts. It's worth running for.

Mile one came quickly. *Great, only 12.1 more to go,* I told myself. Miles two, three, four, five, and six passed uneventfully. My pace slowed a bit on seven and eight. Then, at eleven and twelve, I realized this was a mental game. My mind was saying: *You can't do this. You can't run this far. This is not what you usually do. How do you know you can even do this? You have done it before, but not today, not with illness and exhaustion. I don't think today is a good day for this...*

Right then, I knew the challenge was not physical. The activity could not be any simpler. It's step, step, step, step. Running is so basic; it is almost comical. So, what's the hard part? The mental game. Mentally keeping yourself in the race when it feels overwhelmingly arduous is the challenge. When these feelings kick in, I immediately start encouraging every single runner I see. I mean it. I will say, "Good job, stay strong, hang in there, you look great," anything to prod them on. It looks like I am doing something for *them,* but anyone will tell you that the one doing the talking benefits the most. I cannot entertain decelerating when telling everyone else they can do it.

Throughout the race, I pushed myself and return to my pace if I noticed I was slowing. Then, I noticed I was not returning to baseline pace from mile eleven to twelve. When I tried to go faster, my body betrayed me and refused. My thoughts drifted to: *These are really the wrong shoes. I need better shoes. There are too many uphill climbs on this course. There is not enough shade. I want a triathlon where I can swim and bike, not all this endless running, running, and running.*

I Knew this was all thought trash that I needed to throw out. I recalled a client of mine, Alex. He's an extremely gifted Pro-Am golfer. When we started working together, he was having troubles with his golf game. I asked, "What is the hardest thing about golf?"

"Hands down, putting," he instantly replied.

I said, "Oh, putting, I love putting," with sincere enthusiasm.

We came up with a plan. Alex was to say at least five times a day, "Putting is easy." Whenever his mind wandered to all the difficulties with putting, he repeated, "Putting is easy." This message activated a part of his brain called the reticular activating system, or RAS. You can think of this part of your brain like a net around it that only lets certain information through. If you noticed every little sound and distraction, you would not be able to function very well. So, your RAS helps edit down to five or six critical pieces of information for your brain to follow. Your name is called out, and the scream of a child in distress will always get a fast pass to your brain. That leaves you with four other pieces of information to focus on simultaneously. The different inputs remain outside your awareness.

Think about it. If you have ever been looking for a specific type of car, and suddenly, everywhere you look, that car starts popping up. You didn't see those before. It's not a coincidence. You train your brain on what information is essential at any given time. When you start looking at that car, researching that car, reading articles about that car, test driving the vehicle, and talking with friends about that car, your RAS says, "Right now, red Range Rovers are very important." It lets all of them into your awareness.

The same thing happened with Alex and his putting. Putting did not magically become easy. However, with this constant input into his RAS, he started noticing subtle nuances in his putting game. He saw the story his brain told him about putting, and he combated the negative messages. Alex hired a putting coach. He purchased a new putter and read books about putting. He read books on trusting his game and the mental fortitude needed to succeed in golf. In a few months, guess what? Putting was easy and has been ever since.

In my case, from mile eleven to the finish line, I started telling myself, "This is easy." The more my mind told me this distance was too long, that I was too sick and too stressed to do this, the more I talked. I started saying aloud, "This is easy. It's all easy from here." It was an out-and-back course. I was traveling back to the finish line, and I told runners going the opposite way, "It's all easy from here. Just get to the turnaround and it's so easy." I was okay with my time at this point. I didn't think I could go any faster. Staying at this pace to the finish would be doable.

In the string of runners heading out to the turn, a person suddenly appeared on the ground. I thought of my New Jersey triathlon when I saw a man crash his bike. At that time, there were multiple emergency vehicles and personnel attending to him. There were also a few lanes of highway traffic going both ways between us. I needed to make a split-second decision. I thought about all the help he was receiving, my family members waiting, our tight schedule to get to Philly to a plane on time, and decided to continue with the race. However, I have felt a couple of pangs of guilt about not stopping to help him. That would be my natural response. I will never know what that choice held. That is the thing about life: in a decisive moment, taking one path necessitates abandoning the other.

When I saw this guy on the ground, I knew I had a choice to make. I immediately told myself, *This is not some highway in New*

Jersey where I have no idea where I am or where I am going. I am on a country road in Kansas. My total run time is not that important. If this guy needs help, I am stopping. NO QUESTION.

I realized he was sitting up and rubbing his ankle as I approached. I shouted, "Are you okay? Do you need help?"

"No, I am good," he said.

I also noticed another man was standing to the side with him. In my quick assessment, this teenage male was in good physical health. He was oriented and responsive. He was in no immediate danger— possibly just a hurting ankle and needing to sit for a few minutes. There was a constant parade of runners and pacers traveling on both sides of the road. If he decided he needed help, there was plenty of opportunity. With a clear conscience, I continued with mile twelve and reached mile thirteen.

There was a long stretch, then a right turn to the finish line. I did not count on a woman sprinting up from behind me at the turn. She looked older than me, and she did not look like a stereotypical runner. I was not about to give up my place in the standings to anyone. Suddenly, I found another gear. I gathered speed and truly gave it my all. She came up beside me for a few steps and passed me to cross the line seconds before me.

It was just obnoxious to stage a little mini race right here at the finish, where everyone is watching. The announcer said, "It's going to be a close one. Here they come!" The chagrin of 'losing' by two seconds in this evil plot was palpable and tasted like a spoonful of dry dirt in my mouth. It was like she planned it all along. She must have been running behind me for some time and just set her sights on me as the target to pass. I cannot stand that. I asked myself why this was so bothersome.

Maybe because Nick stood there watching and cheering, "Go Mom, you got this!" I wanted to beat her for him. I wanted him to see me *win*. For all the times I have experienced the joy of his accomplishments, I wanted him to have the opportunity to feel proud of his mama. And let's face it, I wanted to win for myself; to show I was still a formidable competitor. My pride and ego were injured, and I was having a crybaby tantrum in my head about it. Saying, "That wasn't fair. A race isn't fair if you don't even know you are in one until ten seconds before the finish line."

I walked over to the church on the grounds of the run property and prayed:

Thank you, God, for the great race. Thank you that I finished and felt great the entire way. Thank you. I felt absolutely normal in the end. I didn't fall over in exhaustion or anything like that. Thank you.

Then, I heard a still, small voice in the church's silence. It said, "*You could have gone further. I mean, right now you're not tired. You feel completely normal and healthy. You are not hurting. You could have gone at least two or three more miles, no problem.*" It was a loving voice stating a fact, not a pejorative.

I thought back to my feelings about the finish line. I know one thing for sure: winning looks fun and ecstatic. It's a feel-good reward. But the despair, the regrets, the pain of losing is its own tutorial. Winning elevates and losing humbles. I became teachable in that moment. I went on my discovery phase in the trial of me vs. me for 13.1 miles. I thought of all the times I slowed down to have Gatorade or water. Then there was the audacious quantity of minutes spent taking off my sweatshirt and sweatpants. There were times I slowed to look at the spectacular array of bovine beauties along the course. Worst of all was the time I spent in self-doubt and unbelief.

No, this woman was not the guilty party. I stole this race from myself. I perjured myself. I told myself going into the race: *I'm not going for a specific time. I want to keep running and feel good the entire way. I just want to finish. I have not been feeling well, so it's great that I am out here, no pressure. Have a nice day.*

Now I needed to call myself out on that diatribe. There is nothing in there that is true to who I am. No part of me wants to "just finish." Who really wants a 'nice day'? I want to win or at least be overwhelmingly impressive. The truth was that the woman bested me. Now it's the splinter in my foot ever since. There to remind me with little tinges of pain just when I step down on it in a certain way.

The lesson is so basic that I am embarrassed by its content: Everything and every second counts in sports and life. Just as in a race, time counts, whether you are running your fastest or stopping to tie your shoe. I continue to learn this lesson. With all the information I consistently gather to support the precious nature of time, I still waste it.

God, I am so sorry for wasting the precious gift of time. Please forgive me for all the stupid and senseless ways I waste time. I spent time in addiction, but more so in continuing to search for things that will never satisfy. But, God, how tempting are all the luxuries of the world? How they call to me and speak their lies of true happiness and peace. I know that only in You can those things be found. In searching for You, serving You and others, and loving You to the best of my ability. I'm constantly bombarded with the world and its trappings. I know I do not even have the strength to turn away, save for your grace. Please help me discern the use of the amazing gift of time. Even though I have failed countless times, please continue to give me time and more time. With all my heart, I want to use it wisely. Right now, I believe that means using my gifts to benefit others.

I have peace when I write. How do I know it's Your will for me? Because I feel you here right now with me, beside me, guiding me. It's priceless and beautiful. You gave me all my gifts, please help me use them well. Help me focus on what is essential, on doing Your will. May Thy will not mine be done. I love you. Your daughter, Elisemarie

"The strongest athlete isn't the one who finishes first. That athlete is the fastest. The strongest athlete is the one who gets up again every time he falls, the one who doesn't stop when he feels a pain in his side, the one who doesn't abandon the race, no matter how far away the finish line is. That runner is a winner whenever he reaches the finish line, even if he comes in last. Sometimes, not matter how much you want in, being the fastest isn't an option because your legs aren't as long or your lungs as large. But you can always choose to be the strongest. It is up to you. Your willpower and effort. I'm not going to ask you to be the fastest, but I am going to require you to be the strongest." Antonio Iturbe, The Librarian of Auschwitz

"Therefore, since we are surrounded by such a great cloud of witnesses, let us throw off everything that hinders and the sin that so easily entangles. And let us run with endurance the race that is set before us, looking to Jesus, the founder and perfecter of our faith, who for the joy that was set before him endured the cross, despising the shame, and is seated at the right hand of the throne of God." (Hebrews 12: 1-2)

"God cannot give us happiness and peace apart from Himself, because it is not there. There is no such thing." C.S. Lewis

"I have fought the good fight, I have finished the race, I have kept the faith." (2 Timothy 4: 6-8).

SUNSET IX

GOODBYE CARL

BELIEVE THE people I work with in my counseling practice are God's assignments. I genuinely believe in the work I do with them. The time we spend creates a safe and sacred space for healing. On this day, I had an appointment with an individual I have known for fifteen years. Carl competed in sports with my boys. I knew him as a fierce competitor on the course with a kindness always present about him. Because of a tragedy, and by the grace of God, he ended up in counseling with me, which is a privilege and honor.

I want to thank all the parents who sent their kids to me for counseling. Kudos to these great parents who know their children need help. My hat is off to those adolescents and young adults who come so willingly and openheartedly and share with me. Carl is no exception. I work with many elite athletes on the mental, spiritual, and physical aspects of their sport. Carl is one of the most talented athletes with whom I've worked. He is also driven, intelligent, personable, and considerate.

At age 22, he suffered an unthinkable tragedy, and that is how our paths crossed. I am forever better for my time with Carl. In my work, I ask God to use me as a channel for healing. I began praying for Carl long before he came to see me. I hope, pray, and believe I have contributed to his well-being. By the look on his face, God has likely allowed such a miracle to occur.

At the beginning of our work together, Carl would come in looking sullen and depressed. He did not crack a smile, and he shared how incredibly sad he was about the loss of his best friend. As the weeks went by, I saw a transformation occur. After a few weeks had passed, Carl came in with energy and a smile. He talked about hopeful things, which made me feel good because he was thinking about the future and possibilities.

Today was my last meeting with Carl for a while. At the end of the week, he leaves to begin a graduate program. He is highly qualified, and I'm sure he will excel in his work. He has plans to succeed in business and life. I was utterly riveted by what he told me in our last session. I have never heard anyone speak about addiction with such clarity and eloquence. Carl also knows first-hand the severity and depth of the consequences of any action.

I said five sentences during our hour, which is out of character for me. I didn't want to talk. I wanted to give him all the space he needed to get everything off his chest. Carl described his suffering, and I was riveted by his honesty. He grew up suddenly because of the devastation he witnessed and the clamor in his head that told him life would never be good again. Today, I was feverishly writing down his every word. I knew I would want to look back at this treatise on life, addiction, and loss. Carl lost his best friends in a car accident. There was a girl named Annie and his best friend, Sam, who both died.

Carl said, "Annie's mom messaged me today on Instagram."

"What did she say?" I responded.

"She just wanted to talk about the accident and Annie's final moments. I just told her I was not in a place to discuss it. She found out that Annie died when her neck broke in multiple places. I don't want to talk about it. When I do, it makes it all real. The feelings come back, as do the visions and the fear. The weight of it all sets in. It's hard, and it's scary."

"What's scary?" I asked.

"Those vivid images. I feel like I am there again." Carl paused. "When I talked to John this week, he asked, 'So do you think we got the worst end of the stick? We are the ones still here.' I told him, "No, no, man. Are you alive? If you are, you didn't draw the short end.

"When we got in the ambulance, those were the worst moments of my life—sitting there processing it. The finality of death, grasping the weight of it. Those two were dead at 18 and 19 years old. You never think it's going to be you, seeing your friends die in front of you. I watched my best friend die in an accident. I was calling his name, thinking he may still be alive. But there was nothing in him anymore. I knew he was gone, and his spirit had left him. There is so much weight to it.

"There is deeper stuff I don't want to address. Walking away with no proper goodbye sucks. I wish I got to say goodbye to Sam."

"What would you have wanted to say to Sam?" I asked.

Without hesitation, Carl replied, "Thank you, thank you for everything, for being my friend, for standing by me, for believing in me when others didn't." With tears, he added, "I love you, and I hope to see you on the other side." His voice cracked, and he was silent for a moment.

"I don't want to go that deeply into it. I don't want to start smoking weed again. Smoking helped suppress all that. I am in a good place, and I've worked hard to get here. I don't want to run back to it."

"But you're not running back to it. You are getting through this without the pot," I encouraged.

"Pot made it easier, but I had no goals. It wasn't good for me. I associate it with my friends and comfort. People don't understand how real this all is."

"No, they don't," I confirmed.

"They don't get how devastating it can be. It's terrible; it destroys mental stability. They don't understand how suddenly I was in complete darkness. Right there, all the good times ended. I felt a horrific spiral of negative feelings and anger. It's hard to see something that horrible. You don't even think people could witness something like this. I witnessed the mass casualties of my friends.

"My best description is a feeling of deep sorrow and utter despair. I felt, 'This is something that cannot get better.' Destiny has chosen to end the best part of my life. It felt like a sign that good times end, and the uncertainty of the future is now. I got a very big, 'This is the end of your time with these people.' Was part of this sending me a message? What do you think about all of that?"

I took a deep breath and responded, "Well, we have free will. No one forced anyone into the car that day. I can feel better when I look at where I am responsible. What part did I play in this, even if it's minuscule? I need to see it because then I will have some power in the future. I think God gives us free will. He doesn't force the good upon us. He does not force us to choose it. Certain people may have made decisions that day that were not in line with His good and perfect will. I believe that since you are here, you have a responsibility to find what God wants you to do with all of this. You can use it for good in finding your purpose."

"I don't know what my purpose is," Carl admitted.

"That's okay. You don't have to know now," I added.

"I feel this pressure like I cannot fail in life. I just can't, not now," Carl observed.

"What does it mean to you to fail? What would that look like?" I asked.

"I just see all this Gen Z stuff. Everything is failing. Failing means not being able to make it and have a family. I have lived a life of a constant loser, like my destiny was to lose. I want to be a winner. I let it all get out of hand; my running and everything suffered. For the first time, I'm going out on my own. I have nothing from college left because the people are gone. I'll be on my own now. I'm not giving up. I want the confidence that will come from living as an adult." Carl was vehement about this.

"You are already a winner. You have quit doing drugs. Do you know how many people your age possess the insight to do that? Not many, and you are doing it at the hardest time of your life. You may feel like you are doing nothing, but you are staying sober and healing. That's enough," I added.

"No one also understands how difficult it is to give up pot. It's so difficult. No one wants to quit. It's nice getting high all the time. It's nice not having to deal with the B.S. It's so easy, and that's why people don't quit. Things seem easy. I'm not doing anything. I am not getting anything done in life. But it's okay because I'm high. Sometimes, I think I'm still not doing anything anyway, so I might as well be high."

"But you're not smoking pot. I'm so proud of you for quitting. So why are you not smoking?" I questioned.

"I would do it all the time, even when I had shit to do. Then it got bad; life got bad. It started to destroy relationships, and it affected other people. I didn't grow as a person, so that's why. I was living high. It's like a different state of mind. My whole life was about getting high. My single goal was figuring out where and how to get high. I started using people, like hanging out for three hours with someone I don't even like, and just preying on them and waiting for them to smoke. I was hoping they would take it out and offer me some. That's just pot etiquette. You can't just smoke and not offer to share.

"I took advantage of that with multiple people. It's a toxic mindset, always wanting to get high. A day was shitty if I did not get high. There was constant pressure to get high. You feel powerless to it. You must get it. It becomes a need like food or water. Then you know it's an issue. The real needs are food, water, shelter, and companionship. But I began to feel that pot was a necessity. I could not do anything without it. I couldn't function and got restless and irritable until I could get my fix. Without it, I was afraid."

Carl paused and added, "I am scared about the highway. What if these are the last four days of my life because we're going to get in an accident on the way to Duke?"

"What if you are? What would you do? " I queried.

"Spend all my money, go down my bucket list. I would go sky-diving, and that would be fun."

"As we found in our research, the prevalence of fatalities in motor vehicular accidents is 0.010752% over a lifetime, which is minimal. One can only guess that the probability of being in a second accident of this nature is infinitesimally smaller," I added.

"But what do you tell me because I know it can happen?" Carl insisted.

"Yes, you were living invincibly. That is a common belief from the age of fifteen to twenty-five years old. Why do you think car insurance rates are so high at that age? Your mentality was 'nothing bad will ever happen to me.' Now, your brain has this other massive piece of information. It's telling you that terrible things, although rare, do happen. That's the truth. Your brain now has a competing belief. Horrific things can occur, and you have plenty of evidence to support that case.

"I acknowledge I can't control everything, but there are some things I can do to make myself safer. What can I do to make it less dangerous? Drive during the day, wear a seatbelt, drive with sober people, let someone older drive, limit distractions, and obey the speed limit. All these things reduce your chances of being in an accident. Control the factors you can. Know that you can't control everything. That's just the truth."

Carl seemed satisfied with that explanation. He glanced down at his phone to check the time. We had about three minutes left in our session. "With the last few minutes, I just want to thank you for seeing me. You have helped me so much, thank you."

I was moved by his genuine expression of gratitude. "Thank you. I have enjoyed our meetings, too. I am so proud of you for putting down the vape and the pot. That isn't easy, but you are doing it. You are facing the truth. You are already a winner, and I wish you all the best at Duke."

Although fearful, Carl was able to pursue his dream of winning at life. He looked his fear straight in the eye and got in the car anyway to leave for his graduate program. He has my deepest admiration and best wishes.

"You gain strength, courage, and confidence by every experience in which you really stop to look fear in the face. You must do the thing which you think you cannot do." Eleanor Roosevelt

"A man with outward courage dares to die; a man with inner courage dares to live." Lao Tzu

"The Lord is near to the brokenhearted and saves the crushed in spirit." (Psalm 34:18)

Mama Bear's New Year's Day

MOST PEOPLE in the medical field will tell you there are two times a year when you absolutely must not go to the emergency room. Those are New Year's Day and the Fourth of July.

The Fourth of July has the apparent setbacks: fire, alcohol, sunburn, drunk water sports, and dehydration. Couple that with the fact that most medical residency training programs begin on July 1st. By July 4th, these 'green' doctors have exactly three days of 'practicing' medicine. I prefer they practice on someone else. This is reason enough to think twice before lighting a sparkler and handing it off to a nearby toddler. On what other day of the year would we regard fire in the hands of children as sane.

As for New Year's Eve, 5:00 pm on New Year's Eve until 5:00 pm on New Year's Day is a cautionary tale. Even those with the strongest 'white clouds,' a term used for those doctors who always seem protected from heavy workloads, are doomed on this otherwise auspicious night. The shift that brings one year to a close and ushers in the next is marked by chaos. Hospitals commonly fill beyond capacity. The 'lucky' cases are urgently triaged and transported to surgery and other services. But if you find yourself just shy of death's door, you get an all-day pass to the circus also known as the ER waiting room. While under the Big Top, hopes rise as a few patients are called back behind the massive automatic doors that leave plenty of room for a gurney and a gaggle of attending physicians. You may innocently think, "They are going to call me soon" But just then, someone shows up with chest pain or shortness of breath, and you are bumped down another hour.

Why the sudden influx in ER traffic? First, people are beginning to show up in the ER from their germ-filled, people-packed indoor holiday gatherings. Second, every newcomer to partying and drinking seems to believe that December thirty-first is the perfect time to try new recreational drugs. The collateral damage ends up in emergency departments throughout the United States. As a result, the waits are exorbitant, and out of necessity, the care is often perfunctory.

There simply isn't time to dote on sniffles, fevers, aches, strains, and sprains when the stakes are much higher on these two special days. The goal is, as always, to keep everybody alive, or "Don't kill too many people," as one of my medical school attendings liked to say. So, it's triage and move, push them through like cattle being herded to pasture on a dark night. Send them on, like those cattle, into the safe confines of the hospital's fence.' But feeling as alone, confused, and scared as those cows. ER docs are slammed, and the supply of broken bones and hearts seems endless. The lesson here is obvious. If you can hold off for just fifteen hours and see a primary care physician, you are golden.

I was telling Jacob the week before New Year's Eve, "You don't sound very good. I hear you coughing in the night, just hacking. Maybe you should make an appointment at Dr. Smith's office."

Note to self: In my own home, my medical knowledge is completely disregarded. For example, one of my sons had an ear infection, and the more I pushed for him to be seen, the farther away the otoscope got. Finally, when he was seen, they were threatening some fire and wax voodoo procedure as the only hope for the advanced inner ear damage.

Jacob's illness still required a chest x-ray. Since I was fresh out of in-home x-ray machines I resorted to demands disguised as requests for medical attention.

Jacob protested, "I don't need to go to the doctor. Really, I didn't even know that I was hacking last night. I'm feeling better, just my throat, some chills, aches, and sweats, but I feel okay. I'm going to head to the gym."

I can't exactly complain about Jacob minimizing physical discomfort and taking the actions of a healthy person even when ill. This is practically my creed, so I did not argue with him. However, as much as I appreciated the optimism, I wasn't buying the 'feeling better' storyline. I know that New Year's Eve holds particular significance for my son. Not because he likes to party, but, on the contrary, he has been sober since he was sixteen. It's important to him because he pours everything into making the night amazing for a group of newly sober young people.

The preparations begin about two in the afternoon on the thirty-first as they fill a net with hundreds of balloons to drop at the stroke of midnight. There is a spread of food, a bevy of support meetings for teens and their parents, and a host of counselors available for backup. If Jacob was seen by a medical professional, beyond Drs. Mom and Dad, his plans might be curtailed, so he is presenting the 'feeling better' Jacob. The question remained: feeling better than what? A soggy, wet blanket, a half-eaten oyster, a lobster thrown in boiling water?

The night went off well for Jacob and the sober crew. This group has this down to a science, and he finally arrived home, clean and sober, at about 5:00 am.

At 1:00 pm, Jacob casually mentioned, "I think I need to be seen. Is there a good urgent care around here?" This was cute. We have lived in the same house in the same neighborhood for twenty-one years. Yet this fresh-as-new-baby idea popped into his mind, and he asked where to go. It's like the person who asks, "How long do I microwave this?" You know they have their own answer; they just want the reassurance of asking someone with experience who seems to know.

I knew Jacob would not seek medical attention unless his tail was totally falling off, so I immediately provided him with my best recommendations.

"What made you decide to go now?" I inquired.

"I had a little trouble breathing, so I thought I'd better see someone."

In my mind a bright red light was flashing with an accompanying intercom voice saying, "*Shortness of breath, medical emergency, seek treatment, STAT*".

Every doctor, paramedic, EMT, and nurse is taught the essential ABCs—airway, breathing, and circulation. Oxygenation is essential for sustaining life. As breathing deteriorates, so does survival. Difficulty breathing requires an assessment, even on the dreaded January 1.

Jacob said, "I am fine going by myself."

This is boy-mom code for, "I am not going to ask for Mommy to go with me. I don't want to look like a baby. I can go to the ER alone. I'll figure it out, I think."

And since I knew the subtext of what Jacob was saying, I just punched my ticket for a round trip to the hospital and flushed my New Year's Day family bowling plans down the drain. When I arrived at the ER to meet Jacob, he was all checked in, sitting in the waiting area. It appeared that there were a few people ahead of him. Then I noticed a well-dressed woman checking in. A few minutes later, a man with two different shoes on his feet. It turned out that he dropped a chainsaw on his foot, and that was the reason the shoe looked mangled. The man looked surprisingly well for having been out two-steppin' with a chainsaw. The well-dressed woman seemed to jump to the side to let Old Chain Saw Foot through. This is when I noticed that the woman was Lily, a friend of mine from church. She was saying, "Shouldn't *he* go first?" as she gingerly stepped to the side.

Then both my friend Lily and the chainsaw victim made their way to the chairs next to Jacob and me. This was when I got a much closer look at the foot and saw that the man's sock was completely crimson and saturated with blood.

Then there was my Jacob with his sniffles and chills. I knew that he would take a back seat to chest pain, so I made sure he was stocked with water and snacks. I scanned the strip mall behind us and found a twenty-four-hour workout facility. I knew I could not sit waiting for three hours, so I said, "Jacob, there is a gym just across the parking lot. I am going to go for a run. Call me when they call you to be seen." With our plan solidified, I went and ran a 5K and did some weights.

When I returned, Jacob was still sitting in his exact same chair, and the room was replenished with more sickly patients. Hours slipped by. I said, "Jacob, did you tell them you were having trouble breathing?"

"No, Mom, not exactly, but it's fine. I can wait."

"What did you tell them?"

"That I had fever, aches, and a runny nose. Mom, it's fine, I will just wait."

I thought, *Child, you have no idea. Fever, aches, and a runny nose will likely earn you the Least Likely To Be Triaged Award. No one will view any part of that as an emergency. You might as well grab a pillow and a sleeping bag. They will definitely see you before you turn thirty.*

Golden piece of information here: You must tell a professional what is honestly going on with you if you need medical attention. There is no need to minimize what you are experiencing. If you need help, ask for it. That is what these people are here for, and they cannot read your mind. Please step up and advocate for yourself and your needs. If my son was not going to do this for himself, I was, and the front desk was only a few steps away.

The front desk employee is in a position of power. I know that I cannot afford to overexert myself in this type of situation.

Instead of saying, "Excuse me, I am a doctor. Do you not understand that my son is experiencing difficulty breathing? Is there anyone with a pulse back there that can even slap a pulse ox on his finger? Isn't that the least you can do?"

What came out of my mouth was, "Hi, how are you? My son, Jacob Metzner, was having trouble breathing earlier today. I don't know if he told you that, so I just wanted to make sure you are aware."

"No, he did not mention that. He has not appeared to have trouble breathing since he has been here."

"You're right, I don't think he has. I was just wondering if anyone did a pulse ox on him, just to see if his sats are okay?"

"I don't think so but let me check. I'll let them know. They should be bringing him back shortly."

I thanked her and walked back over to Jacob and the other lambs sweetly sitting in pen labeled "I'll wait all day to be seen." I was now wet with sweat, and cold with the chill of ten-degree weather outside. I said, "Jacob, if you are not taken back in three minutes, I need to go shower and come back."

That was at 4:38 pm. At 4:41 pm those huge institutional doors flung open, and they called, "Jacob!"

Immediately, the pulse ox was on his finger. All of Jacob's vital signs looked good. The nurse started asking him questions

"Do you drink?"

"No," I said, along with Jacob

"Do you smoke?"

"No," we both answered simultaneously.

She politely turned to me and said, "These questions are for *him*."

I thought, *clearly, she does not know me very well. Although you are not interested in my answers to these questions, I need to say them, and my answers better match my kid's.* Still, I took this as my cue to shut up.

She continued, "Have you ever smoked?"

"Yes, I did for about a year, but I quit five years ago."

"Quit what? Vaping or smoking?"

"All of it. I'm sober."

"That's great."

"Yes, he will be five years sober next month." I could not resist chiming in on that accomplishment. I am so proud of Jacob. I knew that was enough from Mama Bear, so I got quiet again.

The nurse then asked, "What about your home? Do you feel safe in your home?"

With this, I stepped just outside the door jamb to give them privacy.

She then asked Jacob, "Do you have any thoughts of harming yourself?"

"No."

I suddenly flashed back to taking Jacob to the ER during his freshman year of high school. He had just broken his arm at lacrosse practice. The nurse asked me to step out of the room. I heard her ask, "Do you have any thoughts of harming yourself?"

He deflected and said, "No, my family would suck without me."

Days later I learned he was in a serious depression. What I did not know then was that Jacob was battling an addiction. Addiction is like wearing a mirrored shield that immediately reflects all light away from the soul it inhabits. It's like walking around in your own personal slice of hell. Only darkness is absorbed as it seeps under the shield and directly into the flesh of its victim. The pain-filled days seem eternal.

Not this time. I know my son better now. He has faced his demons and dealt with them as a courageous warrior entering battle in the dark of night. One day at a time, he defeats his dragons.

People meet Jacob and immediately feel drawn to him. They always have. With all his talent, intellect, and accomplishments, he manages to be genuinely humble. Not false humility, where a person secretly thinks they are better than the guy next to them. It's truly in his fabric to know that every person has incredible value, and it shows. He's so bright, yet warm and inviting to hang out with. Business owners want to hire him. Coaches wish to him to captain their teams. Admissions counselors roll out the red carpet for him. Friends enjoy his company.

As a mother, he's a delight. I told all of my children when they were very young. "If I could have sat with God before he knit you in my womb, and asked for everything I wanted in my child, I would have sold myself short," and I meant it. I honestly couldn't conceive of individuals this wonderful.

So how did Jacob reach such a desperate place?

I thank God that Jacob no longer lives in such a terrible place, and neither do I. We walk in the "sunlight of the spirit." We have both traveled a great distance from that now unrecognizable darkness.

Back in the ER, I was satisfied that Jacob was getting the care he needed. His test results showed: pneumonia, negative, COVID-19, negative, influenza, positive. The resulting treatment plan and prognosis were good. Jacob had thirty-six hours to recover, pack for college, and begin his twelve-hour drive back to Tuscaloosa.

Later, my friend Lily from the ER texted me, "Your son is a delight." I did not even know they interacted, but I am sure Jacob was very much centered on her and how she was doing. You feel you can trust him because you can. He's going to be a fantastic doctor one day.

Later that evening, we settled in to do our extra-hard level crossword puzzles, and Jacob said, "Thank you for going to the hospital with me."

"No problem, love you."

The next day, Jacob said, "I feel a lot better. Maybe staying up all night contributed to how terrible I felt yesterday."

"Yes, rest is crucial."

Saturday morning, he loaded his things into his car to head out for Tuscaloosa. I said, "I miss you when you're gone. On the bright side, you only have one and a half semesters to go at 'Bama."

"You mean one and a half *years*," he corrected.

Can't keep a girl from wishing, I knew I said it as I wanted it. I felt a piece of my heart leave as I stood at the front door, waving. That is one incredible young man.

Please, God, keep him safe. Thank you, God.

"Children are the living messages we send to a time we will not see." John F. Kennedy

"Any man can learn anything he will, but no man can teach except to those who want to learn." Henry Ford

"Jesus said to them, 'A prophet is not without honor except in his own town, among his relatives and in his own home.'" (NIV, Mark 6:4)

Here's Looking at You, Kid

F EBRUARY 9, 2025, marked thirty years since my father's death.

For many years following his loss, I hated February 9th. I see that date looming out larger than life on the calendar every year. January was already not my favorite. It's cold as the tundra here in Kansas, with almost constant cloud cover. I long for the rays of the sun. While they occasionally penetrate the white skies, the next incoming snowfall swiftly obliterates the light. January also seems painfully long. It just drags on endlessly for thirty-one full, dark, wet, cold, icy, and snowy days, only to be met by the dreaded first nine days of February, with the anniversary of Dad's death hanging there like an abandoned swing blowing in the wind.

I wish I could take a break and cry. Yesterday, I saw that Tiger Woods withdrew from one of the major golf tournaments. His reason? He is grieving the death of his mother. He tried to play through it, saying, "I thought she would have wanted me to compete. But I am just not able to continue."

No one faulted him for it. Even Ann, one of my die-hard sports fan friends, said, "Oh, of course. That's so hard." But who is looking after a mom who says, "No, I just can't parent right now. I can't be a super-wife right now. Kids and family, you are on your own as I process things."

No one.

Especially when this February 9th fell on Superbowl Sunday, with the Chiefs going for an unheard of 'three-peat' Superbowl win. Instead of going into my room to journal, pray, rest, or maybe have a warm bath, it was a "let's get psyched up for football and pizza" day at my house. I shoved down my tears to celebrate this momentous occasion. The Chiefs matched my mood exactly. They were so lackluster and truly not themselves. I only watched a few minutes of the game as I recognized the feelings behind their lost expressions. The players' faces that said, "Why is this happening? How did it all go so badly? What happened? We practiced, we were psyched up, we were ready. Why are we getting absolutely slammed?" There were no fist bumps or chest-pounding moments in the endzone, only deflated expressions of players seated on the bench. There was only one word for it: misery. I could not watch the ongoing suffering. It exactly mirrored mine, so I needed to turn away. I deflected the game like the opposing pole of a magnet.

I felt their pain.

I hate that my dad is gone. I didn't want to be a Debbie Downer, but I did tell my son, Will, "It's the thirtieth anniversary of Papa D's death."

"Oh, Gosh, I'm sorry, I'm really, really sorry."

I sensed his immediate concern for me, and I was grateful. I quickly moved on from the topic to avoid bringing him down as well. Still, the whole thing stung like a bee on a hot summer day.

I ascended the stairs from the game that was ringing out on the lower level. I busied myself with daily tasks: folding clothes, washing dishes, preparing uniforms, packing lunches, filling swim bags, and more.

I forced myself to get into the 'here and now' and focus on the time I could spend with Will. Since he moved out, I don't have the luxury of hanging out with him often. Although my emotions were unsettled, I refused to let them hinder my time with him. I needed to put myself aside. Being emotionally drained, this took sheer willpower on my part. Just as Will left for the night, Nicholas was in the kitchen, reading me an essay he was working on. If you have teenage boys, you know that you do not get the luxury of choosing to hang out with them whenever. No, you must constantly be available and ready for the five--, ten--, or twenty-minute blocks of interaction that they alone allocate.

I felt further emptied like a cereal bowl with only a few drops of milk clinging to the edges. I hoped it would be enough to quench Nick's thirst. Next, I continued to wipe down the countertops, clear the table, and tidy up for as long as I could hold my eyes open. Finally, I crawled under my blanket, which covered me like a thick layer of snow. The sheer weight of my grief silenced me to sleep. Motionless, I rested deep in my loss, thoroughly defeated.

Monday was no better, and I had difficulty tolerating Madison's regular demand for gourmet foods and snacks on the way to her after-school activities. I responded to her out of exasperation, and I was sorry.

I preached, "I brought you apples, oranges, and pretzels; if you were hungry, you would eat an apple."

"I am not hungry for those things. I am hungry for McDonalds or Starbucks," she protested.

"Well, maybe you could be thankful I brought you anything as I take you to this class that costs thousands of dollars. You could have packed your own snack!" I snapped.

"That's it. When we get there, I am not going. I am not getting out of the car," she declared. She showed she meant it as I stood in the eighteen-degree weather, insisting she exit the car. We battled, and she kept her door locked as I continued to press the unlock button on my fob. By sheer force of will, I won that battle.

As we finally walked into her class, our conflict was evident. Brian, ever the cheerful songbird at the front desk, chirped, "How is it going today?"

I didn't feign pleasantries and said, "Not very well. It's rough. How are you?"

I departed, grasping for forty-three minutes of sanity. My only salvation was to do what has always saved me. I dragged my body to the gym, up the stairs, and onto a treadmill. Completing my run required me to say *aloud*, "Just keep going. Don't stop now," and "Finish this." It may have been annoying to have my positive self-talk coming out of my mouth as I ran, but I needed it, so I made sure the guy next to me had earbuds in, and I professed my own encouragement. I needed rest, but I needed this burst of endorphins more, and I would get it no matter what.

Tuesday was rock bottom. I had a meeting with Karen, my beloved editor. The work I presented to her was a dismal mess, and I deserved the critique I received. I bawled through our meeting. I told her it was because I was tired, which was true, but I was destroyed by how unsolid I felt overall. My writing was not where I wanted it to be. I was not where I wanted to be. The safe haven of my writing was now like a mirage in a desert. The more I ran toward it, the farther it eluded me. I was devastated. Would I not be granted even a sip of the one clear and accurate water that runs through my life? No. Not today. I remained parched, my lips chapped, cracked, and peeling. I dismally plodded on.

Karen said, "You know all that talk you give others about self-care? Maybe it's time to take your own advice and try some."

I knew she was right, but I still felt utterly unable to do so.

She sweetly suggested I rest. I knew that the demands of my day would keep coming, and there was no space on my plate for rest. I needed to pick up Madison soon.

Later, I received a call back from Diane, my sponsor and rock for almost thirty years. We had one of the most challenging conversations we have had in a long time, which prompted another problematic conversation with Jeff. I knew the day would continue like this *ad infinitum,* so I did the only thing I knew to do. I said goodnight to the world. I got under my covers and hoped for the best. Good night.

My last words of the night remained steadfast: *I love you, God.*

At that moment, a revelation came to me. I had forgotten to pray for myself in all my prayers for others, which constantly occupied my every waking moment. It was as if I did not feel worthy of prayer. It felt selfish to ask for the same peace, joy, hope, and happiness I readily requested on behalf of others.

But my life is so good. Why pray for me? Why? Because I need it. I need a prayer right now. It's okay, I told myself.

God, I have forgotten to pray for myself. I am trying to do everything on my own strength. I'm so down. You know my pain. I cannot do this on my own, God. Please help me.

With those words, I immediately fell asleep.

I awakened clear-minded and relieved. My circumstances had not changed, but I had changed. I felt in my soul that all was well. I was fearless. I knew that I was okay and that I was well if I had God and my truth. I burst forth into the day. It was a snow day for my children, and I was delighted. The snow softly fell for a few hours, providing a picturesque background for our morning work in the kitchen. We made waffles, signed valentines, and created artwork with white pencils outlining wintry scenes. The menu featured snow ice cream. Madison's best friend, Colette, came over to go sledding and be nourished by a warm grilled cheese sandwich. They read stories, cut hearts from thick ivory-colored paper, and adorned them with red and pink hearts. The girls shoveled the driveway, and I paid for their labor in quarters and other coins. We exchanged warm conversations and little hugs and kisses throughout the day.

I returned several phone calls and saw my problems from new vantage points. Everything seemed lighter. Even the snow, usually heavy and wet, was light powder. I effortlessly removed the sugar-like blanket covering my car. The darkness of the previous days seemed foreign to me. I returned to a constant meditation of Hail Marys running in my mind and aloud throughout the day. The storm in my mind passed entirely, and calm remained. My task list lost its overwhelming importance. Reviewing Madison's papers from school, I was filled with chagrin that my daughter, a writer's daughter, did not know how to punctuate conversation correctly. I took time to teach Madison how to punctuate direct quotes by having a silent and written conversation with her on a dry-erase board. It was a sweet little conversation I wished I had preserved with pen and paper, but it was only for that moment.

Once my children's cups were full, self-care became an immediate priority. I ran a few fast miles, bathed for longer than three minutes, and dressed for my big date night with my son, Will.

Will purchased tickets to see the movie *Casablanca*, one of his favorites, to be shown accompanied by the Kansas City Symphony. He firmly declared, "People dress up for this. I will be wearing a suit, so dress up. I will come by to pick you up at 5:30, be ready."

Always a man of his word, Will showed up promptly at 5:30 dressed to the nines and looked very handsome. I love how he takes care of himself, which shows in his clear skin and muscular physique. We had a lively conversation on our way downtown. He told me about every starring actor. He shared their birth and death dates, career arcs, significant accomplishments, and personal lives. Will has a steel trap of a mind for this sort of information, and I wish I had taken notes. When we sat down, his excitement was palpable. I looked at him for a moment, reminding myself to take this in through his eyes. He was here to watch *Casablanca* with the symphony. I was here to watch him and be a part of his experience.

Will works for a security company at the Kaufmann Center on Friday nights, so he knew many men and women working throughout the building. He enthusiastically introduced me, "This is my mom, Elisemarie!" To feel that he was proud of me was beyond rewarding.

The symphony was equally as rich and did not disappoint, playing the French national anthem above the roar of the Nazis singing the anthem of the Third Reich. Will informed me that the famous line by Humphrey Bogart, "Here's lookin' at you, kid," was improvised before it became common vernacular.

Serendipitously, I realized that a dear childhood friend of mine and his wife were sitting at the end of our same row. We greeted Joe and Martha Johnson at intermission. They told us their daughter was also with them, "sitting in the cheap seats." We met up with her and her boyfriend, who was none other than Will's high school band instructor, Justin Carnes. Delighted by this coincidence, we had a lovely conversation. They all joined us in our happy row for the show's second half.

If you do not know the story of *Casablanca*, it's worth seeing. It showcases the humanity of characters finding themselves in the dilemmas only war and love can provide. At the final line, "Louis, I think this is the beginning of a beautiful friendship," I felt Will swallow hard as tears momentarily welled in his eyes.

"I'm sorry. That got me," Will explained.

Will feels things in himself, and in others. This makes him one of the most wonderful people to spend time with. He is present, aware, and cares as only a rare few can do. My time with him was an answer to my unspoken prayer.

I cannot say how much I enjoyed this evening with Will. How can I be so blessed to have this gorgeous, thoughtful, strong, intelligent son who would buy me a ticket to a fantastic event in a breathtaking venue where we run into friends new and old? It was beyond a joy to watch Will breathing in all his favorite scenes. Before departing, we took a few pictures in the Kaufmann Center for the Performing Arts, with its glass walls overlooking the city. We reviewed all our favorite parts of the show on our drive back home.

I told him, "Thank you, Will. I love you."

"I love you more," he replied, besting me at my own game.

I was filled with gratitude, and just before bed, I texted, "Thanks a million. Love you.

Will's reply, "Here's looking at you, kid."

Thanks for the reminder, Dad.

"There is no charm equal to tenderness of heart." Jane Austen

"Be kind and compassionate to one another, forgiving each other, just as in Christ God forgave you." (Ephesians 4:32, NIV)

"A sacrifice to be real must cost, must hurt, and must empty ourselves. Give yourself fully to God. He will use you to accomplish great things on the condition that you believe much more in his love than in your weakness." Saint Mother Teresa

"If I find in myself a desire which no human experience in this world can satisfy, the most probable explanation is that I was made for another world." C.S. Lewis

My Sherpa

SINCE FEBRUARY 1995 I wanted to write this book. If I were explaining this on *Shark Tank*, Mr. Wonderful would jump in with disgust, saying "What have you been doing between 1995 and now?"

My response? I have been writing the entire time. Why do I have no book to show for it? It was because I was trying to do it on my own. After all, I'm writing about my life. Who else was available for the job?

Enter my friend, Sharon, who said one day, "I've got to go; I have a meeting with my editor."

Why didn't I have an editor? How could I get one of those? So, in January 2024, my belly was full of fire for this project. Nothing was going to stop me this time, and if I needed an editor, then so be it. I was at Sharon's house. She had already offered to set up a meeting between her editor and me. This time, I needed to have it arranged. Sharon introduced us on a group text, and I set up a meeting with Karen, her editor, from Satiama Writers Resource, a division of Satiama Publishing. I thought an editor would help fix some of the mistakes I missed. I happily sent Karen my book and waited to hear how much she liked it.

When I met with Karen, I was not sure she had read my book at all. She explained that this would involve writing and rewriting each chapter at least three to four times. I thought, "THREE TO FOUR TIMES! No way!" However, as I started working with Karen, my writing began to transform. She told me, "You have a wonderful writer's voice. Some people take years to find their voice or never find it, but you have a voice, and it's quite good."

That honestly meant the world to me. I have longed to share my voice in my writing and jumped this hurdle with ease. What next? We began the process of going through each chapter word for word. It was a fine-tooth comb discovery process. I learned that I would say the same thing five different ways to really drive a point home. Karen would gently say, "Let's cut that...heard that...said that..." or "let's not belabor the point."

In our first meetings, there was a good deal of "cut it, move it, restate it, explain it, choose another word for it," all of which were entirely necessary. I thought we were going to lock this sucker up over in a couple of weeks, and then magically, a book would pop up like a piece of toast ready for consumption. I learned it's a journey. It takes place daily, even hourly, and minute by minute. I needed to carve out the time at 2:00 am, 4:00 am or 11:00 pm I respectfully declined invitations for fun and invested time in my writing.

Karen gave me much more than an editor running through my work with red ink. She received my messages and provided a sounding board for their delivery. She was an accountability partner that I was determined not to let down. My meetings with Karen are written in ink on my calendar and boxed in for emphasis. As soon as one ends, I am feverishly preparing for the next.

On day I was running around, throwing in a load of laundry, taking my daughter to school, cleaning up the dishes, sweeping up some broken glass, feeding my dog and my bunny, and dealing with the crisis of the day. I was ten minutes late for my meeting with Karen. When I joined the Zoom call, she said, "You are late!" She did not look happy at all. I made no excuses. I didn't want to use up any of our precious time. I didn't want to let Karen down, and I don't want to be late again.

Karen and I laughed together at truly humorous moments and were brought to tears by others. I don't hide in my writing, so this was a vulnerable place for us. Karen has made it safe for me to say anything. She even picks up when there is something I'm not saying that needs to be addressed. In contrast, she lets me know if I go on a rant in my writing that is inconsistent with a message of strength, hope, and triumph with God.

After a thorough dissection, we cut a few chapters entirely. I am thankful they are gone. Others have taken their place with new vision and beauty. I appreciate how Karen knows my voice. She told me, "There is a difference between *good* writing and *great* writing. The mark of *good* writing is that you are captivated by it when you are reading. Later, you may forget the details but remember that it was a good book overall. *Great* writing stays with you, and you think about the stories and details a day, a week, or a year later. That's what happens when I read your writing. I think about it over the weekend or wake up thinking about it. It stays with me."

At one point, she said, "You have really become an excellent writer. I mean it. I think you will be shocked when you look back at some of the earlier chapters and see how far you've come."

When assembling the final book, I cringed at some of my word choices or the sentence structures I initially used. I realized I could keep rewriting for greater perfection, which could go on *ad infinitum.* Then, my work would never get out in the world. So, my caveat is that I am releasing this work, knowing it has imperfections, and that as soon as I finish, I will realize there are ten critical messages that I missed sharing with you, and that's okay. In hand is my first book, but not my last. I believe God will continue to teach, and I will continue to write about His lessons.

These are the messages I have now, and I am sharing them to the best of my ability. They are only a beginning. They represent a slice of understanding I have at this moment. I am confident that more will be revealed to me, and as that happens, I will share it. I hope you feel inspired to become your best self and see life's value, especially the gifts that often come from times of suffering. I hope you will know deep in your being that everything can work for good. I hope you will seek the help you need for your mind, body, soul, and life.

Karen is my sherpa who has guided me up this steep mountain one step at a time. She has encouraged me to trudge forward when I was hurt and disappointed by life and the brokenness of the world. She has accentuated the areas where I am blessed beyond belief. Together, we have trampled some troublesome foes and ignored others entirely. We have focused on the light and the love that always has the last word.

Sherpas have an intimate knowledge of the terrain ahead, incredible strength, and the ability to navigate obstacles. The reason I didn't have this book before? No sherpa.

Karen, thank you for being the best sherpa I could ever hope for.

My work here is a success if you enjoy it with even a percentage of the joy, pain, laughter, tears, and love that went into its creation. Thank you for reading and making my work meaningful. After all, art is only art once it's shared.

"Here are five powerful lessons borrowed from those tough-as-nails, yet compassionate, expedition leaders: Your real job is to lead others to the top. Sherpas are successful by helping those around them reach their full potential." Josh Linkner

"Bottom-line, having a Sherpa is critical to navigate a treacherous expedition or journey (think Mt. Everest). These Sherpas, or guides, are incredibly focused, resilient, and tough, yet possess a great deal of empathy." Frank Belen

"The value of a Sherpa goes far beyond their ability to carry gear; they are the guardians of the mountain and the protectors of those who dare to climb it." Author unknown

"The Spirit of the Sovereign Lord is on me, because the Lord has anointed me to proclaim good news to the poor. He has sent me to bind up the brokenhearted, to proclaim freedom for the captives and release from darkness for the prisoners." Isaiah 61:1

THE GOD CAVEAT

I N THIS BOOK, I use the words God and Jesus. Although our beliefs may differ, this is my understanding of the Infinite. I was raised an Irish-Italian Roman Catholic, so I'll use the word God; you fill in what works for you. Please do not let my word choice impede your mental, spiritual, or emotional growth.

On Prayer

Prayer is an essential ingredient of my life. Over the years, prayer has taken many forms as I searched for a personal relationship with God. I read about prayer becoming integrated into life to the extent that all life becomes prayer. Washing dishes is for God, and cleaning the house is for God. Almost anything done with purpose and awareness can be for God. I hope my life is a prayer that you can relate to. You certainly do not need to pray as I do. I do hope that you find your way to connect with this power I call God. I hope you will know Him as the Creator of inexpressible joy and a comfort your times of despair.

I say a litany of Catholic prayers every day, including the rosary. The rosary is a meditation that brings me peace and calms my soul. I also pour my heart out to God and let him know every area where I need His help. He already knows I need His help. I need to acknowledge that I am powerless on my own. I place my requests for myself and others at the feet of Jesus and Mary. I pray in song. I pray as I serve others. I pray when there is conflict in my life. I pray in thanksgiving when all is well. I pray and let God know how very much I love Him. Sometimes, I find myself in a situation I did not choose and cannot change. Today is one of those days, so I say:

God, I don't like this. It seems wrong, unkind, and unjust. The people involved have great power, and I am no match for them. I trust in you, Father, to help me. I feel alone and scared. I know you are still with me. I take great comfort in knowing you see it all. Nothing is hidden from you. I hate to see my children in pain. I would do anything to spare them their suffering. You, God, love with a greater love than any parent has ever known. You love me more than I can imagine. I know you do not take the mistreatment of your children lightly, and this case is no exception. The Bible teaches that vengeance is of the Lord. I cannot seek revenge, for that would only poison my soul. I trust you will make all things right in your time. For now, please help me to understand my lesson in this situation. The people involved are teaching me who I want to be or do not want to be. Father, what would you have me learn? God save me from my anger. Help me be of service.

The Bible contains truths regarding God. One of my favorites is that "God is Love." Have you ever felt love for something or someone? Have you ever received love? Then you have known God. Can you make the sun rise or stop the ocean tides? If not, there exists a power greater than yourself. I choose to call my unending source of strength, goodness, and light God. I can go anywhere if I am on an errand for God. My intention is that I become so in tune with the Creator that my entire life is a prayer. I constantly ask for His discernment and His wisdom. I want His ideas and His will to happen. I ask for Him to lead and help me along the way.

Of all the places I have lived, schools I have attended, jobs I have worked, men I have dated, friends I have made, and callings I have followed, there is only one constant: God. I can follow that one unbreakable thread from my birth to today. God has been my shelter in every storm, shoulder with every tear, and cheering section with every achievement. I have much to be thankful for; I believe it all comes directly from God or indirectly through His children. Sometimes, I call him God, or Holy one, Lord, Jesus Christ, or The Lord God Almighty. Mostly, I call him Father.

I will soon end this day as I do each day. I will pull the blankets around my shoulders and place my head on my soft pillow. I will say to God what I most need to hear from my children: *Thank you, God. I love you so much.*

I will rest easy, knowing that God is handling everything. The answers come even as I sleep.

God can redeem the darkness, bring beauty from the ashes, and anchor my life in hope.

I am blessed and grateful.

Good night, Father. I love you.

"So whether you eat or drink or whatever you do, do it all for the glory of God."

(NIV, 1 Corinthians 10:31)

"Do not take revenge, my dear friends, but leave room for God's wrath, for it is written: 'It is mine to avenge; I will repay,' says the Lord." (Romans 12:19)

"Dear friends, let us love one another, for love comes from God. Everyone who loves has been born of God and knows God. Whoever does not love does not know God, because God is love." (1 John 4: 7-8)

Prayers I Know As Friends

A Prayer For You

God, please bless every person who reads these words. Help them receive what they need, even if it's not on the page. Please help them to feel inspired and transformed. Most of all, I pray they will know your deep and everlasting love for them. And knowing that love, that they will never allow anything to separate them from You, not trouble, hardship, or suffering. Help them see you are closer than ever in the darkest times. You never leave us. You are there in the victories and in the devastating defeats. You are there when we feel everything is lost. You are there in abundance and lack. You are there when we are betrayed and mistreated. You experienced all these things when You came to Earth.

When I ask, 'Why must I suffer like this?' I have heard you say, 'I allowed My own Son to suffer to the point of death. Do you not think the same would be true for you? Of course, I love you. I see you as an eternal being. You see one line from one page in the book of your life, but I know the end from the beginning. I exist in all time. Present circumstances do not constrain me. I know all is well and will work out for good. Keep your eyes on Me, my sweet child. Keep your eyes on Me."

I pledge to keep praying for you and hope to meet you along the journey. May you be blessed with a trusted guide who has weathered the path and can illuminate the way for you. If you will but look, and keep your eyes on God, He will provide.

"The Lord bless you and keep you; the Lord make his face shine on you and be gracious to you; the Lord turn his face toward you and give you peace." (Numbers 6:24-26, NIV)

But Jesus immediately said to them: "Take courage! It is I. Don't be afraid."

"Lord, if it's you," Peter replied, "tell me to come to you on the water."

"Come," he said.

Then Peter got down out of the boat, walked on the water and came toward Jesus. But when he saw the wind, he was afraid and, beginning to sink, cried out, "Lord, save me!" Immediately, Jesus reached out his hand and caught him.

"You of little faith," he said, "why did you doubt?" (NIV Matthew 14:27-31)

The Prayer of St. Francis of Assisi
This prayer is often attributed to this saint, who lived a life of prayer and poverty devoted to God. However,

the prayer is not contained in his writings. The prayer,
also known as the Peace Prayer, suggests doing things
I feel incapable of doing. I chunk it down into small
bite-sized pieces. I decide, just for today, I will try to
understand rather than being understood. On another
day, I will try to love instead of being loved. I find
that even one stanza of this prayer challenges me to
the core.

"Lord, make me an instrument of your peace.
Where there is hatred, let me sow love;
Where there is injury, pardon;
Where there is doubt, faith;
Where there is despair, hope;
Where there is darkness, light;
Where there is sadness, joy.
O Divine Master, grant that I may not so much
seek to be consoled as to console, to be understood
as to understand, to be loved as to love.
For it is in giving that we receive, it is in pardoning
that we are pardoned, and it is in dying that we
are born to eternal life." Attributed to St. Francis

"I have been all things unholy. If God can work through me, He can work through anyone." St. Francis of Assisi

"Preach the Gospel at all times. Use words if necessary." St. Francis of Assisi

"The deeds you do may be the only sermon some persons will hear today." St. Francis of Assisi

"The only thing ever achieved in life without effort is failure." St. Francis of Assisi

The Serenity Prayer

God, grant me the serenity to accept the things
I cannot change,
Courage to change the things I can, and the
wisdom to know the difference.
Living one day at a time;
Enjoying one moment at a time;
Accepting hardship as the pathway to peace.
Taking, as He did, this sinful world as it is,
not as I would have it.
Trusting that He will make all things right if I
surrender to His Will;
That I may be reasonably happy
in this life, and supremely happy with Him forever in
the next.
Amen

REINHOLD NIEBUHR (1926)

Prayer For The Day

"My Lord God, I have no idea where I am going. I do not see the road ahead of me. Nor do I really know myself, and the fact that I think that I am following your will does not mean that I am actually doing so. But I believe that the desire to please you does in fact please you."

Do It Anyway

People are often unreasonable, illogical, and self-centered.
forgive them anyway.
If you do good, people may accuse you of selfish, ulterior
*   motives;*
do good anyway.

*If you are successful, you will win some false friends and
    some true enemies;*
succeed anyway.
Honesty and frankness make you vulnerable;
be honest and frank anyway.
*What you spend years building, someone could destroy
    overnight;*
build anyway.
If you find serenity and happiness, there may be jealousy;
be happy anyway.
The good you do today, people will often forget tomorrow;
do good anyway.
*Give the world the best you have, and it may never be
    enough;*
give the world the best you've got anyway.
You see, in the final analysis, it is between you and God;
it was never between you and them anyway.

Saint Mother Teresa placed this prayer on the wall of her home for children in Calcutta, India. Although many attribute it to her, it was written by **Keith M. Kent.**

"When I love God with all my heart, my relationship with him becomes the axis of my activity, the magnet that brings order and dynamism into all the otherwise scattered shards of my life, the organizing principle around which every other element is arranged," **Fr. John Bartunek**

Night Prayer

"Jesus Christ, my God, I adore You and thank You for all the graces You have given me this day. I offer You my sleep and all the moments of this night. I place myself and all my loved ones, wherever they may be, in Your sacred side and under the mantle of Our Blessed Mother. Let Your holy angels stand watch and keep us in peace. Amen." **Fr. Matlak**

Guardian Angel Prayer

Angel of God, my guardian dear, to whom God's love commits me here, Ever this day be at my side, to light, to guard, to rule, and guide. Amen.

God Help Me, Thank You God

Thank you God.

God, I love you so much. I love you, God.

Help me be a better mom, a better wife, a better daughter, a better doctor, a better friend, and a better person. Help me help in the situation. Please help this person through me. Please find the one who is lost. Please hold my loved ones in health, peace, and prosperity. Help me to be brave, strong, kind, and loving. Help me love the people who hurt me the most. Help me see them as you see them. Please don't let one word of unkindness pass my lips. Help me encourage the gifts I see in others. Keep me humble with the gifts you have given me. I owe it all to you, God. I am nothing by myself. Help me remember your instructions, "to those it has been freely given, freely give." Help me be grateful for all the gifts showering me daily, my sight, my hearing, my breathing, my mind, my ideas, my perfectly functioning body. I didn't earn these. No, you gave them to me as grace, freely given. Hold my hand on this path of life because I never want to do it without you. I love you.

ACKNOWLEDGEMENTS

THANK YOU to my eldest son, Jacob, who saved my life by letting me know how my illness was affecting him and has taught me more in his 21 years than I could hope to teach him in my lifetime.

Thank you to my second son, Will, who leads with a strength, determination, boldness, and joy that inspires me. Thank you for cheering me on.

Thank you, Nicholas, my youngest son, who is one of the best people I know. Your intelligence, humor, fun, and kindness make me want to be a better person every day.

Thank you to my sweet girl, Madison. We choose you and we are blessed beyond words with your spirit, curiosity, energy, determination, and compassion.

To my mom, LeeLee, thank you for everything. I love you more than yesterday and less than tomorrow.

To my dad, Papa D, I hope I make you proud. Miss you and love you forever.

Thank you to Jeff, my devoted husband, and to the entire Metzner family, including his amazing parents, Linda and Richard, who have consistently given me unwavering support.

Thank you to my cousin, Kathleen, whom I love having in my life.

Thank you to my niece, Alaina. Your vulnerability and beauty are unsurpassed.

Thank you to my niece, Nicole, you have brought me joy from the moment of your birth, and I could not love you more.

To my entire family of origin and extended family, brothers, sisters, cousins, aunts, uncles, nieces, and nephews, thank you for all the love and lessons along the way. I would not be the person I am today without you. I am grateful to you.

I love you all.

I want to thank my therapist, Doctor Barney Prentice, who helped me through the toughest grief of my life. I cannot say enough about my sponsor, Diane. She is a spiritual giant, and her instructions for life and sobriety saved my life many times. Thank you to Saint Mother Theresa for your beautiful life and example. Thank you, Chris Sjogren, for tending my soul and caring for my babies.

To the talented individuals and works that have inspired me:

Saint Joseph Edition of The New American Bible, Catholic Book Publishing Company, 1991

Holy Bible, New American Standard Bible, Zondervan Publishing, 1995

Holy bible, New International Version, Zondervan Publishing House, 1984

Thomas à Kempis, *The Imitation of Christ*

Jane Austen, *Pride and Prejudice, Emma, Persuasion*

Louisa May Alcott, *Little Women*

Dr. Martin Luther King, *Letters From a Birmingham Jail*

Harper Lee, *To Kill A Mockingbird*

J. D. Salinger, *The Catcher in the Rye*

Charles Dickens, *A Christmas Carol*

John Donne, *No Man is An Island*

Robert Frost, *The Road Less Travel*

Gerard Manly Hopkins, *God's Grandeur*

Og Mandino, *The Greatest Miracle in the World*

Tuesdays With Morrie, Mitch Albom

Peg Kehret, *Small Steps*

Lopez Lomong, *Running For My Life*

Tara Westover, *Educated*

Jen Sincero, You *Are a Badass at Making Money: Master the Mindset of Wealth*

Laura Hillenbrand, *Unbroken*

Mel Robins, *Five Second Rule*

Eddie Pinero, Your World Within (Podcast)

Kahlil Gibran, *The Prophet*

David Goggins, *Never Finished*

Amanda Frances, *Rich as F****

Karen Stuth, *A Speckled Stone; The Wisdom of Tula*

Bill Wilson, *The Twelve Steps of Alcoholics Anonymous,* and *The Big Book of Alcoholics Anonymous.*

Eddie Pinero, *Your World Within* (Podcast)

Thank you, Mary, for being the loving Mother of all. Thank you for placing me, my children, and all your children under your mantle of protection always.

Thank you, Jesus, for showing us the way to live a life of perfect trust, courage, and love in all circumstances.

Thank you, God, for this life, for the opportunity to share, grow, and inspire others. I love you.

I hope I will hear from many of you on your journeys to healing and triumph. I will continue to pray for you daily. I thank God for you.

"How lucky am I to have something that makes saying goodbye so hard." A.A. Milne

"Every life is noted and is cherished, and nothing loved is ever lost or perished." Madeline L'Engle

"That it will never come again is what makes life sweet." Emily Dickinson

"Therefore go and make disciples of all nations, baptizing them in the name of the Father and of the Son and of the Holy Spirit, and teaching them to obey everything I have commanded you. And surely I am with you always, to the very end of the age." (Matthew 28:19-20)

"May the God of hope fill you with all joy and peace as you trust in Him, so that you may overflow with hope by the power of the Holy Spirit." (Romans 15:13)

About The Author

LISEMARIE DICARLO, M.D., is a Mental Health Counselor, author, motivational speaker, presenter, executive director, and founder of Talk 2 Me – A Program of Hope. She has dedicated much of her adult life to serving and advocating for those who need a hand-up for a wide range of reasons, particularly with mental health needs. She also has a passion for physical health and growth through positivity. In her counseling practice, she helps clients to define success for themselves and to develop action plans to accomplish their goals.

Elisemarie specializes in working with people suffering from anxiety, depression, addiction, chronic pain, self-harming behaviors, and negative thoughts. She works with clients ranging from children to geriatric populations. She enjoys working with elite athletes, primarily in golf and swimming, to accomplish peak performance. Her clients consistently elevate to having top-tier experiences and more freedom than they ever imagined.

Elisemarie grew up in the Midwest. After living in Boston and a convent in New Jersey, she also lived in Brooklyn, Manhattan, Milan, Los Angeles, and Omaha. She returned to live in Leawood, Kansas, where she has resided for the past twenty years. She is a devout Roman Catholic and strives to live an authentic and transparent life. *Running Into Me* was inspired by her intention to use every tragic and challenging event in her life to help others. She is a devoted wife and mother of four wonderful children: Jacob, Will, Nicholas, and Madison. They provide her with constant learning opportunities and inspiration. Her relationship with God is paramount and crucial in her circumstances, as it enables her to see beyond the current unfairness of life and rise to an eternal perspective.

Elisemarie is exceedingly grateful for those God has placed in her life. She is dedicated to improving and challenging herself. She draws strength from the tremendous lessons of her friends and family, especially her mother and father, and seeks to honor their wisdom with her life.

She would be glad to hear from you and learn how her book may have impacted your life journey. Feel free to reach out to her at Elisemarie@talk-2me.com.

ABOUT TALK 2ME

THE MISSION of Talk 2 Me—A Program of Hope is to help people connect, heal, and thrive. The charity was founded in 2019 by Elisemarie DiCarlo and her sons, Jacob, Will, and Nicholas. Her family was concerned about the epidemic levels of mental health problems occurring among young people and felt the need to respond immediately to tragic outcomes.

It was apparent that young people needed the tools to advocate for their own mental health. The stigma and silence surrounding mental health needed to be broken. Talk 2 Me strives to make mental health a safe conversation for everyone. We promote physical health, mental health, and suicide prevention.

Talk 2 Me keeps the lines of communication open so young people know where to turn to get help. We give mental health presentations to elementary and high school groups, mentoring groups, concerned parents, and corporations. We teach coping skills, stress reduction, and self-care. We provide options for what to do if you or a loved one is in a crisis. We offer grants to counseling and created the Talk 2 Me Mental Health Advocacy Scholarships for rising college freshmen. We provide grants to inner city mentoring groups for girls ages six to eighteen that specifically focus on esteem building, confidence, professionalism, and college readiness. We sponsor runs and events to gather peers, get outside, and strive for meaningful change in our communities.

We know it takes courage to admit when you're hurting. That is why we promote 988, the national mental health crisis line. Anyone can call at any time and talk to a trained professional, usually within their area. Ultimately, talking to just one other person can save your life. We have seen it happen time and time again: problems brought into the light and spoken suddenly lose power. There is strength in vulnerability and sharing.

If you or anyone you know needs help immediately, please dial 988 or proceed to any emergency room. All you need to say is, "I am not okay. I need help." It's okay not to be okay; just don't keep it to yourself. If you need help, it's ready and waiting. Please don't spend another day carrying your pain by yourself. You are not alone. Never give up. There is always hope.

To learn more, visit us at www.talk-2me.com.